Samuel Taylor Coleridge

Samuel Taylor Coleridge

Basil Willey

Honorary Fellow of Pembroke College and
King Edward VII Professor Emeritus of English Literature
in the University of Cambridge

1972

W. W. Norton & Company, Inc.

New York

ISBN 393 07467 6

Contents

Acknowledgments

For permission to quote from the *Collected Letters of S. T. Coleridge* I am indebted to the courtesy of Professor E. L. Griggs and of The Clarendon Press. The extracts from Coleridge's *Notebooks* are reprinted, by kind permission of the editor, Professor Kathleen Coburn, and of the Bollingen Series, Princeton University Press and Routledge & Kegan Paul (London): vol. 1, 1957; vol. 2, 1961; vol. 3, 1972. I am especially grateful to Miss Coburn, not only for general encouragement, but for her kindness in lending me the proof sheets of vol. 3, which was still unpublished when I was writing.

I should like also to mention that a summary of parts of this book appeared in the essay 'Coleridge and Religion' in the volume called *S. T. Coleridge* ('Writers and their Background' series) published in 1971 by G. Bell & Sons. For permission to use this material I am grateful to Messrs. Bell and to the editor, Professor R. L. Brett. Lastly, I want to thank the Principal and Council of University College, Cardiff, and Professor Gwyn Jones, for their kind invitation to me to lecture as Visiting Professor in Cardiff during the academic year 1970-71. Five of the six lectures I gave there were extracted from the present work.

Preface

What excuse can there be for another book on Coleridge
at the present moment (February 1967)? An enormous mass
of critical commentary already exists; his sources, and every
aspect of his life, thought and art have been exhaustively
treated; and books about him are still frequently appearing.
Above all, *The Collected Coleridge*, one of the greatest scholarly
projects of this century, is in preparation under the general
editorship of Professor Kathleen Coburn, whose masterly
editions of the *Notebooks* have already shown us how much
new knowledge we are to expect. With so much new material
in the offing, with the certainty that before long we shall be
absorbing the rich feast of Coleridgean scholarship and
interpretation to be provided by Miss Coburn and her army
of sub-editors and researchers, what possible justification
can there be for writing another book *before* all this becomes
available?

I can only excuse it on personal grounds. I first read the
Biographia Literaria fifty years ago, when I was a subaltern
in France; Coleridge enlarged and irradiated my mind then,
and he has been a constant stimulus and inspiration to me
ever since. I am now in my mid-seventies, and if I am ever
to discharge a fraction of my debt to him I had better try
and do it now. I cannot, at my time of life, afford to wait for
the new era of Coleridge studies; someone else, perhaps in
twenty years' time, will have to write the magisterial book
which may then be possible.

So much, then, for the personal motive, which can be of no
interest to anyone but myself. I am however bold enough to
hope that by tracing, in however desultory a manner, the
outline of Coleridge's intellectual and spiritual biography, I
may be able to draw the attention of some others to a development which is not only fascinating in itself but possesses a
relevance for all time, and not least for our own time.

ABBREVIATIONS

CL :   *Collected Letters of S.T.C.*, ed. E. L. Griggs (Clarendon Press, 1956-9, 4 vols.).

L :   *Letters of S.T.C.*, ed. E. H. Coleridge (2 vols., 1895).

CN :   *The Notebooks of S.T.C.*, ed. Kathleen Coburn (Routledge & Kegan Paul, 1957-62, 2 vols. Vol. III now in preparation).

WEL :   *The Early Letters of William and Dorothy Wordsworth*, ed. E. de Selincourt (Clarendon Press, 1935).

WMY :   *The Letters of W. & D. Wordsworth, The Middle Years*, revised by Mary Moorman (Clarendon Press, 1969).

PW :   *The Complete Poetical Works of S.T.C.*, ed. E. H. Coleridge (Clarendon Press, 1962 ed.).

AP :   *Anima Poetae*, ed. E. H. Coleridge (Heinemann, 1895).

BRF :   *The Friend*, ed. Barbara Rooke (The Collected S.T.C. Routledge & Kegan Paul, 1969).

BL :   *Biographia Literaria*, ed. J. Shawcross (Clarendon Press, 1907).

C. & S.:   *On the Constitution of the Church and State*, ed. H. N. Coleridge (Moxon, 1852).

UP :   Unpublished Letters of S.T.C., ed. E. L. Griggs (Constable, 1932).

CHAPTER I

CHILDHOOD

'A MAN'S religion', said Carlyle, 'is the chief fact with regard to him.' This statement may seem absurd today, when most people have no religion at all; but it was abundantly true of Coleridge, and in the sense intended by Carlyle. The quest for religious truth and the establishment of religious faith formed the master-current of his life, to which all his other myriad interests were but tributary rills. Thus any study of Coleridge in only one of his many guises —as literary critic, as poet, as political thinker, as philosopher etc.—is bound to be incomplete and misleading. 'How shall he fully enjoy Wordsworth', Coleridge once asked, 'who has never meditated on the truths which Wordsworth has wedded to immortal verse?'[1] Similarly one cannot understand Coleridge, or see him in true proportion, unless one has meditated with him, and tried to follow the line of his thought, on those truths to whose vindication he devoted the central energy of his life. It is precisely this that I am attempting to do in the present book. And in so doing we may, I hope, find ourselves getting glimpses of his other interests, with due subordination of each to each 'according to their relative worth and dignity'. For Coleridge was one to whom 'the unity of all hath been revealed', and no subject, for him, existed in isolation from the central theme or from all the others.

The pattern in the Coleridgean carpet is unbelievably complex, but I mean to try and follow chiefly the line which leads from the Unitarianism of his Cambridge and Somerset days to the full Christian orthodoxy of his mature years. First, then, how and why did he become a Unitarian? What was it like to be a Unitarian in the 1790s? And why did he come to reject Unitarianism?

[1] *Omniana*, Oxford ed., p. 386.

11

In 1797, when he was in his 25th year, Coleridge began a series of five autobiographical letters to Thomas Poole; and it is from these that we learn most of what is known about his childhood. A clear picture emerges of this youngest of ten children (of his father's second marriage), the darling of his parents' declining years; hated, despised and admired in turn by his next-elder brother Francis; a precocious boy, gifted far beyond any of the rest except the father, taking no pleasure in 'boyish sports', reading incessantly and filling his ardent imagination with Arabian Nights 'spectres'—his 'memory and understanding forced into almost an unnatural ripeness'. 'Before I was eight years old', he says, 'I was a *character*—sensibility, imagination, vanity, sloth, and feelings of deep and bitter contempt for almost all who traversed the orbit of my understanding, were even then prominent and manifest.'[1]

His father, the Rev. John Coleridge, Master of the Grammar School and Vicar of Ottery St Mary in Devon, was 'a profound Mathematician, and well-versed in the Latin, Greek, and Oriental Languages', and author of 'Miscellaneous Dissertations' on the Book of Judges, and of a 'Critical Latin Grammar'. 'My Father', he says, 'was not a first-rate Genius—he was however a first-rate Christian . . . in learning, good-heartedness, absentness of mind and excessive ignorance of the world, he was a perfect Parson Adams.'[2] 'He was an Israelite without guile; simple, generous, and, taking some scripture texts in their literal sense, he was conscientiously indifferent to the good and the evil of this world.'[3] It was from this father (whom, as he wrote in 1808, 'I confess I have a feeling, one third pride and two thirds tenderness in being told that I strongly resemble . . . in person and mind')[4] that he received his first religious impressions. There is a passage in the third autobiographical letter to Poole which memorably describes the relationship between father and son; it has often been quoted from, but I must give it in full because it shows the child's mind in process of assuming the shape and propensity which, despite ephemeral and superficial changes, it never afterwards lost:

. . . my father was fond of me, and used to take me on his knee, and hold long conversations with me. I remember, that at eight years old I walked with him one winter evening from a farmer's house, a mile from Ottery—and he told me the names of the stars—and how Jupiter was a thousand times larger than our world—and that the other twinkling stars were Suns that had other worlds rolling round them—and when I came home, he showed me how they rolled round—. I heard him with a profound delight and admiration; but without the least mixture of wonder or incredulity. For from my early reading of Faery Tales, and Genii etc. etc.—my mind had been habituated *to the Vast*—and I never regarded *my senses* in any way as the criteria of my belief. I regulated all my creeds by my conceptions not by my *sight*—even at that age. Should children be permitted to read Romances, and Relations of Giants and Magicians, and Genii?—I know all that has been said against it; but I have formed my faith in the affirmative.—I know no other way of giving the mind a love of 'the Great', and 'the Whole'. —Those who have been led to the same truths step by step thro' the constant testimony of their senses, seem to me to want a sense which I possess.—They contemplate nothing but parts—and all *parts* are necessarily little—and the Universe to them is but a mass of *little things*—It is true, that the mind *may* become credulous and prone to superstition by the former method—but are not the Experimentalists credulous even to madness in believing any absurdity, rather than believe the grandest truths, if they have not the testimony of their own senses in their favor?—I have known many who have been *rationally* educated, as it is styled. They were marked by a microscopic acuteness; but when they looked at great things, all became blank and they saw nothing—and denied (very illogically) that any thing could be seen; and uniformly put the negation of a power for the possession of a power—and called the want of imagination Judgment, and the never being moved to Rapture Philosophy!—[1]

The questions with which I started, and with which this whole book is to be concerned, are here already answered;

[1] *CL*, 210.

here are the deep-laid foundations of his philosophy and his religion: of his philosophy and his Unitarianism, in this sense of the Great and the Whole; and of his Christianity in the association of both with the faith and character of his father, with 'that venerable countenance and name which form my earliest recollections and *make them religious*'.[1]

At Christ's Hospital he became a 'playless day-dreamer, a *helluo librorum*', devouring the contents of a City circulating library to which he was given access (in the words of E. K. Chambers) 'by a kindly stranger, with whom he collided as he thrust his way down the Strand in the character of Leander swimming the Hellespont, and who at first took him for a pickpocket'. Always apt, in his early developing years, to take his intellectual colouring and enthusiasms from his recent reading or his most admired associates, he was 'converted' to free thought at the age of 15 by reading Voltaire's *Dictionnaire Philosophique* together, it seems, with various medical books lent him by his brother Luke (then a young surgeon at the London Hospital). The immediate effect of this emancipation was to make him resolve to become a shoemaker instead of a parson. Accordingly, he persuaded his shoemaker friend to call on the schoolmaster James Bowyer and apply for him as an apprentice. ' "'Od's my life, man, what d'ye mean?" said Boyer [*sic*], and thrust Crispin out of the room. Coleridge pointed out that he was an infidel. And then, he tells us, he had the one just flogging of his life-time.'[2] 'But', said Coleridge on the heights of Highgate many years later, 'my infidel vanity never touched my heart. With my heart I never did abandon the name of Christ.'[3] And just as, later, his head was with Spinoza while his heart was with Paul and John, so now—while he was excited by Voltaire he was also feeding upon the Neo-platonists and 'conjuring' over Boehme's *Aurora*[4] (in William Law's translation). 'I had translated the eighth Hymn of Synesius from the Greek into English Anacreon-

---

[1] *L*, II, CCXL (May 19, 1825).
[2] E. K. C., p. 12. The authority is Gillman, p. 23.
[3] Gillman, *Life of S. T. C.* (1838), p. 23.
[4] See letter to Tieck, July 4, 1817; *CL*, IV, 1067, p. 751.

tics before my fifteenth year', he wrote in the *Biographia Literaria*.[1] It is to this latter side of him that Lamb bears witness in the oft-quoted passage:

Come back into memory, like as thou wert in the day-spring of thy fancies, with hope like a fiery column before thee—the dark pillar not yet turned—Samuel Taylor Coleridge—Logician, Metaphysician, Bard!—How have I seen the casual passer through the Cloisters stand still, intranced with admiration (while he weighed the disproportion between the *speech* and the *garb* of the young Mirandula), to hear thee unfold, in thy deep and sweet intonations, the mysteries of Jamblichus, or Plotinus (for even in those years thou waxedst not pale at such philosophic draughts), or reciting Homer in his Greek, or Pindar—while the walls of the old Grey Friars re-echoed to the accents of the inspired *charity-boy*![2]

[1] *BL*, I, p. 170n.
[2] *Elia*, Christ's Hospital Five-and-Thirty Years Ago.

CHAPTER II

CAMBRIDGE

1 Unitarianism

WHEN Coleridge went up to Cambridge (he began residence at Jesus College in October 1791, three terms after Wordsworth took his B.A.), it was with the general idea of becoming a parson—which was what his father, and his school, had always intended. But Jesus College was then in a ferment of 'left-wing' ideas and influences, and Coleridge's youthful impulse was always to be with the *avant-garde* or, shall we say, to associate himself eagerly with whatever ideas seemed to him most stirring and most true. Late in life, when men thought him reactionary, he knew (and said) that this was only because he had got so much ahead of them, and could see so much further. He had been right through Unitarianism, seen through it, and 'come round to the other side'.[1] But for the time being Unitarianism, as represented in Cambridge by men like Gilbert Wakefield and William Frend, was as much one of the new, true 'causes', to which every ardent and advanced undergraduate sought to be 'committed', as C.N.D., War on Want, anti-*apartheid*, or perhaps Communism, are today.

To be a Unitarian at that time meant also, almost as a matter of course, to be—if not an avowed republican in politics, at least a warm sympathiser with the French Revolution and a foe to aristocracy and the Established Church. Radicalism in politics and rationalism in religion went hand in hand.

There is no need to repeat here the familiar story of the birth and growth of Unitarianism from Faustus Socinus (1539-1604)—or Jesus Christ himself, if we may believe some Unitarian historians—to Joseph Priestley, whom Coleridge came to regard as the founder of modern Unitarianism.

[1] *Table Talk* (Oxford ed.), p. 308.

It was a part of the great leftward drift in theology which began (as we may roughly say, though historical 'beginnings' can always be pre-dated) in the sixteenth century, and culminated in the era of the French Revolution. During those centuries the de-mythologizing of religion was proceeding steadily wherever thought was free; mystery, miracle, and finally the whole supernatural basis of the Christian faith were being eliminated. Naturally, in England, it was amongst the Dissenters and radicals that this process went furthest; many of the Presbyterian and Independent congregations evolved during the eighteenth century into Unitarianism. But in that age, when the heavens seemed to declare the glory of God more obviously than the Scriptures, a deistic turn of thought was very common even within the established Church, and prevailed widely outside all Churches. In such a theological climate the more mysterious of the orthodox tenets, such as the Incarnation, the Atonement, and above all, the Trinity, began to perish of cold. A religion which rested upon the veracity of certain miraculous stories was bound to suffer in a century whose leading thinker exploded all miracle as so improbable that no testimony could be strong enough to establish it. Most Anglican clergymen, indeed, found no special difficulty in retaining their orders and benefices even if their views had veered, since ordination, towards Arianism, Socinianism, or even pure deism. But there were some striking examples, of whom Theophilus Lindsey and William Frend are the best-known, of resignation from Church livings by clergymen who had ceased to believe in the Trinity. To the average non-theological or non-ecclesiastical reader of today, this may seem a strangely technical reason for courting 'martyrdom'. He may, however, be reminded that the real point of issue was vital enough: it was whether or no Jesus of Nazareth was Almighty God. The disinclination to credit any supernatural breaks in the chain of physical and historical causation had become so strong in the eighteenth century, that many could only preserve their 'Christianity' by removing from it all that had hitherto distinguished it from 'natural' religion, and particularly by reducing Jesus to the status of a good man—perhaps the best of men, but a human being and no more. Men like Lindsey and Frend took their beliefs so seriously, and were so concerned about intellectual honesty, that they felt obliged to dissociate themselves from a Church which accorded divine worship, and offered prayer, to one (though the noblest) of God's creatures.

ii William Frend

It is not surprising, I think, that Coleridge as an under-graduate should have been caught up in this current of opinion. He had left school with an 'inferiority complex', and indeed both then and for years afterwards he was in-clined to regard most other men as his superiors. With a mind so fluid that it could hold Boehme and Synesius in suspension with Voltaire, and flow afterwards so rapidly into a succession of philosophic moulds—Priestley, Hartley, Godwin, Berkeley, Spinoza, Kant—he naturally adopted at Jesus College the viewpoint of those he most admired, and whose convictions, political and religious, seemed to have the sharpest cutting-edge. All Coleridge's biographers, begin-ning with Gillman, attribute to William Frend the greatest influence over him at this time:

> as, through the instrumentality of Frend, with whom an intimacy had now taken place, he had been converted to what in these days is called Unitarianism, he was too conscientious to take orders and enter the Established Church.[1]

It will therefore be worth while, if we want to feel the spiritual ethos of Coleridge's College, to take a closer look at Mr Frend, and see what manner of man he was.

William Frend (1757-1841) was a man of thirty-four when Coleridge came up (aged 19). He had already been deprived of his Tutorship at Jesus for his heretical opinions, though he was still a Fellow of the College. Frend was the son of a leading tradesman and former mayor of Canterbury. He graduated at Christ's College as 2nd Wrangler, and thereafter became Fellow and Tutor of Jesus. He took

[1] Gillman, p. 65.

Holy Orders, and from 1780 to 1787 he was Vicar of
Madingley near Cambridge. At that time, at first, he tells
us: 'I conceived myself a believer in the Trinity.'[1] But in
his quiet vicarage at Madingley, within sight of the magnificent Elizabethan hall, with its lake and its cedars, he
began a course of study by no means in harmony with the
feudal spirit of that scene. He read many books of contro-
versial divinity, ending with the famous Rakovian Cate-
chism, based on the thought of Socinus and largely drawn
up by him. Of this book (published at Rakov in Poland in
1605) it has been said that 'it did more than any other book
ever published (except the New Testament) to spread
Unitarian ways of thinking about religion.'[2] Frend's views
soon became more radical than those of the father of
Socinianism; he came to deny entirely the divinity of Christ,
whereas Socinus himself, while rejecting the Trinity, held
somewhat ambiguous opinions about Christ. Christ, he
taught, was truly man, yet not a 'mere' man, for he was
miraculously born, worked many miracles himself, and was
miraculously raised from the dead. Socinus, unlike most of
his own followers, even allowed prayers to Christ, on the
ground that Christ was divinely commissioned to lead
mankind, through faith, to knowledge of God and reconciliation with him. All this seems remote from the non-
miraculous *psilanthropism* (Coleridge's word, meaning 'mere-
man-ism')which began to prevail at the end of the eighteenth
century. But the denial of the Trinity was enough to convince
Frend that he had no business to hold office in a Church
which professed this doctrine, 'the great errour of the
christian world'.

He resigned his living, and turned his attention to agi-
tating for the abolition of the Subscription to Religious
Tests, then and for long afterwards imposed by the University of Cambridge upon candidates for the B.A. degree.
He supported the Grace promoted by Dr Edwards to this
effect. When this was rejected, Frend published his *Thoughts*

1 Frend, *A Sequel to the Account of Proceedings* etc., 1795, p. 104 ('Account
of the Author').
2 See H. Gow, *The Unitarians* (1928), p. 20.

on Subscription (St Ives, 1788), and it was for this that he was deprived of his Tutorship.[1] In this pamphlet he argued that it was wrong to make young men subscribe to propositions they had not studied and could not possibly understand at that stage. This was what had happened in his own case, and it was only after he had become a parson that he had discovered, by laborious study and thought, that the scriptures did not teach the doctrine of the Trinity. He had then, of course, had to undergo the humiliation of resigning his benefice. He went on to urge that the admission of Dissenters to the University would cause no danger to Church or State. The imposition of tests was traceable, not to zeal for Christian orthodoxy, but to a desire to exclude a set of men who were suspected to be politically unsound. Yet Dissenters are 'Men and Englishmen!—look at Priestley, the greatest ornament of this Country; he whom every learned Society in Europe is proud to enroll among it's members, debarred by the absurd prejudices of superstition, from a place in our Universities'.

In the same year (1788) Frend also published *An Address to the Inhabitants of Cambridge and its Neighbourhood, exhorting them to turn from the false worship of Three Persons, to the worship of the One True God.* 'The Lord our God is one Lord'—but do you really, he asks the inhabitants, worship the God of whom Christ speaks? No: in worshipping the other Persons, and the Trinity itself, you are bowing down to other gods—and he quotes some of the familiar Old Testament denunciations of idolatry. 'How then say ye, in express contradiction to Scripture, and to common sense, that Jesus Christ is God, making no difference between the great Being, who sent, and the man who was sent . . . ?' 'Consult common sense. Could God lie in the womb of a woman? could God expire on the cross? could God be buried in the grave? shocking suppositions!' Like all the Unitarians (and indeed all the sectarians) of his time, Frend claimed that Scripture was on his side:

---

[1] 'It has indeed been said, that by depriving me of the office of tutour, the master cleared his way to a bishoprick.' *Sequel*, p. 107.

Search the Scriptures; point out one single passage, in which Jesus Christ declared himself to be God. Point out one, in which the Apostles declared him to be God . . . etc.[1]

In *A Second Address* etc., published the following year (1789), Frend adduces the prayers of Jesus to the Father—as if, he says, Jesus as man could pray to himself as God! Where are the Trinitarian liturgical forms to be found? Not in Scripture, but in Mass Books, Prayer Books and the like suspect sources. 'We give Christ all due honour, but we cannot without blasphemy make him equal to our Maker'; 'the whole doctrine of the Trinity is a libel on the Scriptures, and an insult on the understanding of mankind'.

The Unitarians of Frend's time were in a cleft stick: basing their arguments essentially on common sense, nature, reason and conscience (the real creed of the eighteenth century), they were yet committed to the authority of a scriptural revelation which was full of miracle, and which everywhere implied the supernatural origin and status of Jesus. Their efforts to explain away the texts which did not support them were ingenious, but unconvincing to outsiders. It would have been safer and more consistent to have appealed to a tribunal higher even than Scripture; but the time was not yet ripe for this.

At the outbreak of the French Revolution, Frend was travelling on the Continent. His reaction was like that of the young Wordsworth in 1790: 'I rejoiced', he says, 'at the prospect of general freedom in Europe; I heard with pleasure that the chains of despotism were broken', etc. A few years later, in 1793 when Coleridge was up at Jesus College, Frend published the book which led to his trial by the University and banishment from Cambridge. It was called *Peace and Union recommended to the Associated Bodies of Republicans and Anti-Republicans*, and was an attempt, he explains, to steer a middle course between French extremism and the British Constitution. He starts from the agreed position that our Constitution is the best in Europe: very well then! Do not overthrow it, but improve it; improve it,

1 *Address* (St Ives, 1788), p. 8.

for example, by reforming our electoral system, abolishing rotten boroughs, having triennial Parliaments, reforming our laws, and so forth. But it was his criticisms of the Church of England, and of orthodoxy in general, which gave the real offence. He first weights the scales by inserting a rhetorical denunciation of the 'harlot' Rome and her tyranny, and by calling the Church of England an instrument of policy rather than of religion. The liturgy of our Church, he goes on, is:

> a composition derived from the Mass Book of Rome, over which, if it has in some respects a manifest superiority, it is very far from that standard of purity in its arrangement, language, or doctrine, which is required from such compositions.[1]

On this question of liturgy Frend's proposals are very moderate, though shot with irony. He suggests that a modernized version should be drawn up, as an optional alternative; this, after 'a few centuries', might perhaps prove acceptable. Religious tests, and tithes, are to be done away with. The thought of tithes sets him off on the passage which most incriminated him in the eyes of authority:

> The . . . priest in every age, whether he solemnizes the orgies of Bacchus, or solemnizes the rites of the Eucharist, will, should either his victims or his allowance fail, oppose in either case every truth which threatens to undermine his altars, or weaken his sacerdotal authority.[2]

What further need have we of witnesses? Behold, now ye have heard his blasphemy! He has placed the Bacchic orgies on a level with Holy Communion. But he has not quite finished; there are still the theological abuses to be denounced: the neglect of the doctrine of 'only one god' [sic]; the unlawful association of 'created beings' with the worship of 'the god and father of Jesus Christ'; the pride and exclusiveness of the sacerdotal orders, their ranks, tithes and dress—all so 'repugnant to the spirit of Christianity'; and

[1] *Peace and Union* (Cambridge, B. Flower 1793, 2nd ed.), p. 41.
[2] *Ibid.*, p. 50.

the 'superstitious prejudices' which admit priestly inter-
ference in domestic affairs—marriage, christening, burial.

On the strength of this book, Frend was brought before
the Vice-Chancellor's court, on the charge of defaming the
Church, its hierarchy and liturgy, ridiculing the eucharist,
and calling its worship idolatrous. Undergraduates attended
the trial in large numbers, and demonstrated in Frend's
favour—conspicuous among them, for his loud applause of
Frend's self-defence, being Coleridge. Frend's own *Account
of the Proceedings*[1] is almost verbatim. It is swollen to huge
size, as the trial itself was to great length, by the pitiless
ingenuity of Frend, who challenged his adversaries on every
legal quibble he could possibly start up, e.g.: he had never
been *proved* to be the author of *Peace and Union*, the court
was irregularly constituted, the prosecution malicious, and
the Statute obsolete and inapplicable. One cannot help
admiring, as Coleridge and his set did, the spirited way in
which Frend defended himself. But one's heart sinks as one
recognizes in him a type all too familiar in academic (and
other) affairs: cantankerous, fanatical, embittered, obstinate
and wrong-headed. But no doubt he had in him something
of the stuff of martyrs, and to the young men of 1793 he
seemed a noble champion of religious and political liberty.
Coleridge, writing in January 1792 to his orthodox brother,
the Rev. George, and evidently trying to allay misgivings
in that quarter, said 'Mr Frend's company is by no means
invidious. On the contrary Pierce himself [the Master,
usually spelt Pearce] is very intimate with him'.[2] Well!
so it may have appeared from a freshman's level, a year
before the trial. But Coleridge goes on in a vein intended, it
seems, to reassure his clerical brother still more, but likely
(one suspects) to have the opposite effect: 'No! Tho' I am
not an *Alderman*, I have yet *prudence* enough to *respect* that
gluttony of Faith waggishly yclept Orthodoxy.' If so, he
showed little sign of it for the next three or four years.

Before bidding farewell to Frend, who after Cambridge
days played no personal part in Coleridge's life, let us do him

[1] Published by B. Flower, Cambridge, 1793.
[2] *CL*, 11.

the justice of listening to his *confessio fidei*, spoken at the trial and recorded in the *Account of the Proceedings*:[1]

> Sir, I have been represented as an heretic, deist, infidel, atheist. Shall that man be called an atheist, who firmly believes in the existence of one God, the parent, the protecter [*sic*], and governer of the Universe? . . . But, Sir, I may be considered if not an atheist, yet as an infidel. Shall he, Sir, be deemed an infidel, who, for the second article of his creed, grounds his hope of salvation solely on Jesus Christ? Who looks upon his saviour as *a person sent from heaven to be the means of the greatest happiness to mankind* [my italics]? Is he an infidel who declares his saviour to be the great mediatour between god and man, that his saviour gave himself as a ransom for all, and through whom alone is eternal life, the free gift of god, bestowed upon a sinful world?

His third tenet, he adds, is 'universal benevolence'. What is my 'sect'? 'Jesus Christ is the head of my sect.'

Such, then, was the man from whom the undergraduate Coleridge acquired much of his intellectual tone and direction. But Unitarianism did not affect him through this one contact alone, nor merely through his living in the College which was 'the hotbed of Cambridge radicalism'—the College in which R. Tyrwhitt had nourished a group of 'young firebrands' including G. Wakefield, W. Frend and T. Edwards.[2] It affected him as a prevailing wind of doctrine in a revolutionary era; and in this wider sense it can be seen penetrating his thoughts and writings until he was twenty-five (his own estimate, according to Gillman); but also as present there in a negative sense until the very end, since in later life he never ceased to criticise the creed of his youth and to explain, in detail and in depth, why it no longer satisfied him. I do not think, therefore, that merely by glancing briefly at William Frend we have breathed in the Socinian air deeply enough to feel the full force of its influence on Coleridge. To do that, I am going to present brief and partial portraits of the two leading figures in eighteenth-century Unitarianism: Theophilus Lindsey and,

[1] p. 88.
[2] See B. R. Schneider, *Wordsworth's Cambridge Education* (1957), p. 119.

Joseph Priestley. Priestley is well known as one of Coleridge's early heroes; he read his work and his edition of Hartley, and greatly revered his character and intellect. He worked up ideas from Priestley's *Disquisitions Relating to Matter and Spirit* (1777) in his own *Religious Musings*. Lindsey, so far as I am aware, he only once refers to,[1] but no better representative could be found of the spiritual, pastoral and humane side of Unitarianism, which Coleridge met and admired amongst the Unitarians of Bristol and elsewhere; moreover, in his *Historical View of Unitarianism* (1783), Lindsey gave a scholarly account of the doctrinal and historical foundations of the movement, and of its later evolution—material to which Coleridge in his later years continually recurs.

iii Theophilus Lindsey

Theophilus Lindsey (1723-1808) was a close and lifelong friend of Joseph Priestley, but unlike him was a Churchman by upbringing and an Anglican clergyman by vocation. He was in sympathy from the start with the liberalizing spirit within the Church of England, and in 1772 he joined with his wife's step-father Archdeacon Blackburne and others in a Petition for Relief from Subscription, begging Parliament to release the clergy from any requirement 'to acknowledge by subscription or declaration the truth of any formulary of religious faith or doctrine whatsoever beside Holy Scripture itself'.[2] The Petition was of course defeated, but Lindsey's conscience was not appeased, and in 1772 at the age of fifty, he resigned from the living of Catterick in Yorkshire and began a new life as minister of the first church opened on avowedly Unitarian principles—the Essex Street Chapel in London. It is remarkable that, although his secession was based on a denial of the Godhead of Jesus, he yet conceived of it as 'giving up all for Christ'—a sacrifice made in the cause of 'pure and uncorrupted Christianity', a coming-out from 'Babylon'.

---

[1] *CL*, 447, July 26, 1802.   [2] Gow, *op. cit.*, p. 91.

In his *Apology on Resigning the Vicarage of Catterick*,[1] Lindsey tells how in his early struggles with his conscience he was satisfied for a time with the Trinitarian formula of the Rev. Dr Wallis, Savilian Professor of Geometry at Oxford for over fifty years (1649-1703). What do we mean, asked Dr Wallis, by a divine 'person'? Only a mode, or respect, or relation of God to his creatures. 'He beareth to his creatures these three relations, modes, or respects, that he is their Creator, their Redeemer, their Sanctifier: this is what we mean, and all that we mean, when we say God is three persons. He hath those relations to his creatures, and is thereby no more three Gods, than he was three Gods to the Jews, because he calleth himself the God of Abraham, the God of Isaac, and the God of Jacob.'[2] It was an explanation which would have been congenial to Coleridge at one stage of his struggle back towards a Trinitarian theology. But Lindsey, as an Anglican priest, realised that this was *not* what was meant, or all that was meant, by the orthodox creeds; and not what was understood by his congregation when they recited them. The Church taught that Jesus *was* the second 'mode, or respect, or relation', and Lindsey therefore, 'upon the most calm and serious deliberation . . . and weighing of every circumstance' felt 'obliged to give up my benefice, whatever I suffer by it, unless I would lose all inward peace and hope and God's favour and acceptance in the end'.

In his *Historical View of the State of the Unitarian Doctrine and Worship* (1783), published the year after Priestley's *History of the Corruptions of Christianity*, Lindsey aims to clear away the 'rubbish of ages' by showing (as Priestley had also tried to do) that all Christians up to about A.D. 300 were Unitarians, whether of the Arian school (holding the pre-existence of Christ, but as a 'creature' of God) or the Socinian (holding his 'mere humanity' but retaining his miraculous origin and powers). Claiming, as he does, that the Unitarian doctrine is the only truly scriptural one, he has to deal straight off with the many texts usually cited to prove that Jesus was God. This he does with varying degrees

[1] References are to the 2nd ed., 1774.
[2] Quoted by Lindsey, *op. cit.*, pp. 212-13.

of unconvincingness. All is plain sailing with 1 John v. 7 ('For there are three that bear record in heaven, the Father, the Word, and the Holy Ghost: and these three are one'), for Erasmus long ago showed the spuriousness of this crucial passage, and is duly praised by Lindsey for having done so.[1] Jesus, he says, was in all respects a human creature: 'as if God could be an infant!' he exclaims with almost the crudity of Frend, though he greatly surpasses the latter in spirituality; 'as if God could die!' To the orthodox mind, it should here be remarked, those paradoxes, which to Lindsey and his school seemed merely absurd, were of the very essence of the Christian faith—adorable mysteries. Orthodoxy agrees that Jesus was indeed 'a human creature', but believes that the divine nature was incarnate in him also. It would have been legitimate for Lindsey to ask how, according to the received teaching, the God in Christ was manifested. If the reply were 'in the Scriptures', he would answer 'No! That is to misinterpret the Scriptures'. If the reply were 'by the miraculous circumstances surrounding his advent, by his own miraculous deeds, by voices from heaven, by his Transfiguration, Resurrection and Ascension'—what could Lindsey say?—for all these were recorded in the Scriptures he claimed to accept as his sole authority. He could only have reached consistency if, yielding wholly to the rationalism of his time, he had denied the authenticity of these stories; or if, more boldly still, he had challenged the hitherto unquestioned authority of the Bible as divinely inspired. But neither Lindsey nor any other Unitarian at that time was prepared to go so far, and he was therefore left with the unsatisfactory task of picking out what seemed to him the shakiest of the 'Trinitarian' texts and 'explaining' them away.

A few examples will suffice, and they will serve to illustrate the sort of thing that Coleridge had in mind when, later on, he accused the Socinians of distorting the plain sense of Scripture.

'God was in Christ' (2 Cor. v. 19) and 'the Father in me' (John xiv. 10): these texts, he says (not unplausibly) do not

1 It is omitted for the same reason in the *New English Bible*.

affirm *identity*, but merely the spiritual presence and activity of God in his chosen servant. Sometimes, as with 1 John v. 7, he is plainly right; as again in his comment on Philippians ii. 6 where, after observing how important it is for the Bible to be accurately translated, he points out (correctly) that 'thought it no robbery to be equal with God' should be 'not grasping, or greedily ambitious to be like unto God'.[1]

It is in his uncritical struggles with passages like John i. 3 ('All things were made by him, and without him was not anything made that was made') that his weakness appears. He tries to shift the stress here back to God and away from the demiurge-Logos: it was by the *Wisdom* of *God* that all things were made; and that wisdom *entered into* Christ. Instead of recognizing the Fourth Gospel as an essay in Logos-doctrine (which of course he could not have been expected to do), he places it exactly on a level with the Synoptics. Because the latter treat Jesus largely as a man, John must have thought of him in the same way; therefore, the Logos cannot be the pre-existent Christ.

I had wondered, in reading Lindsey's book, how he would evade (if he mentioned it at all) the cry of doubting Thomas, when confronted with the risen Christ (John xx. 28), 'My Lord and my God!' Sure enough, we come to it at last:[2] Thomas 'did not intend Christ himself'! What then *did* he intend? Just an ejaculation? No, he was *praising God* for having raised Christ from the dead. As Dr Lardner has rightly said, being raised from the dead is not a proof of divinity.

The doctrine of Three Gods in One is, he says, a metaphysical abstraction and refinement; 'such philosophy, 'tis to be hoped, will in time give way to common sense, and the plain meaning of the Scriptures.' To 'common sense', very likely; but how extraordinary to assume its necessary agreement with Scripture! We have seen how 'plain' meanings had to be 'coloured' to achieve it. Scripture was indeed a terribly awkward authority for eighteenth-century Unitarians to have to acknowledge; their nineteenth-century

[1] *New English Bible* has 'did not think to snatch at equality with God'.
[2] *An Historical View*, etc. (1783), p. 394.

successors, who replaced Scripture by reason ('common sense') and conscience, were much more comfortably placed.

Turning briefly to the historical part of Lindsey's argument, we notice first his dubious attitude to Socinus himself, the reputed founder of the sect. Of course Jesus was its real founder, so no exaggerated reverence need be paid to Socinus. 'It was', he says, 'a circumstance much to be regretted' that the sixteenth-century Socinians retained the *worship* of Christ. Socinus himself was induced to retain it through having been involved in a contest with his fellow-Unitarian 'Davides' (Francis David, 1510-79), the apostle of Transylvanian Unitarianism. Both men regarded Jesus as a man, with no heavenly pre-existence; but Socinus thought he had scriptural authority for the worship of Christ on the score of the great powers bestowed upon him. David retorted that Socinus had misinterpreted his texts (!), and that there was no express command from God to this effect. The view of Socinus, however, was that we *might* (not *must*) pray to Christ. Lindsey is very severe on Socinus for his cruelty to David and Palaeologus, and cannot forgive him for denying the name of Christian to those Unitarians (e.g. the Transylvanians) who would not worship and pray to Jesus Christ.

Much of the book is devoted to accounts of the sufferings and martyrdoms endured by early Unitarians, from Servetus (who died in the flames acknowledging Christ as son of the Eternal God, but not the *Eternal Son* of God); to Legatt and Wightman, who were burnt alive in 1611 (the year of the Authorized Version); and John Biddle of Magdalen, who, near the end of Charles I's reign, narrowly escaped the same fate at the hands of the Presbyterians. With Thomas Firmin, an Anglican layman, rich, philanthropic and theologically liberal, we meet (at the end of the seventeenth century) another of the attempts to rationalize Trinitarian doctrine. Firmin devised a 'Unitarian Trinity' which enabled him—and, he hoped, might enable others—to hold Unitarian views and yet retain Trinitarian forms of worship and remain in the Church of England. According to his formula, the Trinity stood for three internal relations or respects of the Infinite Mind to itself. Thus, the First Person is the prime sovereign agent and author of all things; the Second: the same as manifesting himself by Christ; the Third: the same as manifesting himself by his holy spirit, or extraordinary power in the establishment and propagation of the gospel. Why not adopt this formula, then, and so avoid schism? But no, the same objection applies to this as to Dr Wallis's rationalization: we must not worship along with others who are understanding the words in their traditional sense.

The great Dr Samuel Clarke, who had drawn up a 'Unitarian' liturgy which Lindsey used at Essex Street Chapel, is treated, along with Bishop Hoadly and others, as a painful example of that class of good clergymen, who, though Unitarians, stayed in the Church of England. Clarke was in fact an Arian, holding that Christ was a dependent created being, but that he existed before all worlds, was the deputy of God in the Creation, and was incarnate as in St John's gospel, ch. i. Sir Isaac Newton, too, was perhaps an Arian, or maybe a Psilanthropist, but certainly a Unitarian, though too timid to say so.

Abraham Tucker, author of *The Light of Nature Pursued*, was another Unitarian conformer. Some of the most revealing of Lindsey's phrases slip out unawares when he is speaking of these men; for instance here, while explaining Christ's redeeming, atoning and mediating offices, he gives warning that 'even his death and passion will avail only such, who strive to *imitate his endurance in a good cause*' [my italics]. Similarly, during the discussion on S. Clarke he speaks of 'his [Christ's] *unwearied efforts in the cause of virtue, and for the good of mankind*' [my italics again]. It would be an interesting exercise in theologico-literary Practical Criticism to analyse those italicized phrases and show why, to the ordinary Christian reader, they seem slightly absurd.

Lindsey died in 1808, four years after Priestley, and fourteen years after the latter's emigration to the banks of the Susquehanna. Of Lindsey's last years, his biographer Thomas Belsham speaks in phrases replete with period overtones: 'His retrospects were most gratifying, his anticipations delightful, his principles most rational and consolatory, his circumstances easy.'

iv Joseph Priestley
(1733-1804)

Many years ago, in a book about the eighteenth century,[1] I quoted the following remark of Coleridge (in the *Table Talk*[2]): 'I think Priestley must be considered the author of the modern Unitarianism.' He goes on, 'I owe, under God, my return to the faith, to my having gone much further than the Unitarians, and so having come round to the other side' (cf. above, p. 16). The latter sentence will be the text for most of the present book; as for the former, I feel exonerated, by having already written about Priestley, from offering more now than a few sketchy outlines.

In the life, character and work of Joseph Priestley, the Socinian moonlight of the English eighteenth century shines most brightly. His evolution from strict Calvinism to 'genuine and rational' Christianity—or as Coleridge afterwards put it 'the generation of the modern worldly Dissenter was thus: Presbyterian, Arian, Socinian, and last, Unitarian'[3] —was a true epitome of the history of Dissent (excluding Methodism, which was not originally 'dissent' at all) in the eighteenth century. Priestley himself was greatly influenced by David Hartley, whose *Observations on Man* (1749) he edited (1775); and Coleridge in turn, as everyone knows, was for a while the ardent disciple of both. In 1794, when he was drafting *Religious Musings*, Hartley and Priestley were his bright particular heroes. What attracted him about both was the union in them of scientific enlightenment with a confident, optimistic theism. In the France of the *philosophes*, enlightenment was paired with infidelity; not so in England! When Priestley was dining with Turgot in Paris (1774), he was told by the 'philosophical persons' present that he was 'the only person they had ever met with, of whose understanding they had any opinion, who professed

---

[1] *The Eighteenth Century Background* (1940), p. 181.
[2] *Table Talk*, p. 308. June 23, 1834.   [3] *Table Talk*, p. 311. June 28, 1834.

31

to believe Christianity'. Coleridge was born with a believing temper and a questing intellect, and the tension between these two elements in him (the heart and the head, as he so often called them) determined the whole pattern of his life and thought. He longed to find a mental clue to the mighty maze of things, and tried system after system before his own self-knowledge taught him that deep thinking without deep feeling, repentance and faith led only to pantheism and spiritual pride. In his youth, as with all brilliant young men, the intellect predominated, and he eagerly absorbed any philosophy which seemed to explain the universe—particularly any which, like Hartley's and Priestley's, supported his own innate sense of an underlying and omnipresent divine energy. In the thought of those two writers the blend of scientific precision with warmth and certainty of religious conviction stirred him to hero-worship, and it was not until bitter experience had revealed his own insufficiency that their essentially limited and prosaic quality became manifest to him. Hartley taught that life itself, through the beneficent workings of the Law of Association, automatically built up 'the being that we are', and led us on by stages from the pleasures of sense to the love of God. How delightful, and how reassuring!—especially to one who shrank from self-direction and the disciplines of the active life. Priestley taught that 'Nature's vast ever-acting Energy'[1] was the energy of God himself, everywhere and always causing, impelling and sustaining. How glorious!—especially to one who longed to know all things, and know that God was in them. Coleridge's favourite phrase 'and what if—?' is a sign, wherever it occurs, that one of these great thoughts has quickened his mind and set the whole universe a-tremble with life and meaning.

> And what if all of animated nature
> Be but organic Harps diversely fram'd,
> That tremble into thought, as o'er them sweeps
> Plastic and vast, one intellectual breeze
> At once the Soul of each, and God of all?[2]

[1] *The Destiny of Nations*, l. 461.   [2] *The Eolian Harp*, ll. 44-48 (1793 and later).

This is pure Priestley, though that good man could not have expressed the thought so eloquently. But how much of Coleridge's after-development is foreshadowed in the lines that follow, where he assigns to Sara the role of the affable archangel in *Paradise Lost*, checking Adam's inquisitiveness:

> Solicit not thy thoughts with matters hid,
> Leave them to God above, him serve and fear.[1]

In *The Eolian Harp*, Sara, in language full of Miltonic echoes, reproves Coleridge for his speculative flight.

> But thy more serious eye a mild reproof
> Darts, O belovéd Woman! nor such thoughts
> Dim and unhallowed dost thou not reject,
> And biddest me walk humbly with my God.
> Meek daughter in the family of Christ!
> Well hast thou said and holily disprais'd
> These shapings of the unregenerate mind;
> Bubbles that glitter as they rise and break
> On vain Philosophy's aye-babbling spring.

It is typical that Coleridge, with his submissive temper and his tendency to look up to everybody, should at this early stage transform Sara's very imperviousness to ideas into a sign of spiritual superiority. And looking into the future, we may find it ironic that he should return to 'abstruse research' as a way of escape from domestic infelicity. The Icarus-flight, the warmth and glow of the intellectual Sun! Then the melting wings, and the return to earth; later, other flights—horizontal perhaps, or downward, rather than heavenward, and painfully sustained rather than with rapture; finally, the long attempt to combine head and heart in a Christian philosophy adequate to the modern world— this is the outline of Coleridge's history, so early glimpsed in *The Eolian Harp*.

In *Religious Musings* he is very far from regarding the thoughts of Hartley and Priestley as 'dim and unhallowed', or as 'shapings of the unregenerate mind'. Here is Hartley:

[1] *Paradise Lost*, Bk. VIII, l. 168.

[The Soul] From Hope and firmer Faith to perfect Love
Attracted and absorbed: and centered there
God only to behold, and know, and feel,
Till by exclusive consciousness of God
All self-annihilated it shall make
God its Identity: God all in all!
We and our Father one![1]

—and Coleridge adds the footnote 'See this *demonstrated* by Hartley. . . .' And again, after salutes to Milton and Newton (both Arians, by the way):

and he of mortal kind
Wisest, he first who marked the ideal tribes
Up the fine fibres to the sentient brain[2]

—referring to Hartley's account of the origin of ideas in vibrations of the nerves and brain. Immediately following this comes Priestley:

Pressing on his [Hartley's] steps
Lo! PRIESTLEY there, Patriot, and Saint, and Sage,
.   .   .   .   .   Him from his native land
Statesmen blood-stained and priests idolatrous
By dark lies maddening the blind multitude
Drove with vain hate.[3]

—referring to that 'effervescence of the public mind' (as Pitt called it) when

on occasion of the celebration of the anniversary of the French Revolution, on July 14, 1791, by several of my friends . . . a mob, encouraged by some persons in power, first burned the Meeting-house in which I preached, then another Meeting-house in the town [Birmingham], and then my dwelling-house, demolishing my library, apparatus, and, as far as they could, everything belonging to me.[4]

Three years after this, Priestley set sail for America intending to join 'the large settlement for the friends of liberty in

[1] *Religious Musings*, l. 39.   [2] *Religious Musings*, l. 368.
[3] *Ibid.*, l. 372 (1796 version).   [4] Priestley's *Memoirs*.

general, near the head of the Susquehanna'. Two months later Coleridge was planning with Southey and others for the establishment of 'aspheterism' or Pantisocracy on the banks of the same delightful river, which was recommended to him for 'its excessive Beauty, and its security from hostile Indians'.[1] He has just had breakfast with George Dyer, who 'is intimate with Dr Priestley—and doubts not, that the doctor will join us'.

Priestley had indeed 'pressed on Hartley's steps'; he had gone beyond him, abolishing the distinction between matter and spirit, and teaching a full necessitarianism. What appealed to Coleridge about Priestley's materialism was that it made the best of both worlds; it offered all the attractions of materialism without the stigma. 'Matter' turned out to be a kind of energy (God's energy), and so (as Priestley said) it was as 'immaterial as any person can wish for', and 'the reproach of matter is wiped off'. For Priestley himself (less for Coleridge, though he went the whole way with Priestley for a short time) the main advantage of this doctrine was that it enabled him to dispose of all notions based on 'the soul' as an immaterial substance distinct from the body, above all, of the pre-existence of Christ the demiurge. The separable, immortal soul was one of those heathen fables, Greek and Oriental, which were absorbed by Christianity as it spread amongst the nations, and which corrupted its primitive (Unitarian) purity. It is only, says he, 'by purging away the whole of this corrupt *leaven*, that we can recover the pristine simplicity, and purity of our most excellent and truly rational, though much abused, religion'.[2]

Matter is not to be considered merely inert; it has 'attraction' and 'repulsion', and these are 'powers'—not to be attributed, as by Bruno and Baxter, to the direct action of God, but God-given none the less. Its power of 'resistance' is due, not to any fictitious 'solidity' or 'impenetrability' but to its 'power of repulsion'. Then how does matter differ from spirit? It is not for me, says Priestley, to show that it *does*! We ought not to think of it as something 'base' or

---

[1] *CL*, 55 (Sept. 1, 1794). And cf. my *Eighteenth Century Background*, p. 193.
[2] *Disquisitions Relating to Matter and Spirit* (1777), Preface.

'sluggish'; it should 'rise in our esteem'. There is no reason why matter, thus rehabilitated, should not think and perceive. These powers have never yet 'been found but in conjunction wih a certain organized system of matter'; destroy the brain, and all thought is destroyed too. The Platonic notion that 'death is an advantage with respect to thinking' is sheer absurdity.[1]

Priestley, like Milton and Hobbes, was prepared to accept a full 'mortalism'; soul and body being indistinguishable, the death of the body means the death of the whole man. How, with his unabated deference to Scripture, could he maintain such a thing? 'We have no hope of surviving the grave', he says, 'but what is derived from the scheme of revelation.' What do we so derive? Let us briefly watch him dealing with this problem.

> It is a great advantage attending the system of materialism, that we thereby get rid of a great number of *difficulties*, which exceedingly clog and embarrass the opposite system; such, for instance, as these, *what becomes of the soul during sleep*, in a *swoon*, when the body is *seemingly dead* (as by drowning, or other accidents), and especially *after death*; also *what was the condition of it before it became united to the body*, and *at what time did that union take place?*[2]

Here Priestley allows his fancy to riot pleasantly amongst absurdities:

> Must the divine power be necessarily employed to produce a soul, whenever the human species copulate? Or, must some of the preexistent spirits be obliged, immediately upon that event, to descend from the superior regions, to inhabit the new-formed embrio?

And then, what of animals: have they immaterial souls, too? Some of them have more right to claim it than 'ideots' or those human beings who die in infancy. How and where are they to be disposed of after death? Above all (coming back to full seriousness, and to the central issues), what happens to the soul between death and Resurrection at the Last Day? Does it range 'the empyrean for some thousands of years'? There is no Scripture warrant for this speculation (and

[1] See *Disquisitions*, Sects. I to III.   [2] *Disquisitions*, p. 41.

purgatory is a purely ecclesiastical invention). What Scripture does teach, and what Priestley and all of us must therefore believe, is that there will be a general resurrection on the Day of Judgment, when God, who originally gave life and thought to the departed, will, by a miracle perhaps no greater, restore them to life and immortality.

The Scripture teaching, then, according to Priestley, is the sleep of death until the General Resurrection. Thus it is not true—it is the reverse of the truth—that the Scripture doctrine of resurrection depends on the natural or inherent immortality of the soul. There is no mention, in either the Old or the New Testament, he says, of 'soul' as separable from 'body'. Where the language of Scripture seems to imply such separation, it must of course be 'interpreted' to mean something else; and Priestley has this Unitarian technique always ready for use. 'The spirit shall return to God who gave it'? Oh, this *must* mean 'breath' or 'life'. 'Fear not them which kill the body, but are not able to kill the soul'?—here soul *must* mean the future life! Scripture is silent on the immortality of the soul, not because this is an obvious or demonstrable doctrine, but because it is not true.

If we base all our hopes of a future life on an event so far-off, however divine, as the General Resurrection, are we not making it very precarious? So any one of us might question Dr Priestley, as we read his book. Yes, indeed; and surely that is the very reason why proofs of the soul's 'natural' immortality have been, and still are, so eagerly sought after. The Resurrection, the Last Trump, the Great Assize—are these not parts of an exploded mythology? And if so, if we have no other grounds for expecting a life hereafter, what hope have we? Priestley would reply that if we think like that we do err, not knowing the Scriptures. He was still at the stage when Scripture authority could be used as decisive against any doubts or oppositions. And he thought he had Scriptural support for the view that we are 'extinguished' at death, and remain dormant until 're-composed' at the Last Day.

After a long historical survey, in which he tries to show how the early 'Unitarian' Christianity became infected with

Oriental and Greek fables of the soul; and how, in particular, the 'reproach of the Cross' was countered by promoting Jesus to the rank of Logos, or demiurge, or first-emanation, Priestley goes out of his way to demonstrate the great reverence which he yet feels towards his Man-Christ. He accepts, as indeed a Scripturalist cannot but accept, the miraculous Birth and the Resurrection of Jesus. He appears also to exempt Jesus from the sleep of death: 'I go to prepare a place for you'—that is, Jesus does not await the Last Day, like all other men. It may be said, I think, that his Psilanthropism enables him to give the Resurrection of Christ a meaning which it lacks (as I have often felt) in the orthodox view—that is, if the orthodox view is that the Resurrection was a *unique* event which occurred *because* Christ was God incarnate. St Paul's argument against the Sadducees in 1 Corinthians 15, that 'if there be no resurrection of the dead, then is Christ not risen' has always seemed to me difficult to reconcile with what I have called the 'orthodox view', for surely the unique God-man might well have been raised from the dead though no other man were—and his Resurrection was the principal evidence that he *was* no ordinary man. St Paul's point, however, becomes a source of hope for us ordinary men precisely on the ground alleged by Priestley, since it is then possible to argue that, Christ being a man like the rest of us, his Resurrection is a pledge and promise of what may be in store for us all.

v The Doctrine of Philosophic Necessity (1777)

Since Coleridge at one time (letter to Southey, Dec. 11, 1794) declared himself 'a compleat Necessitarian', it will be worth while briefly to examine Priestley's argument on this subject.

Priestley labours earnestly to prove that we are *not* exempt, as orthodox free-will doctrine claimed, from the chain of causation whose first beginning is in the hands of God. But he seems to me, first, to set up a wrong antithesis, viz.: between (1) a will which is always determined by the strongest motive, and (2) one which is arbitrary and not determined by motives at all; and then to assume that the defenders of free-will mean it in sense (2). Yet, as his argument proceeds, he gradually introduces the notion of *good character*, i.e. a habitual disposition to be determined only by the *best* motives; and he assumes, further, that by reflexion and self-discipline we can acquire a good character. Is not this all that the free-will doctrine means to claim? We are so made that, unlike the animals, we can shift our allegiance from one system of determinism to another—to a higher system, if 'good character' is our aim. Something in us enables us to see our former motives as contemptible, so that we cease to take pleasure in what formerly determined our will. We have realised (if we have been 'converted') that God's service is perfect freedom, and that freedom from God means enslavement to self and sin. What sort of force is it, on the necessitarian theory, which has wrought this conversion?

Priestley considers the objection that Necessitarianism might paralyse the will in fatalistic resignation. Surely it 'ought' to do so? But no, he says, not if we realise that our will is itself part of the chain of causes. If I am fated to starve, it is because I am also fated to be lazy; or conversely, if I am fated to be rich and successful it is because I have also been fated to work hard and exert all my powers. There seems to be a catch somewhere in all this. We do not know what fate's decree for us is, hence we are bound to exert ourselves in any case. Priestley speaks as if Necessitarianism simply meant: 'Your exertions will never fail of their necessary result'. Very reassuring, but in practice a full emotional commitment to Necessity often can, and does, unstring the will; or alternatively, the principle of Necessity may be adopted as a way of rationalizing and excusing inaction. On the latter ground, it must have had a fatal attraction for a man like Coleridge.

Priestley admits that men are often 'staggered' when told that nothing could have been otherwise than it has been, and that God has caused it all, good and evil alike. Are they not right to be 'staggered' at this—at least, if the corollary holds good, that 'all things will be what they will be, no matter what we do now or don't do'? Perhaps the first is admissible, and not the second? Later, he admits—or rather claims for Necessitarianism as a merit—that it 'must tend to diffuse a joyful serenity over the mind, producing a conviction that notwithstanding all present unfavourable appearances, whatever is, is right. . . .' 'The connection that all persons and all things necessarily have, as parts of an immense, glorious and happy system . . . with the great author of this system makes us regard every person, and every thing, in a friendly and pleasing light. I cannot, as a necessarian, hate any man, because I consider him as being, in all respects, just what God has made him to be.'

What an ecstasy of acceptance, not to say complacency! What a pleasant exercise of hope and joy rivalling—on its lowly and prosaic level—the 'chameleon' imagination ('negative capability') of Shakespeare, whereby he could rejoice as much in Iago as in Imogen. And yet, immediately after this lotus-vision, this trance uninduced by Muse or drug, Priestley—content with nothing less than the best of both worlds—faces right-about and becomes the evangelist again. I cease to blame bad men, he says, but I must be all the 'more earnest and unwearied in my endeavours to reclaim them'. Why must I? On what principle can I presume to amend the Creator's productions, and distort the perfection of 'whatever is'? It is because, he now says, men's disposition 'is capable of being changed for the better'. God is now admitted to be the 'Author of sin'—but this is only, of course, to secure the greater good in the end. Priestley thinks that even the wicked, after the General Resurrection, will attain final happiness; and he quotes, in confirmation, the conclusion of Hartley's *Observations*, where the glorious prospects are celebrated. In the (inevitable) section of Scripture citations he adduces Philippians ii, 12-13, 'Work out your own salvation . . . *for it is God that worketh in you* both to will and to do', without commenting, as a profounder thinker would have done, on that pregnant paradox.

It is curious, when Priestley comes to comparing and contrasting Necessitarianism and Calvinism, that although he sees they have much in common, it is to Necessitarianism that he gives the credit of producing in men a sense of dependence upon their own efforts. A necessitarian, he argues, will not rely, like the Calvinist, upon divine election and fore-knowledge. I find it hard to see, however, how his principles as such can incite him to make the required efforts; whereas the Calvinist, however illogically, did in practice feel obliged to prove to himself that he *was* one of the elect. Priestley tells us that, brought up himself in strict Calvinism, he had rejected the whole 'scheme'—original sin, inherent depravity, atonement etc.—and come to rest in the opprobrious Socinianism; that is, 'the simple and unadulterated doctrine of revelation' (but 'predestination' is a Pauline teaching!). His innate good sense, however, triumphs over the theological chaos when he says that, given a good heart, speculative principles don't much matter; and he can conclude with a charming tribute to the saintly Calvinist aunt who brought him up.

CHAPTER III

PANTISOCRACY;
BRISTOL LECTURES; MARRIAGE

SUCH, then, was the climate of opinion which was shaping the mind of Coleridge during his undergraduate years, though one must remember that he had already dipped into Neo-platonism, and 'conjured' over Boehme's *Aurora*, at Christ's Hospital; and that on February 22, 1792, in a letter to Mrs Evans (mother of his first love, Mary) he could describe himself as 'Reverend in the future tense' though still 'Scholar of Jesus College in the present tense'. According to Gillman: 'as, through the instrumentality of Frend...he had been converted to what in these days [1838] is called Unitarianism, he was too conscientious to take orders and enter the Established Church.'[1] 'Be not startled, courteous reader!' says Gillman, after mentioning that Coleridge himself had admitted to being a Socinian till the age of 25 (i.e. 1797). To comfort the said reader he quotes this from Coleridge: 'After I had read Voltaire's Philosophical Dictionary, I sported infidel! but my infidel vanity never touched my heart...With my heart I never did abandon the name of Christ.' True indeed, but we shall see through what successive phases his 'Christianity' had to evolve.

This is not a biography, and it will thus be enough to recall here that in December 1793 Coleridge, in panic at his College debts and perhaps distracted too by his love for Mary Evans, ran away from Cambridge and enlisted in the 15th or King's Light Dragoons. Has the enormity of this action ever been sufficiently remarked?—enormity, I mean, for an advanced left-winger of the time, who must have been pro-French and to whom service in the armed forces of 'tyranny' would be, as one might suppose, anathema? Either his crisis must have seemed desperate, or his political principles were as yet only skin-deep; perhaps both are true.

[1] *Life* (1838), p. 65.

42

In any case, my reason for referring to the escapade is that during his (roughly) four and a half months' military service Coleridge wrote a series of letters to his brother George, which reveal a good deal of his religious feeling at this time. One must of course allow, in reading them, for the fact that George Coleridge was a parson (he succeeded their father as Chaplain Priest at Ottery St Mary later in 1794); for Coleridge's own chameleon-habit, which lasted through life, of adjusting his mental tone and colour to that of his correspondents; and for the *in loco parentis* relationship of George to his very unsatisfactory younger brother.

In a letter dated February 11, 1794, mainly concerning the question of getting his discharge, he says:

> What my future life may produce, I dare not anticipate—Pray for me my Brother—I will pray nightly to the Almighty Dispenser of good and evil, that his Chastisements may not have harrowed up my heart in vain!—Scepticism had mildewed my hope in the Saviour—I was far from disbelieving the Truth of revealed Religion, but still farther from a steady Faith.[1]

We are not concerned here with his confessions of idleness, drunkenness, debauchery and near-suicide (Feb. 23, 1794), except in so far as they illustrate the mood of repentance and self-abasement in which his religious testimonies are made. Of these, I think the most revealing is the following (March 30):

> I long ago theoretically and in a less degree experimentally knew the necessity of Faith in order to [?] regular Virtues—nor did I ever seriously disbelieve the existence of a future State—In short, my religious Creed bore and perhaps bears a correspondence with my mind and heart—I had too much Vanity to be altogether a Christian—too much tenderness of Nature to be utterly an Infidel. Fond of the dazzle of Wit, fond of subtlety of Argument, I could not read without some degree of pleasure the levities of Voltaire, or the reasonings of Helvetius—but tremblingly alive to the feelings of humanity, and susceptible of the charms of Truth my Heart forced me to admire the beauty of Holiness in the Gospel, forced

[1] *CL*, 34.

me to *love* the Jesus, whom my Reason (or perhaps my *reasonings*) would not permit me to *worship*—My Faith therefore was made up of the Evangelists and the Deistic Philosophy—a kind of *religious Twilight*. . . . Faith is neither altogether voluntary, or involuntary —We cannot believe what we choose—but we can certainly cultivate such habits of thinking and acting, as will give force and effective Energy to the Arguments on either side—[1]

After being discharged from the Dragoons as 'insane' (April 10, 1794), and being duly admonished before the Fellows by the Master of Jesus College, Coleridge visited Oxford (June) and there met Robert Southey, then an undergraduate at Balliol. From that time on, though he returned to Cambridge for the Michaelmas Term, his letters are full of new excitements: Pantisocracy ('aspheterism'), the Bristol circle: the Frickers and Thomas Poole, etc.—there is no need to repeat the oft-told tale. What does concern us here is the new tone, the new politico-religious language he now adopts. There is, for instance, the callow 'republicanism' of letter No. 50, written to Southey on July 4 while on the way to Wales with Joseph Hucks, which begins 'S. T. Coleridge to R. Southey—Health and Republicanism', and contains the well-known passage:

> It is *wrong*, Southey! for a little girl with a half-famished sickly Baby in her arms to put her head in at the window of an Inn— 'Pray give me a bit of Bread and Meat'! from a party dining on Lamb, Green Pease, and Sallad—Why? Because it is *impertinent* and *obtrusive*! I am a Gentleman!—and wherefore should the clamorous Voice of Woe *intrude* upon mine Ear!?
>
> My companion is a Man of cultivated, tho' not vigorous, understanding—his feelings are all on the side of humanity—yet such are the unfeeling Remarks, which the lingering Remains of Aristocracy occasionally prompt. When the pure system of Pantocracy [*sic*] shall have aspheterized the Bounties of Nature, these things will not be so—! I trust you admire the word 'aspheterized' from α non, σφέτερος proprius!

He calls Monarchy 'a *monster* generated by *Ingratitude* on

[1] *Ibid.*, 44.

Absurdity', and adds a poem he has just composed, entitled 'Perspiration, a Travelling Eclogue', opening with

> The Dust lies smothering, as on clatt'ring Wheels
> Loath'd Aristocracy careers along

(he and Hucks, it will be recalled, were on a walking tour).

Soon after, from Wrexham, he is upbraiding Southey for suspected backsliding from the standards of 'stern simplicity' required by 'republicanism'. Southey is actually contemplating ordination: 'For God's sake', cries Coleridge with (probably) unconscious irony, 'enter not into the church'.

Next, he is back in Bristol getting involved with the Frickers, alas! getting engaged to Sara while his heart is with Mary Evans; in London breakfasting with George Dyer, who 'doubts not that the Doctor [Priestley] will join us' on the banks of the Susquehanna; meeting 'a most intelligent young Man' from America who extols the Susquehanna à la *Martin Chuzzlewit* ('literary Characters make *money* there'); intending to learn 'the theory and practice of agriculture and carpentry'; and sending 'to Lovell [already married to Mary Fricker] and Mrs Lovell my *fraternal* love—to Miss F. *more*'.[1] Still in London (on Sept. 11) he asks Southey again, to say 'to etc. [!] all the *tender* things'—though he doesn't write to her himself. The same letter refers to Godwin, who '*thinks* himself *inclined* to *Atheism* . . . I set him at Defiance'—and he adds that he is to be introduced to him 'sometime or other'.

Back at Cambridge in later September, he is in a fever of recollection (of the tremendous events of the summer), anticipation of America, and factitious 'love' for Sara:

> Since I quitted this room what and how important Events have been evolved! America! Southey! Miss Fricker!—Yes—Southey —you are right—Even Love is the creature of a strong Motive— I certainly love her. I think of her incessantly and with unspeakable tenderness—with that inward melting away of Soul that symptomatizes it.[2]

---

[1] *CL*, 54 and 55.   [2] *CL*, 59.

The stalwart capitals of SHAD GOES WITH US. HE IS MY BROTHER! are meant to be a republican defiance of class-prejudice, for 'Shad' (Shadrach Weekes) was man-servant to Southey's aunt, Miss Tyler. Much more serious were his misgivings about Sara: as he said three months later, he had mistaken 'the ebullience of *schematism* for affection'[1]—and he still yearned for Mary Evans. Meantime Southey reproaches him for not having written to Sara; Coleridge makes excuses: he *has* written to her now, and Southey, with his 'undeviating Simplicity of Rectitude' must not judge him too hastily. The same theme appears with redoubled pathos in letter No. 65 (Oct. 21), where he quotes (to Southey) an impassioned appeal from Mary against 'rash Schemes':

> You have doting Friends [she says]. Will you break their Hearts? There is a God—Coleridge! Though I have been told (*indeed* I do not believe it) that you doubt of his Existence and disbelieve a hereafter.—No! you have too much Sensibility to be an Infidel. You know I never was rigid in my opinions concerning Religion—and have always thought *Faith* to be only Reason applied to a particular Subject—In short, I am the same Being, as when you used to say—We thought in all things alike.

A truly Coleridgean letter, even anticipating his later insights about Faith and Reason. What a wife she might have made him! No wonder Coleridge cries 'I loved her, Southey! almost to madness', and adds that though his 'Resolution has not faltered', he has failed to transfer his affections to 'her, whom I do not love—but whom by every tie of Reason and Honor I ought to love'. He has misgivings, too, about *égalité* in America: Southey, it seems, wants the master-servant distinction to be observed even there. 'Of course it is each Individual's *duty* to be Just, *because* it is his *Interest*' but it is not enough merely to perceive this 'as an abstract proposition': 'The *Heart* should have *fed* upon the *truth*, as Insects on a Leaf—till it be tinged with the colour, and show it's food in every minutest fibre.' Thus early did Coleridge realize the difference between mental assent and heart-knowledge.

---

[1] *Ibid.*, 73.

Similar uneasiness appears again in the next letter (No. 66, Oct. 23). The women!—will not 'the *Mothers* tinge the Mind of the Infants with prejudications?' And the children, '*your* Brothers', for instance:

> Are they not already *deeply* tinged with the prejudices and errors of Society? *How* can we ensure their silence concerning *God* etc.—? *That* Mrs. Fricker—we shall have her teaching the infants *Christianity*,—I mean—that mongrel whelp that goes under it's name—teaching them by stealth in some ague-fit of Superstition!—[1]

Writing to his Reverend brother George (No. 69, Nov. 6, 1794) he tries, excusably enough (though perhaps a trifle disingenuously), to disclaim the label 'Democrat'. No! don't mistake 'the ebullitions of youthful disputatiousness' for 'fixed Principles'! And if, in *The Fall of Robespierre* (published in Cambridge this same autumn), Jacobin sentiments are expressed, what was this but dramatic necessity? Even so, do not 'my own feelings' appear, in defiance of dramatic propriety, in such lines as

> And Hebert's atheist Crew, whose maddening hand
> Hurl'd down the altars of the living God
> With all the Infidel's Intolerance?

Solemnly, my Brother! I tell you—I am *not* a Democrat. I see evidently, that the present is *not* the *highest* state of Society, of which we are *capable*—And after a diligent, I *may* say, an intense study of Locke, Hartley and others who have written most wisely on the Nature of Man—I appear to myself to see the point of *possible* perfection at which the World may be destined to arrive—But how to lead Mankind from one point to the other is a process of such infinite Complexity, that in deep-felt humility I resign it to that Being—'Who shaketh the Earth out of her place and the pillars thereof tremble'. . .

There is no need to doubt his sincerity—indeed, it is borne out by his subsequent teaching—when he replies to the question: 'what the friend of universal Equality *should* do'? —' "Talk not of Politics—*Preach the Gospel*"—Yea! my Brother! I have at all times in all places exerted my powers

[1] *CL*, 66 and 68.

in the defence of the Holy One of Nazareth against the Learning of the Historian, the *Libertinism* of the Wit, and (his worst Enemy!) the Mystery of the Bigot'. This same letter contains the familiar piece of self-knowledge in the lines on the death of Smerdon:

> To me hath Heaven with liberal hand assign'd
> Energic Reason and a shaping Mind,
> The daring ken of Truth, the patriot's part,
> And Pity's Sigh, that breathes the gentle heart
> Sloth-jaundic'd all!

He left Cambridge without a degree in December 1794, never to return. Writing to Southey from London (No. 73, Dec. 9) he again rebuts the charge of neglecting Sara, but admits that he is self-betrayed and miserable. 'However it still remains for me to be externally Just though my Heart is withered within me.'[1]

Letter No. 74 to Southey (Dec. 11) says nothing about Pantisocracy, but is full of acute critical remarks about the verses of Southey, Lovell, Bowles, Lamb and himself. Of himself he truly (at this time) remarks 'I cannot write without a *body* of *thought*—hence my Poetry is crowded and sweats beneath a heavy burthen of Ideas and Imagery!' More to our present purpose, however, is this:

> I am a compleat Necessitarian—and understand the subject as well almost as Hartley himself—but I go farther than Hartley and believe the corporeality of *thought*—namely, that it is motion—

Yet, how seriously is this to be taken?—for Coleridge only brings it in so as to quote a parody of this very doctrine which he has just written (in a letter to Favell). One must never forget that Coleridge was at that time, and indeed for years to come, a quick-change artist, delighting to don one intellectual suit after another, and to speak and think in the appropriate dialect. To set ideas dancing and systems revolving, and to watch the outcome, was for him an end in itself, a self-justifying activity ('and what if?'—). However,

---

[1] See also *CL*, 77: 'To *love her* [i.e. Mary Evans] Habit has made unalterable . . .' but '*I will do my Duty*'.

this suit is still on him twelve days later (No. 77, Dec. 29), when he refers to Charles Lamb 'who like me is a Unitarian Christian and an Advocate for the Automatism of Man'. Writing to Dyer from Bristol (No. 81, Feb. 1795) he says of Southey: 'He is truly a man of *perpendicular Virtue*—a *downright upright Republican*! He is *Christianizing* apace—I doubt not, that I shall present him to you right orthodox in the heterodoxy of Unitarianism'. Possibly; but meanwhile Southey, having been urged by his uncle Hill to take Orders, consulted Coleridge. He must have known what advice he would get: 'But you disapprove of an Establishment alto-gether—you believe it iniquitous—a mother of Crimes!—It is impossible that *you* could uphold it by assuming the badge of Affiliation.'[1] Southey took the advice.

In the new year of 1795, soon after arriving in Bristol, Coleridge gave 'three political Lectures' there. He met with the same sort of opposition as is now encountered in some Universities by certain visiting speakers—only it was from the contrary wing—the 'Aristocrats' as he still calls them: 'Mobs and Mayors, Blockheads and Brickbats, Placards and Press gangs'; so that he fears 'the Good I do is not proportionate to the Evil I occasion'.[2] I will remark briefly on these lectures.

The first, called *A Moral and Political Lecture*, was alleged to contain 'Treason', but in fact was very mild and sedative, echoing almost verbatim certain passages from recent Letters I have been quoting. The 'oppressed'? Yes, of course they need championing; but we must plead *for* them, not *to* them. 'Go preach the GOSPEL to the poor'!—and, 'uniting the zeal of the methodist with the views of the philosopher', live personally among them. The doctrine of Necessity is here invoked in its benigner aspect: vice is the inevitable effect of 'surrounding circumstances'; so, don't blame the sinner, but alter the circumstances. Nor is it

---

[1] *CL*, 87 (early Aug. 1795).

[2] These lectures were published the same year, but are most readily found in *Essays on His Own Times* (1850), vol. i: *Conciones Ad Populum*; and now best of all in the 'Collected Coleridge', I, *Lectures 1795 on Politics and Religion*, ed. Lewis Patton and Peter Mann (1971).

enough to have once swallowed these truths; 'We must feed on them, as insects on a leaf, till the whole heart is coloured by their qualities, and shew its food in every the minutest fibre.' [cf. *CL*, No. 65.] Necessitarianism had been put to similar use by Godwin, but Coleridge is already on guard against 'that proud philosophy, which affects to inculcate philanthropy while it denounces every home-born feeling by which it is produced and nurtured'. Next year (1796) he will be condemning Godwinism still more roundly.

The second, *On the Present War*, is more hysterical and inflammatory. The 'Establishment', religious and political, is blamed for bloodshed abroad and police-state miseries at home. The real enemy is 'not the religion of peace . . . of the meek and lowly Jesus . . . but the religion of mitres and mysteries . . . the £18,000-a-year religion of episcopacy', etc. In an interesting footnote, after quoting 'that pattern of Christian meekness, Bishop Horsley', and Bishop Pretty-man's remark that the same 'busy spirit' leads both to Unitarianism and to republicanism', Coleridge parodies Burke's famous outburst on the age of chivalry: 'the age of priesthood will soon be no more', and all its associated horrors—tyranny, repression, slaughter, etc.—will pass away.

The third, called *The Plot Discovered*, attacks the repressive Acts and the State Trials. It will suffice to give a specimen of its rhetoric:

> The cadaverous tranquillity of despotism will succeed the gener-ous order and graceful indiscretions of freedom—the black moveless pestilential vapour of slavery will be inhaled at every pore.

It is a wonder that Coleridge escaped prosecution for this speech (rather than the first), for it contains amongst other things this apostrophe to the country with which we were then at war: 'France! whose crimes and miseries posterity will impute to us. France! to whom posterity will impute their virtues and their happiness.'

During the same spring (February 1795) Coleridge gave in Bristol a series of Theological Lectures, which have remained unpublished to this day (though they are being edited for the forthcoming 'Collected Coleridge').[1]

The wedding of S. T. C. and Sara Fricker took place at St Mary Redcliffe on October 4, 1795. Two days later, S. T. C. wrote to Cottle, from their jasmine-and-myrtle-covered cottage at Clevedon, asking him to send at once a list of household requirements, in which 'a bible' figures in between 'two large tin spoons', and 'a keg of porter'. During this brief idyll his bride was the 'pensive Sara' of *The Eolian Harp*, and he can tell Thomas Poole (Oct. 7, 1795) of his happiness 'united to the woman, whom I love best of all created Beings'.

[1] They appeared in the 'Collected Coleridge' in 1971, after this book was finished and therefore too late for me to do more than refer my readers to this excellent edition (see above, p. 49, footnote 2).

CHAPTER IV

THE WATCHMAN; GODWIN; THELWALL

JAMES GILLMAN tells us, in his life of *S. T. Coleridge* (1838), that Coleridge had 'recorded that he was a Socinian till twenty-five'. But the truth is, I think, that his mind was like quicksilver, and did not set, for the convenience of biographers, into rigid moulds of time or season. Thus, as is well known, he was preaching Unitarian sermons in 1796 and 1797, and as late as January 1798 he preached the Shropshire sermon described by Hazlitt, and was then on the point of entering the Unitarian ministry. But even while his head was most active his heart kept itself alive by feeding upon Boehme and the mystics, and it had never ceased to draw nutriment from the deeper sources of Platonism and Christianity. Coleridge could never have shrunk into any sort of sectarian conformity; and by following his letters and notebooks one can watch his myriad-mindedness at work, bursting one barrier after another on the way to self-knowledge—or, as someone has said, in the process of 'growledge'.

In the *Biographia Literaria* he says of the time when he was preparing *The Watchman* (i.e. late 1795 and early 1796):

I set off on a tour to the North, from Bristol to Sheffield, for the purpose of procuring customers, preaching by the way in most of the great towns, as a hireless volunteer, in a blue coat and white waistcoat, that not a rag of the woman of Babylon might be seen on me. For I was at that time *and long after* [my italics], though a Trinitarian (i.e. ad normam Platonis) in philosophy, yet a zealous Unitarian in religion; more accurately, I was a *psilanthropist*, one of those who believe our Lord to have been the real son of Joseph, and who lay the main stress on the resurrection rather than on the crucifixion. O! never can I remember those days with either shame or regret. For I was most sincere, most disinterested! My opinions were indeed in many and most important points erroneous; but my heart was single.[1]

Gillman throws some light on the *ad normam Platonis* when he explains that Coleridge at this time 'could admit the Logos', while retaining doubts about the accepted doctrines of Incarnation and Atonement. He could accept that God from all eternity had ordained the existence of an emanation from Himself which, in the fulness of time, should be united to a human body, but he could not then abide the idea of vicarious payment or expiation. He later came to believe, says Gillman, that the difference in his *metaphysical* notions from those of most Unitarians was what contributed to his 'final re-conversion to the whole truth in Christ'.[2]

In his letters of January-February 1796, describing the 'Watchman' tour (mostly addressed to Josiah Wade), the 'republican' tone is still predominant. Worcester was hopeless, he says; in this cathedral city, 'the Aristocrats are so numerous and the influence of the Clergy so extensive'. Birmingham, as would be expected, was more responsive; he preached twice there, to about 1400 people, 'and my sermons, (great part extempore) were *preciously peppered with Politics*'. Indeed these 'sermons' must have been thinly disguised *Conciones ad Populum*, for as he tells the Rev. John Edwards[3] (Jan. 29) 'my *Sermons* spread a sort of sanctity over my *Sedition*'. It was at Nottingham that an 'Aristocrat' scoffed at the motto on *The Watchman* prospectus 'That all may know the truth, and that the truth may make us free—A *Seditious* beginning! quoth he—Sir! said Mr. Fellowes—the motto is quoted from another Author— Poo! quoth the Aristocrat—what Odds is it whether he wrote it himself or quoted it from any *other seditious Dog?*'

At Derby he met Dr Erasmus Darwin, 'the everything, except the Christian': the most widely-informed and original man in Europe, in Coleridge's view. Yet on the subject of religion Darwin was a conventional infidel:

[1] *BL*, I, p. 114.   [2] cf. *op. cit.*, pp. 91 ff. and 225.
[3] Unitarian Minister at Birmingham.

I heard all his arguments, and told him that it was infinitely consoling to me, to find that the arguments which so great a man adduced against the existence of a God and the evidences of revealed religion were such as had startled me at fifteen, but had become the objects of my smile at twenty. . . . He boasted that he had never read one book in defence of *such stuff*, but he had read all the works of infidels! . . . Dr. Darwin would have been ashamed to have rejected Hutton's theory of the earth without having minutely examined it . . . but *all at once he makes up his mind* on such important subjects, as whether we be the outcasts of a blind idiot called Nature, or the children of an all-wise and infinitely good God. . . . These subjects are unworthy a philosopher's investigation. He deems that there is a certain *self-evidence* in infidelity, and becomes an atheist by intuition.[1]

How quickly Coleridge's mind was growing and taking shape appears from his changed attitudes to Priestley and Godwin during the spring of 1796. In March he is asking the Rev. J. Edwards:

How is it that Dr. Priestley is not an atheist?—He asserts in three different Places, that God not only *does*, but *is*, everything.— But if God *be* every Thing, every Thing is God—which is all, the Atheists assert. . . . Has not Dr. Priestley forgotten that *Incomprehensibility* is as necessary an attribute of the First Cause, as Love, or Power, or Intelligence?[2]

Not quite 'all the atheists assert', but Coleridge has already perceived how pantheism, so alluring to emancipated minds like his, merges into atheism. If God 'is every thing', without remainder, there is nothing specially divine anywhere; all the atheist wants is to drop the 'if' clause and keep the concluding statement.

As for Godwin, the clearest avowal is the letter to 'Caius Gracchus' (*Watchman* No. V, April 2, 1796) in which he replies to a hostile review[3] by a Godwinian who thought *Political Justice* 'a deep Metaphysical Work though abstruse', tending 'to meliorate the condition of Man'. The

[1] *CL*, 99.   [2] *Ibid.*, 112.
[3] In the *Bristol Gazette*, March 24, 1796.

54

reviewer had been stung by Coleridge's anti-Godwinian article in *Watchman* III entitled 'Modern Patriotism'; here, Coleridge had delivered himself of the following sentiments:

> You have studied Mr. Godwin's Essay on Political Justice; but to think filial affection folly, gratitude a crime, marriage injustice, and the promiscuous intercourse of the sexes right and wise will not make you a Patriot. Your philosophy is the pimp of your sensuality. You must condescend to believe in a God, and in the existence of a Future State![1]

And now, in the letter to 'Gracchus', after some preliminary skirmishing, he repeats:

> I do consider Mr. Godwin's principles as vicious; and his book as a Pander to Sensuality. Once, I thought otherwise—nay, even addressed a complimentary sonnet to the Author, in the Morning Chronicle, of which I confess with much moral and poetical contrition, that the lines and the subject were equally bad.... You deem me an *Enthusiast*—an Enthusiast, I presume, because I am not quite convinced with yourself and Mr. Godwin that mind will be omnipotent over matter, that a plough will go into the field and perform its labour without the presence of the Agriculturist, that man may be immortal in this life, and that Death is an act of the Will!!!

He writes like a mature sage admitting the errors of his youth, but in fact it was little more than a year since he had composed that sonnet.[2]

Further light on Coleridge's rapid swing away from Godwin is shed by the Notebooks of 1795-96. In her notes on Notebook entry 174 (G. 169) Miss Coburn says that Coleridge 'repeatedly attacked Godwin' in the (unpublished) Theological Lectures of 1795; and she quotes from Lecture III of this series:

> We find in Jesus nothing of that Pride which affects to inculcate benevolence while it does away with every home-born Feeling by which it is produced and nurtured.

---

[1] *EOT*, I, p. 135.
[2] The last six lines appeared in a letter to Southey, Dec. 17, 1794 (*CL*, 75), and the complete sonnet in the *Morning Chronicle*, Jan. 10. 1795.

Referring to Notebook entry 174 itself, we find, in a list of projected works (? Dec. 1795-Jan. 1796) the following:

> Hymns to the Sun, the Moon, and the Elements—six hymns.— In one of them to introduce a dissection of Atheism—particularly the Godwinian System of Pride. Proud of what? An outcast of blind nature ruled by a fatal Necessity—Slave of an ideot Nature!

Coleridge borrowed Cudworth from the Bristol lending library in May-June 1795 (and again Nov.-Dec. 1796), and this study of the celebrated seventeenth-century champion of 'spirit' against Hobbesian materialism and determinism would inevitably have furnished him with ammunition against Godwin. Cudworth is probably the source of the phrase 'outcast of blind Nature' (cf. the almost identical phrase quoted from *CL*, No. 99 above); and Cudworth, therefore, together with Berkeley (cf. NB 174 again: 'a bold avowal of Berkley's [*sic*] System!!!!!') must be reckoned among the luminaries which were then drawing the growing-point of Coleridge's mind back in its true and native direction.

Coleridge's *Poems on Various Subjects* were published by Cottle on April 16, 1796. Sending a copy to Thelwall (who had been imprisoned in the Tower and tried for treason in 1794), he fears that Thelwall will 'find much to blame in them—much effeminacy of sentiment, much faulty glitter of expression'. But 'I build all my poetic pretentions on the Religious Musings'—which he wishes Thelwall could read with the same pleasure as 'the atheistic Poem of Lucretius':

> A Necessitarian, I cannot possibly disesteem a man for his religious or anti-religious Opinions—and as an *Optimist*, I feel diminished concern.—I have studied the subject deeply and widely —I cannot say, without prejudice: for when I commenced the Examination, I was an Infidel.[1]

One must allow for Coleridge's habit (noted above) of adapting his tone to his correspondent; to Thelwall, 'infidel' would have been congenial, whereas to his brother George

[1] *CL*, 122.

and many others he would not have admitted the imputation. Nor had he ever, except in a superficial sense, been truly an 'infidel', I think. Similarly, after reading the remarks (just quoted) about 'blind Nature' and 'fatal Necessity', one may well question his right to go on calling himself a 'Necessitarian'. But we surely allow some flexibility of opinion to any mortal?—all the more, then, to such a protean mind as Coleridge's.

By May 4, 1796 he is telling Poole that he has two alternative plans for the future. The first is to study German (which he says he has already begun), to translate 'all the works of Schiller', and then to go and study at Jena. He would bring back with him 'all the works of Semler and Michaelis, the German Theologians, and of Kant, the great German Metaphysician'; and finally set up 'a School for 8 young men at 100 guineas each', and perfect them in universal knowledge, and wisdom. The second plan, which came nearer to fulfilment, was, 'to become a Dissenting Parson and abjure Politics and carnal Literature'. Here a scruple nags him: 'Preaching for Hire is not right'; he might be forced to go on professing what he no longer believed, '*if ever* maturer Judgment with wider and deeper reading should lessen or destroy my faith in Christianity'. Evidently he then considered his Christian faith to be unshaken; and, as we know, deeper draughts from the Pierian spring sobered, not intoxicated, him.

In reply to Thelwall, a more formidable critic than the *Bristol Gazette* reviewer, Coleridge is again defending his anti-Godwinian article in a letter of May 13, 1796. He vehemently protests that on Godwin's principles there is no logical ground for condemning adultery and promiscuity, and that to disapprove of such things is no mere Christian or non-conformist prejudice. Suddenly remembering to whom he is writing, he slips in '*Guilt* is out of the Question —I am a Necessarian, and of course deny the possibility of it.' But (luckily) a letter is not the place for 'reasoning'— and anyway he will be publishing a 'Critique on the New Philosophy' at some time unspecified. There are several very interesting asides in this letter, e.g. this on Godwin:

I was once and only once in Company with Godwin—He appeared to me to possess neither the strength of intellect that discovers truth, or the powers of imagination that decorate falsehood—he talked futile sophisms in jejune language.

Or this on poetry:

> . . . but why so violent against *metaphysics* in poetry? Is not Akenside's a metaphysical poem?[1] Perhaps, you do not like Akenside—well—*but I do*—and so do a great many others—Why pass an act of *Uniformity* against Poets?

Which leads to the most interesting thing of all:

> A very dear friend of mine, who is in my opinion the best poet of the age[2] . . . thinks that the lines from 364 to 375[3] and from 403 to 428[4] [of 'Religious Musings'] are the best in the Volume—indeed worth all the rest—And this man is a Republican and at least a *Semi*-atheist.

The important thing about a man is what he is, not what he *thinks*. 'Believe me, Thelwall!' he cries (in a later letter, June 22, 1796), 'it is not his Atheism that has prejudiced me against Godwin; but Godwin who has perhaps *prejudiced* me against Atheism'. 'Let me see you,' he goes on, 'and then I shall be able to show love to an Atheist, as I already do towards Deists, Calvinists or Moravians (By the by, *are* you an Atheist?)'. His postscript to this letter is characteristic:

> PS. We have an hundred lovely scenes about Bristol, which would make you exclaim—O admirable *Nature*! and me, O Gracious *God*!

The religious tone deepens in the letters of September 1796—though this, it is true, may be partly the outcome of two very special events: the birth of his first child, and the

---

[1] Not, of course, in the twentieth-century sense of the term. Coleridge means here 'a poem dealing with metaphysical topics'.

[2] Wordsworth, whom he had met the previous autumn.

[3] About Milton, Newton, Hartley and Priestley.

[4] 'Ebullient with creative Deity', etc. The lines are differently numbered in *PW* I, pp. 123 and 124-5.

tragedy of Lamb's mother. Of the first, he writes to Poole (Sept. 24):

> It's name is DAVID HARTLEY COLERIDGE.—I hope, that ere he be a man, if God destine him for continuance in this life, his head will be convinced of, and his heart saturated with, the truths so ably supported by that great master of Christian Philosophy.

As for the tragedy, one's sympathies are divided between Lamb in the agony of his grief and Coleridge in his daunting task of writing, at his friend's request, 'as religious a letter as possible'. He did his best, and did it with his usual impulsive generosity of heart. If in such an extremity he overdid the religious unction—as Lamb himself came later to feel—he can be forgiven; and Lamb was deeply grateful for the letter (Sept. 28), which, he said, was 'an inestimable treasure to me'.

Along with this deepening of religious feeling came a revulsion from revolutionary politics—indeed, from politics altogether. The pantisocratic dream has faded, and is replaced by a passionate desire for rural seclusion and simplicity—a longing strengthened, no doubt, by Charles Lloyd (now living with the Coleridges), a youth 'greatly averse from the common run of society'. 'I am anxious', writes S. T. C. to Lloyd's father (Oct. 15, 1796):

> that my children should be bred up from earliest infancy in the simplicity of peasants, their food, dress, and habits completely rustic.

Politics and politicians are now viewed as 'a set of men and a kind of study . . . highly unfavourable to all Christian graces'. Accordingly:

> I have snapped my squeaking baby-trumpet of sedition, and have hung up its fragments in the chamber of Penitences.[1]

Later the same autumn (Nov. 13) he tells Thelwall that he is 'daily more and more a religionist'. We can believe

---

[1] Coleridge remembered phrases of his own coining, when they stood for something important to him. The 'baby-trumpet' appears again in *CL*, 238, March 10(?), 1798.

this, while wincing when he also says that his 'Answer to Godwin' 'will appear now in a few weeks'. To the elder Lloyd (Nov. 14) he defends his scheme of rural retirement, which was soon to take shape at Nether Stowey. Lloyd had evidently warned him that such a life might prove 'monastic rather than Christian'; but 'shall I not be an Agriculturist, an Husband, a Father, and a *Priest* after the order of *Peace*? an *hireless* Priest?' I might, he says, be a Unitarian minister or a politician; but 'the Voice within' vetoes both.

One of the best letters of this autumn is that of November 19 to Thelwall, in which he gives a well-known self-portrait including both physical and mental traits:

> my face, unless when animated by immediate eloquence, expresses great Sloth, and great, indeed almost ideotic, good nature. 'Tis a mere carcass of a face: fat, flabby, and expressive chiefly of inexpression . . . my gait is awkward, and the walk, and the *Whole Man* indicates *indolence capable of energies*.—I am, and ever have been, a great reader—and have read almost every thing—a library-cormorant—I am *deep* in all out of the way books, whether of the monkish times, or of the puritanical aera. . . . Metaphysics and Poetry, and 'Facts of Mind'—(i.e. Accounts of all the strange phantasms that ever possessed your philosophy—dreamers from Tauth [Thoth] the Egyptian to Taylor the English Pagan) are my darling Studies. . . . I love chemistry . . . but I *will* be (please God) an Horticulturist and a Farmer. I compose very little—and I absolutely detest composition.

His request to Thelwall to get him books in London shows the trend of his reading at this time: Iamblichus, Proclus, Porphyry, Julian, Sidonius Apollinaris and Ficino's Plotinus. Less than a month later (Dec. 11) he is writing another letter of religious consolation, this time to Benjamin Flower (the Cambridge publisher):

> I have known affliction, yea, my friend! I have been myself sorely afflicted, and have rolled my dreary eye from earth to Heaven, and found no comfort, till it pleased the Unimaginable High and Lofty One to make my Heart more tender in regard of religious feelings. My philosophical refinements, and metaphysical Theories

lay by me in the hour of anguish, as toys by the bedside of a Child deadly-sick.

He then recurs to the oft-promised 'answer to Godwin', which he now hopes to publish 'shortly after Christmas'. It was:

> designed to shew not only the absurdities and wickedness of *his* System, but to detect what appear to me the defects of all the systems of morality before and since Christ, and to shew that wherein they have been right, they have exactly coincided with the Gospel, and that each has erred exactly where and in proportion as, he has deviated from that perfect canon. My last Chapter will attack the credulity, superstition, calumnies, and hypocrisy of the present race of Infidels.

At the end of this letter he mentions, with horror, a recent 'book of horrible Blasphemies' by 'a young man of fortune', who 'after a fulsome panegyric adds that the name of *Godwin* will soon supersede that of Christ—Godwin wrote a letter to this Man, thanking him for his *admirable* work, and soliciting the honour of his personal friendship!!!—' A withdrawal of interest in the destiny of nations, particularly of France, is the natural corollary of this transition: 'I am out of heart with the French . . . my curiosity is worn out'.

Coleridge's letters to Thelwall at this period are of more than ordinary interest. Thelwall held strong views about poetry and about religion, views mostly the reverse of Coleridge's own; and this friendly tension put him on his mettle. He replied in a letter of Dec. 17, 1796 (No. 164) to some carpings of Thelwall's against Bowles, against Old Age and against Christianity. I will not linger over the first two topics, except to mention the admirable aside about his own poetry and how it got written:

> I feel strongly, and I think strongly; but I seldom feel without thinking, or think without feeling. Hence tho' my poetry has in general a *hue* of tenderness, or Passion over it, yet it seldom exhibits unmixed and simple tenderness or Passion. My philosophical opinions are blended with, or deduced from, my feelings: and this, I think, peculiarizes my style of Writing. And like every thing else, it is sometimes a beauty, and sometimes a fault. But do not let us

introduce an act of Uniformity against Poets—I have room enough in *my* brain to admire, aye and almost equally, the *head* and fancy of Akenside, and the *heart* and fancy of Bowles, the solemn Lordliness of Milton, and the divine Chit chat of Cowper.

'Felt thought', often supposed to have been the perquisite of 'Donne and his school' and to have been first detected and defined by T. S. Eliot and his followers, is here already described by Coleridge—quite unaffectedly, and without pomp and circumstance. It is a pity his catholicity of taste is less easy to parallel in our own times.

As for Christianity, it appears that Thelwall had been sneering at it and expressing contempt for it, as a 'mean' religion, teaching 'Morals for the Magdalen and Botany Bay'. First, Coleridge observes gently that contempt is always evil, and 'a good man ought to speak *contemptuously* of nothing'. He then reduces Christian belief to two tenets: that there is a Father in Heaven, and that there is a future state of reward or punishment. 'This is the Christian *Religion*', he says, 'and all of the Christian *Religion*.' If the second half of this statement causes any eyebrow to be raised, one must remember that Coleridge is writing to an embittered left-wing atheist, and is therefore trying to be 'honest to God'. After glancing at the argument by testimonial—'this Religion was believed by Newton, Locke, and Hartley, after intense investigation'—he has no difficulty in scouting the imputation of 'meanness'; he does it, characteristically, first by illustrating the sublimity of Christian imagery from the Book of Revelation, Milton, the Epistle to the Hebrews; and then by arguing for the all-inclusiveness and loftiness of Christian ethics. It is in this same letter that, in a footnote on 'godliness', he uses the phrase (and spelling): 'the most unintelligible Emanuel Kant'.

The next letter to Thelwall (No. 170) was written on Dec. 31, 1796—the very day the Coleridges moved to Nether Stowey. Yet in spite of this upheaval Coleridge's mind is soaring high enough to be capable of a very important distinction: that between two opposed theories of Life:

Dr Beddoes, and Dr Darwin think that *Life* is utterly inexplicable, writing as Materialists—You, I understand, have adopted the idea that it is the result of organized matter acted on by external Stimuli.—As likely, as any other system; but you *assume* the thing to be proved—the 'capability of being stimulated into sensation' as a *property* of organized matter—now, 'the Capab.' etc. is *my* definition of *animal Life.*

'Matter' first, as a primary datum, with 'life' somehow superinduced upon it from without? or an 'Idea' first, a 'capability', expressing itself through 'matter'? Coleridge is already firmly on the side of the second. He soon relapses here, however, into banter and irony, as befits a letter-writer:

Now as to the Metaphysicians, Plato says, it is *Harmony*—he might as well have said, a fiddle stick's end—but I love Plato—his dear *gorgeous* Nonsense! And I, *tho' last not least,* I do not know what to think about it—on the whole, I have rather made up my mind that I am a mere *apparition*—a naked Spirit!—And that Life is I myself I! which is a mighty clear account of it.

CHAPTER V

WORDSWORTH; SHREWSBURY; ALFOXDEN

FROM June 1797 onwards Coleridge's letters, like his life, were quickened and enriched by the friendship and companionship of Wordsworths, William and Dorothy. S. T. C. may have met Wordsworth again at Bristol in March, and Wordsworth visited him at Stowey on the way back to Racedown. But the real beginning of their threefold partnership was on that 6th of June 1797 when Coleridge, having preached at Taunton and thence tramped across to Racedown, 'leaped over a gate and bounded down a pathless field' into the presence of Wordsworth and his sister. If I were writing a biography I should wish here to quote, and enlarge upon, their comments on each other—for this wonderful meeting influenced not only the poets themselves but the whole course of nineteenth-century English poetry. But I must be content with a mere glance at Dorothy's description of Coleridge:

> He is a wonderful man. His conversation teems with soul, mind, and spirit. At first I thought him very plain, that is, for about three minutes: he is pale and thin, has a wide mouth, thick lips, and not very good teeth, longish loose-growing half-curling rough black hair. But if you hear him speak for five minutes you think no more of them. His eye . . . speaks every emotion of his animated mind; it has more of the 'poet's eye in a fine frenzy rolling' than I ever witnessed.[1]

Coleridge's of Wordsworth:

> I speak with heart-felt sincerity and (I think) unblinded judgement, when I tell you, that I feel myself a *little man by his* side; and yet do not think myself the less man, than I formerly thought myself. . . . T. Poole's opinion of Wordsworth is—that he is the greatest Man, he ever knew—I coincide.[2]

[1] *WEL*, 61, June 1797.   [2] *CL*, 190 (to Cottle, June 8, 1797).

—and Coleridge's of Dorothy (written while the Wordsworths were staying with him at Nether Stowey).[1]

> Wordsworth and his exquisite Sister are with me—She is a woman indeed!—in mind, I mean, and heart—for her person is such, that if you expected to see a pretty woman, you would think her ordinary—If you expected to find an ordinary woman, you would think her pretty!—But her manners are simple, ardent, impressive . . . her eye watchful in minutest observation of nature— and her taste a perfect electrometer—it bends, protrudes, and draws in, at subtlest beauties and most recondite faults.[2]

And how did this affect the pensive Sara? It was the end of her brief idyll of married bliss—and, through her, of Coleridge's. Henceforward he will prefer the company of the Wordsworths to any other, and will leave home whenever possible to be with them. Dorothy, in utter innocence, must have been a sore trial to Sara; her mere presence showed up, for the first time perhaps, the true poverty of her relationship with her husband. For Dorothy not only admired (and surely loved) him, but entered eagerly into all those interests and pursuits which she (Sara) could never share.

At Racedown Wordsworth and Coleridge had exchanged readings of their respective tragedies, *The Borderers* and *Osorio*; and it is worth noting that these were the most considerable works written by both before they knew each other intimately and saw each other often. At the same time Coleridge heard what then existed of *The Ruined Cottage*; and it was very soon afterwards that he became capable of a blank verse almost as pure as Wordsworth's. *This Lime-tree Bower* was sent to Southey in a letter (No. 197) of about July 17—a letter in which he also discusses 'natural emotion' *versus* 'buckram' in a young poet's diction, and repeats that 'Wordsworth is a very great man—the only man, to whom *at all times* and *in all modes of excellence* I feel myself inferior'.

A letter to his Unitarian minister-friend at Bristol, the Rev. J. P. Estlin (July 23), shows his politico-religious poise at that moment. In religion, it is 'fruits' that matter,

---

1 They arrived on July 2.
2 *CL*, 195 (to the same, *c*. July 3).

rather than tenets. He cannot 'as yet' reconcile his intellect to the 'sacramental rites', and therefore cannot without hypocrisy perform or receive the Lord's Supper. But he is content to keep quiet about this, and not make it an arguing-point. As for politics, he is wearied with it 'even to soreness' and observes that he 'never knew a passion for politics exist for a long time without swallowing up, or absolutely excluding, a passion for Religion'. To this growing disgust for politics, the attitude of the Somersetshire gentry towards him and Wordsworth must have contributed something; the 'Aristocrats' (as he still calls them when writing to Citizen John Thelwall) 'seem determined to persecute *even Wordsworth*' (No. 202, Aug. 19); and soon after (No. 204, Aug. 21) he writes to Thelwall begging him not to come and live in their neighbourhood:

> Very great odium T. Poole incurred by bringing *me* here—my peaceable manners and known attachment to Christianity had almost worn it away—when Wordsworth came and he likewise by Poole's agency settled here—You cannot conceive the tumult, calumnies, and apparatus of threatened persecutions which this event has occasioned round about us. If *you* too should come, I am afraid, that even riots and dangerous riots might be the consequence —*either* of us separately would perhaps be tolerated—but *all three* together—what can it be less than plot and damned conspiracy—a school for the propagation of demagogy and atheism?

Later (No. 209, Oct. 14) lamenting his inability, through lack of money and influence, to help Thelwall, he says 'I suppose that at last I must become a Unitarian minister as a less evil than starvation'. But he is at once deflected into a rhapsody on the One and the Many, ending characteristically with yearnings for an age-long lotus-dream:

> I can *at times* feel strongly the beauties you describe, in themselves, and for themselves—but more frequently *all things* appear little . . . the universe itself—what but an immense heap of *little* things? I can contemplate nothing but parts, and parts are all *little*—!—My mind feels as if it ached to behold and to know something great—something *one and indivisible*—and it is only in the

faith of this that rocks or waterfalls, mountains or caverns give me the sense of sublimity or majesty!—But in this faith *all things* counterfeit infinity!

One moment, when, 'struck with the deepest calm of Joy', he had attained a vision of unity in multiplicity, had been celebrated in *This Limetree Bower my Prison*—from which he now quotes some lines:

> On the wide Landscape gaze till all doth seem
> Less gross than bodily, a living Thing
> Which acts upon the mind, and with such Hues
> As cloath th' Almighty Spirit, when he makes
> Spirits perceive his presence!

'It is but seldom', he goes on,

> that I raise and spiritualize my intellect to this height. . . . I should much wish, like the Indian Vishna [Vishnu] to float about along an infinite ocean cradled in the flower of the Lotos, and wake once in a million years for a few minutes—just to know that I was going to sleep a million years more.

I am not taking sides here in the dispute about the dating of *Kubla Khan*, but whether (as E. L. Griggs guesses) he had written it just before this letter, or whether (as others think) it was the following year, the kinship of the visionary mood is apparent. It appears again in the following letter (No. 210, Oct. 16), the fourth of the autobiographical series addressed to Poole, in which he tells how in his childhood's reading and star-gazing his mind had been 'habituated *to the Vast*':

> I never regarded *my senses* in any way as the criteria of my belief. I regulated all my creeds by my conceptions not by my *sight*. . . . Those who have been led to the same truths step by step thro' the constant testimony of their senses, seem to me to want a sense which I possess—They contemplate nothing but *parts*—and all *parts* are necessarily little—and the Universe to them is but a mass of *little things* [cf. p. 13 above].

Towards the end of 1797 Coleridge was compelled by sheer lack of coin to face up to the question of a subsistence —the cottage-garden at Nether Stowey, from which he had hoped (or pretended to hope) so much, having proved as delusive as the pantisocratic furore of which it was the last dying ember. Of the three possible schemes that presented themselves, the first—that of running a school with Basil Montagu—came to nothing; and Coleridge was left with the alternatives of journalism or the Unitarian ministry. There were objections to both: newspaper-work was repugnant to 'a man who would wish to preserve any delicacy of moral feeling'; and, as we have already seen, the ministry might compromise a scrupulous conscience and 'warp the intellectual faculty'. But in the event another dilemma confronted him: he received, almost simultaneously, an invitation to the Unitarian ministry at Shrewsbury, and a 'draft' for £100 from the brothers Josiah and Tom Wedgwood to enable him to decline it. After several days of distracted thought he accepted the draft, and then almost immediately returned it on receiving confirmation of the Shrewsbury post. No sooner had he arrived at Shrewsbury and begun his probationary sermons than the Wedgwoods returned to the charge with a more munificent offer: £150 a year for life—or until the shipwreck of their fortunes, which seemed an unlikely event. I am not concerned now with the high-minded casuistry with which Coleridge convinced himself that he could best benefit the human race and serve the cause of true Christianity by accepting the Wedgwood annuity. As we know, he did accept it, with perhaps dubious consequences to his morale. But some interesting points emerged during his debate with his own conscience. In returning the £100 draft—i.e. while he was still opting for the ministry—he made the following statement to Josiah Wedgwood (*CL*, No. 217, Jan. 5, 1798):

> . . . not only without any design of becoming an hired Teacher in any sect but with decisive intentions to the contrary I have studied the subject of natural and revealed Religion—I have read the works of the celebrated Infidels—I have conversed long, and seriously, and dispassionately with Infidels of great Talents and information—and most assuredly, my faith in Christianity has been confirmed rather than staggered. In teaching it therefore, at present,

whether I act *beneficently* or no, I shall certainly act bene*volently*. . . .
The *necessary* creed in our sect is but short—it will be necessary
for me, in order to my continuance as an Unitarian minister, to
believe that Jesus Christ was the Messiah—in all other points I
may play off my intellect *ad libitum*.

After the die was cast, he told Estlin (No. 221, Jan. 16,
1798):

> To the cause of Religion I solemnly devote my best faculties—
> and if I wish to acquire knowledge as a philosopher and fame as a
> poet, I pray for grace that I may continue to feel what I now feel,
> that my greatest reason for wishing the one and the other, is that
> I may be enabled by my knowledge to defend Religion ably, and
> by my reputation to draw attention to the defence of it—I regard
> every experiment that Priestly [*sic*] made in Chemistry, as giving
> *wings* to his more sublime theological works.

It is salutary, I think, when reading modern Coleridge
critics to whom his religion is 'irrelevant', or a tiresome extra,
to remember that to Coleridge himself it was the *raison
d'être* of everything else. And on a very different (and lower)
level of reflexion, it does no harm—as a corrective to critical
over-sophistication—to note the place occupied by *The
Ancient Mariner* in the poet's own thoughts in letter No. 218
(to Estlin, Jan. 6, 1798):

> I am now utterly without money [and I am in debt to the tune
> of £18. 11. 0]. This is all I owe in the world: now in order to pay
> it I must borrow ten pound of you, 5£ of Mr. Wade, and will sell
> my Ballad to Phillips who I doubt not will give me 5£ for it. . . .

Reflect, too, that during the half-year represented by the
correspondence I have latterly been quoting from, *Christabel*
Part I, the *Ancient Mariner* and probably *Kubla Khan* had
slipped into existence.

After deciding in favour of the Wedgwood annuity, he
wrote to Isaac Wood (one of the Shrewsbury Unitarians):

> I have an humble trust, that many years will not pass over my
> head before I shall have given proof in some way or other that active
> zeal for Unitarian Christianity, not indolence or indifference, has

been the motive of my declining a local and stated settlement as preacher of it.[1]

Wordsworth's comment on the annuity may not have expressed quite the same degree of confidence: 'I hope the fruit will be as good as the seed is noble'.[2]

Another point which readers and critics of the present age would do well to notice is that Coleridge, Wordsworth, Thomas Poole—and, shall we say, the whole literary and literate fraternity of that era—took it absolutely for granted, that the only aim of a writer's life was 'to benefit mankind'. This comes out quite unselfconsciously in a remark to Cottle (No. 235, March 7, 1798):

> The Giant Wordsworth—God love him!—even when I speak in terms of admiration due to his intellect, I fear lest tho[se] terms should keep out of sight the amiableness of his manners—he has written near 1200 lines of a blank verse [*The Recluse*], superior, I hesitate not to aver, to any thing in our language which any way resembles it. Poole . . . thinks of it as likely to benefit mankind much more than any thing Wordsworth has yet written.

There can be no doubt that Wordsworth's presence near by, and the constant intercourse between Alfoxden and Nether Stowey, greatly affected the colouring of Coleridge's mind, and the tone of his feelings, during the spring of 1798. If any further evidence be needed beyond what is generally known, we have plenty in the letters of that time. Wordsworthian phrases are recurrent, and the Wordsworthian cast of mind begins to predominate. In particular there are echoes of that part of *The Excursion* Book IV which is known to belong to the Racedown-Alfoxden period (lines 1207-74). For example, 'So build we up the Being that we are' (now line 1264 of Book IV) seems to appear as follows:

1. To Cottle (No. 235, March 7, 1798):

> By past experiences we build up our moral being.

[This phrase occurs just before the passage, just quoted above, about 'the Giant Wordsworth'.]

[1] Cf. *CL*, I, p. 377.   [2] Cf. *CL*, I, p. 377.

2. To John Wicksteed (No. 237, March 9, 1798):

But regret is a waste of our faculties—from the past experiences we constitute the present moral existence.

3. To the Rev. George Coleridge (No. 238, March 10, 1798):

Governments are more the *effect* than the *cause* of that which we are.

But this last letter, to his parson brother at Ottery St Mary, is of more than ordinary interest; it marks a crucial point of transition in Coleridge's thought—a transition, moreover, in accord with the Wanderer's advice for Correcting Despondency. First he dissociates himself from the 'moral and intellectual habits' of the so-called 'Philosophers and Friends of Freedom', both in France and in England. He believes himself 'utterly untainted with French Metaphysics, French Politics, French Ethics and French Theology'. He sees now (as above) that it is an error to attribute to governments any 'talismanic influence' over our lives; we get the governments our frailty, and our Original Sin, produce and deserve; all rulers are as bad as they dare to be. So he repeats, in a much larger context and with a greater weight of meaning, the phrase he had already used in October 1796 in writing to Charles Lloyd's father (cf. above, p. 59):

I have snapped my squeaking baby-trumpet of Sedition.

Feeling alienated now from the complexities of political intrigue, he goes on:

I have for some time past withdrawn myself almost totally from the consideration of *immediate* causes, which are infinitely complex and uncertain, to muse on fundamental and general causes—the 'causae causarum'.

He then paraphrases, and finally quotes from, the reclusedoctrine of the Giant Wordsworth:

I devote myself to such works as encroach not on the antisocial passions—in poetry, to elevate the imagination and set the affections in right tune by the beauty of the inanimate impregnated, as with a living soul, by the presence of Life—in prose, to the seeking with patience and a slow, very slow mind 'Quid sumus, et quidnam victuri gignimur'—What our faculties are and what they are capable of becoming.—I love fields and woods and mountains with almost a visionary fondness—and because I have found benevolence and quietness growing within me as that fondness has increased, therefore I should wish to be the means of implanting it in others—and to destroy the bad passions not by combating them, but by keeping them in inaction.

> Nor useless do I deem
> These shadowy Sympathies with things that hold
> An inarticulate Language: for the Man
> Once taught to love such objects, as excite
> No morbid passions, no disquietude,
> No vengeance and no hatred, needs must feel
> The Joy of that pure principle of Love
> So deeply, that, unsatisfied with aught
> Less pure and exquisite, he cannot chuse
> But seek for objects of a kindred Love
> In fellow-natures, and a kindred Joy.
> Accordingly, he by degrees perceives
> His feelings of aversion softened down,
> A holy tenderness pervade his frame!
> His sanity of reason not impair'd,
> Say rather that his thoughts now flowing clear
> From a clear fountain flowing, he looks round—
> He seeks for Good and finds the Good he seeks.
>   Wordsworth

A further stage in Coleridge's approach to spiritual self-knowledge is marked in a letter to Estlin (No. 243, May 14, 1798). He has just been 'supplying' the (Unitarian) pulpit for Dr Toulmin at Taunton, and a train of thought is started by the tragic death of Toulmin's daughter. The father has borne his grief like a 'true practical Christian' and this leads Coleridge to feel his own backwardness in 'practical religion'—a phrase by which he here means, quite simply, the regular practice of prayer and Scripture-reading as a duty. The most interesting sentence is this:

> But tho' all my doubts are done away, tho' Christianity is my *Passion*, it is too much my *intellectual* Passion: and therefore will do me but little good in the hour of temptation and calamity.

A similar note is struck in another letter, written the same day to Poole, whose brother Richard was on his death-bed:

> I have found Religion and *commonplace Religion too*, my restorer and my comforter.

Prayer for others seems to have scriptural sanction:

> and tho' my Reason is perplexed, yet my internal feelings impel me to a humble Faith, that it is possible and consistent with the divine attributes.

Writing a few days later (May 18) to Estlin, he refers guardedly to the state of Wordsworth's beliefs at that time. After declaring Wordsworth to be 'a tried good man' as well as a great one, he says that 'on one subject we are habitually silent—we found our data dissimilar, and never renewed the subject'. It is Wordsworth's practice:

> to convey all the truth he knows without any attack on what he supposes falsehood, if that falsehood be interwoven with virtues or happiness—he loves and venerates Christ and Christianity—I wish, he did more. . . .

CHAPTER VI

GERMANY; GRETA HALL

ON September 16, 1798, Coleridge, together with William and Dorothy Wordsworth, sailed from Yarmouth for their winter in Germany. Not France now, but Germany: the land of philosophy and theology and science, the land where Englishmen were worshipped, where Nelson's victories were acclaimed, and where national feeling would eventually rise up against French militarism and dictatorship.

I do not propose to dwell upon this adventure. The Wordsworths cannot have derived much benefit from it; they lived in comparative isolation at Goslar, cut off from Coleridge by distance, and from German society by their shyness and ignorance of the language. Coleridge himself learnt little during his ten months' absence which he could not have learnt at home; the foreign travel, the Göttingen lectures, the collecting of materials for a notional life of Lessing, served mainly, one feels, to perpetuate the illusion of work-in-progress, and blind him to the reality of wasted time and dissipated energies. Still, it certainly was important for him to learn German, and this he did, probably with much greater speed and effectiveness in Germany than he could have done anywhere else. But he knew his own weakness:

> That is the disease of my mind—it is comprehensive in it's conceptions and wastes itself in the contemplation of the many things it might do! I am aware of the disease, and for the next three months, if I cannot cure it I will at least suspend it's operation.[1]

'What have I done in Germany?' he asks, in a letter to Josiah Wedgwood not long before his return:

[1] *CL*, 269, Jan. 4, 1799, to Poole.

I have learnt the language . . . attended the lectures on Physiology, Anatomy and Natural History . . . made collections for an history of the Belles Lettres in Germany before the time of Lessing . . . very large collections for a Life of Lessing . . . I chose the Life of Lessing . . . because it would give me an opportunity of conveying under a better name, than my own will ever be, opinions, which I deem of the highest importance. . . . For these last 4 months, with the exception of last week in which I visited the Harz I have worked harder than, I trust in God Almighty, I shall ever have to work again—this endless Transcription is such a body-and-soul-wearying Purgatory!—I shall have bought 30 pounds worth of books (chiefly metaphysics, and with a view to the one work, to which I hope to dedicate in silence the prime of my life). . . .[1]

The effective confrontation with Kant and Schelling, which so powerfully influenced him later (and nineteenth-century English thought through him), did not take place in Germany, but at Keswick when he opened his packing-cases of books. But the intellectual kinship he felt with Lessing is significant, for in Lessing many of the lineaments of the mature Coleridge are already apparent. Like Coleridge, Lessing was in revolt against the aridity of eighteenth-century thought, and pushing forwards to a nineteenth-century standpoint, using *literary* perceptions and experience to fertilize his judgments of philosophical systems. In particular, he laid down many of the positions about biblical interpretation which Coleridge later adopted in *Confessions of an Inquiring Spirit*: he 'invented' the 'Coleridgean' word 'bibliolatry'[2]; he urged that Christianity existed before the New Testament; that the Bible 'contains' what belongs to religion but much else besides, and that no infallibility is to be ascribed to the 'much else'; that Christianity is not true *because* the evangelists and apostles taught it, but that they taught it *because* it is true; and that the authority of Scripture rests, not upon any miraculous inspiration, but

---

[1] *CL*, 283, May 21, 1799.

[2] Though, as the Rev. H. St J. Hart points out, S. T. C. may have met the word in John Byrom (d. 1763), who used it twice. Cf. Hart's introduction to his edition of *Confessions* (1956), p. 7.

upon its own intrinsic truth—that in it which (as Coleridge afterwards said) 'finds' us. Coleridge certainly absorbed these views and made them his own, and they entered so closely into his developing thought that much later, when he came to write the *Confessions*,[1] he seems to have incorporated some material from his Lessing transcripts. The parallels are so close (sometimes almost verbal) that the pious J. H. Green, at the instigation of S. T. C.'s daughter Sara, wrote an introduction in which these are set forth, and Coleridge's originality vindicated (1849—the 2nd edition).[2]

The autumn of 1799 produced little to our present purpose, but I will pick out a few 'landmark' passages and phrases from the letters and notebooks of that period. The fragment to Wordsworth (*CL*, 290, *c*. Sept. 10) is familiar and oft-quoted; it marks pretty accurately the stage Coleridge's political views had now reached, and his sense of Wordsworth's poetic mission to the age:

> My dear friend, I do entreat you go on with 'The Recluse'; and I wish you would write a poem, in blank verse, addressed to those, who, in consequence of the complete failure of the French Revolution, have thrown up all hopes of the amelioration of mankind, and are sinking into an almost epicurean selfishness, disguising the same under the soft title of domestic attachment and contempt for visionary *philosophes*. It would do great good. . . .

Spinoza, the Great Alternative of his pre-Kantian and pre-Christian (i.e. 'orthodox') thought, still has him in thrall. On Sept. 30 he tells Southey that in spite of domestic chaos —floods, fatigue, rheumatics, a fretful child, and the 'hovel' smelling of fumigatory sulphur—he, 'sunk in Spinoza', remains 'as undisturbed as a Toad in a Rock'. This same letter contains one of the early references to his projected *magnum opus*, though he does not here indicate its nature. He is not, he says, 'in a poetical Mood', and moreover is 'resolved to publish nothing with my name till my Great

[1] First published posthumously, 1840, ed. H. N. Coleridge.
[2] See also James Martineau, *Essays, Reviews and Addresses*, vol. I (1890): 'Lessing's Theology and Times'.

Work'. Next month comes another premonitory note: a hint of conjugal infelicity. Considering his state of mind when he married, it is I think remarkable that the first four years had passed with no apparent—at least no avowed—rift. But the magnetism of the Wordsworths, pulling him away from his wife, dragging him (as it may well have seemed to her) right away to Germany; his over-long absence there, including the heartbreaking time of Berkeley's death; and his relapse, after returning, into apparent torpor or drift ('sunk in Spinoza')—all this strained Sara's belief in him to breaking point. And now S. T. C. was clearly hankering after the North, whither his idols had gone. This explains a phrase like this (to Southey, Oct. 15):

> the Wife of a man of Genius who sympathizes effectively with her Husband in his habits and feelings is a rara avis with me. . . .

Less than a week later he was off with Cottle to join the Wordsworths at Sockburn. After this came about a fortnight's walking in the Lake District with Wordsworth. This was S. T. C.'s first sight of Lakeland, and his response was immediate and rapturous. Any notion of Coleridge as 'debarred from Nature's living images' should be finally dispelled by reading his Notebook entries about this and later experiences of northern scenes. He shows, in fact, preternatural sensitiveness of response to natural beauty and accuracy in rendering it; he lives himself into the objects observed with Keatsian intensity, and reproduces them, sometimes as symbols of a mood or a thought, but often simply for their own sakes, 'disimprisoning the soul of fact'. Here are a few examples:

> River Greta near its fall into the Tees—Shootings of water threads down the slope of the huge green stone—The white Eddy-rose that blossom'd up against the stream in the scollop, by fits and starts, obstinate in resurrection—It *is the life* that we live. (*CN*, I, 495.)
>
> The solemn murmur of the unseen river far in the distance behind us—and the silence of the Lake (*ibid.*, 510).
>
> On the top of Helvellin, first the Lake of Grasmere like a sullen

Tarn, then the black ridge of mountain—then as upborne among the other mountains the luminous Cunneston Lake—(515).

Distance removing all sense of motion or sound painted the waterfalls on the distant crags (534).

Brooks in their anger (541).

a little below Placefell a large Slice of calm silver—above this a bright ruffledness, or atomic sportiveness—motes in the sun?—Vortices of flies? (549).

Starlings in vast flights drove along like smoke, mist, or anything misty without volition—now a circular area inclined in an arc—now a globe—now from a complete orb into an elipse and oblong—now a balloon with the car suspended, now a concaved semicircle and still it expands and condenses, some moments glimmering and shivering, dim and shadowy, now thickening, deepening, blackening! (582).

By November 24, 1799 Coleridge was back at Sockburn with the Hutchinsons. That dry statement conveys nothing of the tremendous import of that date for Coleridge. What happened that day affected the whole flow of his emotional life for more than a decade; on that day he fell in love with Sara Hutchinson. Four years later he wrote in a Notebook:

Nov. 24th—the Sunday—Conundrums and Puns and Stories and Laughter—with Jack Hutchinson—Stood up round the Fire, et Sarae manum a tergo longum in tempus prensabam, et tunc temporis, tunc primum, amor me levi spiculo, venenato, eheu! et insanibili,[1] etc (1575).

From that time on, and for many years to come, Coleridge's heart was riven by this hopeless yearning, and there can be no understanding of the story of those years unless we remember this. In November 1799, as he explicitly says, he did not know of the attachment between Wordsworth and Sara's sister Mary.

The first half of 1800 was spent in London: writing

---

[1] ... and I held Sara's hand from behind for a long time; and it was then, then for the first time, that love [pierced me] with its swift arrow—poisoned, alas! and incurable.

political leaders for Daniel Stuart's *Morning Post*, reporting House of Commons debates, translating *Wallenstein*, and staying with the Lambs at Pentonville. In April, and again in June-July, he was paying month-long visits to the Wordsworths at Dove Cottage; by the end of July he and his family were installed at Greta Hall, Keswick. City life appalled him; his house-hunting in Somerset proved fruitless; and the magnetism of the North was finally irresistible.

A letter to Southey and a later one to T. Wedgwood (Dec. 19, 1799 and Jan. 2, 1800, 303 and 309) show that he had been meeting Godwin and Humphry Davy in London. His attitude to Godwin—always a useful barometer of Coleridge's mental climates—is at this time amused and condescending; he despises Godwin as thinker, but relents towards him as a human being. Speaking of Charles Danvers, he says:

> 'God bless him, to use a vulgar Phrase'—This is a quotation from Godwin who used these words in conversation with me and Davy—the pedantry of atheism tickled me hugely.—Godwin is no great Thing in Intellect; but in heart and manner he is all the better for having been the Husband of Mary Wolstonecraft—(303).

To Southey he confides a degree of marital infelicity not self-admitted so openly until he had known 'Asra' (Sara Hutchinson):

> Indoles vero quotidiana, et Sympathiae minutiores, meis studiis, temperamento, infirmitatibus eheu! minime consentiunt—non possumus omni ex parte felices esse[1] (Feb. 12, 1800, 317.)

To the Rev. J. P. Estlin, his old Unitarian friend at Bristol, he writes as if he were still himself an ardent Unitarian (March 1, 1800). He deplores the policy of sending sons of Unitarian Dissenters to the 'Established and Idolatrous Universities'. If they don't learn infidelity there they will certainly learn 'Indifference to all Religions but the Religion

---

[1] But indeed her everyday disposition, and her sympathies in lesser details, are at complete variance with my studies, my temperament and—alas!—my infirmities; [so that] it is not possible for us to be thoroughly happy.

of the *Gentleman*' and 'a deep *Contempt* for those Dissenters among whom they were born'.

> We Dissenters (for I am proud of the Distinction) have somewhat of a simple and *scholarly* formality, perhaps . . . but with the young men at Oxford and Cambridge '*the Gentleman*' is the all-implying Word of Honor—a thing more blasting to real Virtue, real Utility, real Standing forth for the Truth in Christ, than all the Whoredoms and Impurities which this Gentlemanliness does most generally bring with it (323).

The Unitarian tone and stance evidently persisted long after the date given by Gillman (and S. T. C. himself)—1797—but once again one must allow for Coleridge's chameleonism: he was writing to a Unitarian minister. He would not have sent to Estlin what he had written in his Notebook six months before—that incomparable saying:

> Socinianism Moonlight—Methodism etc. A Stove!
> O for some Sun that shall unite Light and Warmth!
> *(CN*, I, 467.)

Who better fitted than himself to unite them! To attempt it was his life's task.

So great was his longing to escape from London ('I would to God, I could get Wordsworth to re-take Alfoxden—') that he told Poole he had refused an offer by Stuart of half shares in the *Morning Post* and the *Courier*, an offer worth some £2000 a year:

> but I told him, that I would not give up the Country, and the lazy reading of Old Folios for two Thousand Times two thousand Pound—in short, that beyond £250 a year, I considered money as a real Evil—at which he stared (328, March 21).

I am, I hope, second to none in my love and admiration for Coleridge, but I cannot be deaf to the faint sound of Skimpolism in this 'heroic' avowal of unworldliness by one who was becoming increasingly dependent on others for the support of himself and his family.

His letters from Greta Hall in late July are full of ecstatic descriptions of the view from his study window: unquestionably the finest in England, and well-fitted—if any scenery could do it—to inspire and incite him. If it did neither, at least it *ex*cited him, as his letters and notebooks (now full of exhilarated and detailed accounts of walks and scenes) abundantly show.

> my God! what a scene—! Right before me is a great *Camp* of single mountains—each in shape resembles a Giant's Tent. . . .
>
> a wilderness of mountains, catching and streaming lights or shadows at all times. . . .

Alas, what actually followed was nine months of recurrent illnesses, variously described as 'gout', 'rheumatic fever', etc., with opium gaining firmer and firmer hold.

And these physical ills were aggravated—who shall say how far caused?—by subtle poisons working in his soul; some consciously avowed, others not. There was the fatal and enduring lack of domestic accord—not much spoken of just now, when the arrival of Derwent was near—there was his longing for the inaccessible Sara Hutchinson. And, though he did not yet allow a whisper to escape him, or perhaps even a thought to form in his mind—there must have been a painful intensification of his sense of inferiority to Wordsworth. He still looked up to Wordsworth with glad self-abasement and true worship, but there are signs of strain (though not a word of criticism) during the summer and autumn of 1800 as it became clear that Wordsworth was going to publish the new two-volume edition of *Lyrical Ballads* under his own name, and finally without *Christabel*. He begins to talk of giving up poetry:

> I abandon Poetry altogether—I leave the higher and deeper kinds to Wordsworth, the delightful, popular and simply dignified to Southey; and reserve for myself the honourable attempt to make others feel and understand their writings, as they deserve to be felt and understood. (To Tobin, 351, Sept. 17, 1800).

The diplomatic reasons for the exclusion of *Christabel* are given in two letters, one to Humphry Davy (Oct. 9) and the other to Josiah Wedgwood (Nov. 1). *Christabel* had grown too long and too 'impressive', and 'was so much admired by Wordsworth, that he thought it indelicate to print two volumes with *his name* in which so much of another man's was included' (*The Ancient Mariner* was retained in Vol. I, though Wordsworth had picked holes in it; also *The Foster-Mother's Tale*, *The Nightingale*, *The Dungeon* and *Love*); moreover, *Christabel* was 'discordant' with Wordsworth's own style, and opposed to the principle of giving imaginative value to 'incidents of common life'. Not a word of the complementary principle (Coleridge's own) of inducing 'suspension of disbelief' in *super*natural incidents. A somewhat franker nuance appears in a remark of Wordsworth to Longman: 'I found that the Style of this poem was so discordant from my own that it could not be printed along with my poems with any propriety'.[1] On Dec. 17 Coleridge tells Thelwall:

> As to Poetry, I have altogether abandoned it, being convinced that I never had the essentials of poetic Genius, and that I mistook a strong desire for original power (369).

Shortly before this he had told Stuart that he had 'not a spark of ambition', and that 'my taste in judging is far, far more perfect than my power to execute'.

> He [Wordsworth] is a great, a true Poet—I am only a kind of a Metaphysician. (To Wrangham, 371, Dec. 19, 1800).

This ebbing of faith in his own powers as a poet is a central theme in our story, since it was partly this which led him to 'abstruse research'—to that plunge into metaphysics and introspection which shaped his later thought. I will therefore pursue the subject a little further before reverting to chronological order.

About a year before the 'Dejection' letter to Asra (April 4, 1802) he is already brooding on the 'see-not-feel' motif in a letter to Godwin (March 25, 1801):

> I have been, during the last 3 months, undergoing a process of intellectual *exsiccation*. In my long illness I had compelled into hours of Delight many a sleepless, painful hour of Darkness by chasing

[1] Quoted by E. L. Griggs, *CL*, I, p. 362n.

down metaphysical Game. . . . You would not know me . . . I look at the Mountains (that visible God Almighty that looks in at all my windows) I look at the Mountains only for the Curves of their outlines. . . . The Poet is dead in me—my imagination (or rather the Somewhat that had been imaginative) lies, like a Cold Snuff on the circular Rim of a Brass Candlestick. . . . If I die, and the Booksellers will give you anything for my Life, be sure to say— 'Wordsworth descended on him, like the $\tau\nu\hat{\omega}\theta\iota$ $\sigma\epsilon\alpha\nu\tau\acute{o}\nu$ from Heaven; by shewing to him what true Poetry was, he made him know, that he himself was no Poet'.

This stream of feeling, running through caverns of the sub-conscious for years, and (more's the pity) reinforced by bitter waters of resentment and jealousy, bubbled up long after in many a place, e.g. in 1818 when he speaks of the Wordsworths'

> cold praise and effective discouragement of every attempt of mine to roll onward in a distinct current of my own—who *admitted* that the Ancient Mariner and the Christabel . . . were not without merit, but were abundantly anxious to acquit their judgements of any blindness to the very numerous defects.[1]

The recrudescence of Coleridge's friendly feeling towards Godwin is a curious fact of this period; since their recent meetings in London his heart had somewhat warmed to-wards the man, though not to his ideas and principles. Some of his best descriptions of the incomparable mountain-view from Greta Hall are sent to Godwin. So is a request for the loan of £10—a mark of true confidence, and one which Godwin, on the principles of *Political Justice*, must have been glad to honour (he did, and Coleridge actually repaid him). But more to our purpose are some moral and philosophical problems he puts before Godwin. The birth of Derwent Coleridge (Sept. 14, 1800) raised the question (until recently it would not have arisen) whether to have him baptized—and Hartley too, while we were about it. In some moods of large tolerance he thinks he can allow it. 'But then another fit of moody philosophy attacks me':

---

[1] Quoted E. L. Griggs, *op. cit.*, p. 631.

> I look down at my doted-on Hartley . . . he is the darling of the Sun and of the Breeze! Nature seems to bless him as a thing of her own! . . . Then I say, Shall I suffer the Toad of Priesthood to spurt out his foul juice in this Babe's face? Shall I suffer him to see grave countenances and hear grave accents, while his face is sprinkled, and while the fat paw of a Parson crosses his Forehead? (352).

A very late example of Coleridge's older anti-establishment rhetoric!—but there is a touch of ironic bravado in it, and after all it was meant for Godwin's eye. In the end Derwent was christened in a hurry, because he seemed likely to die.

He also poses Godwin with some of the profound queries he is beginning to raise about the relations between Thinking, Words and Things: should not the old antithesis between Words and Things be abolished, 'elevating, as it were, words into Things, and living Things too'? But indeed these problems announce themselves in many of the letters of this new year (1801); they are premonitory snatches of the great theme which will soon dominate the Coleridgean orchestra. On religion he addresses Thelwall in the liberal style proper to that correspondent:

> You entirely misunderstand me as to religious matters.—You love your wife, children, and friends, you worship nature, and you dare hope, nay, have faith in, the future improvement of the human Race—this is true Religion; your notions about the historical credibility or non-credibility of a sacred Book, your assent to or dissent from the existence of a supra-mundane Deity, or personal God, are absolutely indifferent to me . . . I hold my faith—you keep your's (Jan. 23, 1801, CL, II, 376).

Could a theologian of the 1960s say more—or less?
On Feb. 1 he writes to Poole:

> I hope, that shortly I shall look back on my long and painful illness only as a Storehouse of wild Dreams for Poems, or intellectual Facts for metaphysical Speculation. Davy in the kindness of his heart calls me the Poet-philosopher—I hope, Philosophy and Poetry will not neutralize each other, and leave me an inert mass. But I talk idly—I feel, that I have power within me; and I humbly pray to the Great Being, the God and Father who has bidden me 'rise

and walk' that he will grant me a steady mind to employ that
health of my youth and manhood in the manifestation of that power
(377).

On the crest of this wave of new hope he tells Davy
(Feb. 3) that his thoughts on 'the affinities of the Feelings
with Words and Ideas' ought to issue in a book about poetry
which 'would supersede all the Books of Metaphysics hitherto written, and all the Books of Morals too. . . . Every poor
fellow [he subjoins] has his proud hour sometimes—and
this, I suppose, is mine.' Perhaps this was self-compensation
for having let slip, into Wordsworth's hands, the writing of
the Preface to the new edition of *Lyrical Ballads*? Though,
as we know, he urged Wordsworth to write it, Coleridge
knew that the Preface was 'half the child of his own brain';
and yet he may also have known that he would have been
incapable of finishing it in time.

CHAPTER VII

KANT; THE 'DEJECTION' ODE

THE spring of 1801 was a crucial moment in the growth of Coleridge's thought; it was then that Kant took hold of him 'as with a giant's hands'. But Kant would never have taken such possession if Coleridge's own mind had not long been gathering momentum for a total break with a (to him) sterile tradition, including his own past self, and his youthful idols and enthusiasms: Locke, Hartley, Priestley, Bruno, Behmen and above all Spinoza. Life had not yet taught him the need for Christian orthodoxy, nor had he yet fully worked out its metaphysical meanings. But he began now to understand why the 'corpuscular' philosophy is the 'philosophy of death', and why all pantheisms, however alluring to the young aspiring mind, turn later to dust and ashes (see above pp. 16-17).

I have called Spinoza (p. 76 above) 'the Great Alternative' in all Coleridge's pre-Kantian and pre-Christian thought, and we saw that late in 1799 he was still 'sunk in Spinoza'. Even when he had rejected pantheism as fatal to true religion and destructive of freewill and moral responsibility, Coleridge continued to revere Spinoza, both for his personal saintliness and for the intellectual grandeur of his system. And not only he, but a cohort of romantic philosophers found inspiration in this once-despised and much-maligned thinker—formerly labelled 'atheist', but now seen as 'the God-intoxicated man'. No wonder—at a time when not Coleridge alone, but all speculative Europe, was smitten with a longing for the Great, the Whole and the Indivisible, hoping to find the One in the Many and the All, and feeling the presence of One Life, within us and without—no wonder that then, Spinoza's majestic vision of One Substance, of which matter and mind are both modifications, proved irresistible. It was Lessing who had said 'There is no other philosophy than the philosophy of Spinoza'. Why, then, would it no longer do?

For Coleridge it would no longer do because it led, by one of the two possible routes (really the same route) to atheism and the death of the Will. To atheism, because where God is everywhere he is nowhere in particular; where he is All in All, he is not transcendent; where he is abstract Law he is not personal or gracious or loving; where he is the author of all things, he is the author of evil as well as good. To the death of the Will, because all is fixed, rigid and fore-ordained in the scheme of divine determinism; God alone Is, and Acts, and Wills—I am naught. Substitute 'Nature' or 'Matter' for 'God', and the same end is reached along the materialist instead of the Spinozistic route. And Coleridge came to believe that the philosophy of Locke and Hartley and Priestley, for all their religiosity, led along this road to dusty death. He must therefore cling to Plato, Kant and Christianity; and his reasons for rejecting Spinoza were akin to his reasons for rejecting Unitarianism. Both were infected with pride and vanity; the pride of intellect and the vanity of the unregenerate heart; both substituted a cold impersonal abstraction—a 'ground of the Universe'—for the living God of Christianity.

> 'Socinianism Moonlight—Methodism etc. A Stove!
> O for some Sun that shall unite Light and Warmth.

So Coleridge wrote twice in his Notebooks (1799 and 1802: *CN*, I, 46 and 1233); this union was to have been the main *motif* of that *opus maximum* of which we begin to hear in 1799, and hear more continually as the years go by.

The early months of 1801 were for Coleridge a period of intense study and metaphysical speculation, partly undertaken to escape from pain, domestic infelicity, and self-reproach for his opium-habit—now acknowledged to be an addiction. Another motive (in addition to this, and his need to overthrow the metaphysical Apollyon) was to satisfy the Wedgwoods that he had not been wasting his time and talents, and their money. The first outcome, then, of his intellectual marathon was a series of four letters to Josiah

Wedgwood (*CL*, 381-4), in which he aims to show that Hobbes, Locke and Hume do not deserve the reputation they have enjoyed. Locke's *Essay*, he claims, is only a prolix paraphrase on Descartes; and his famous attack on 'innate ideas' shows that he was superficial, and misunderstood Descartes' real meaning (which was that we are born, not with a set of ready-made ideas, but with a mind capable of responding to experience in certain necessary ways).

Coleridge summed up the outcome of all this in letters to Poole, written in March (1801). After an interval of 'most intense study', he says,

> I have not only completely extricated the notions of Time, and Space; but have overthrown the doctrine of Association, as taught by Hartley, and with it all the irreligious metaphysics of modern Infidels—especially, the doctrine of Necessity . . . Truths so important, which came to me almost as a Revelation . . . I shall propose to Longman . . . a work on the originality and merits of Locke, Hobbes, and Hume, which work I mean as a *Pioneer* to my greater work.[1]

A week later he writes again to Poole:

> My opinion is this—that deep Thinking is attainable only by a man of deep Feeling, and that all Truth is a species of Revelation. The more I understand of Sir Isaac Newton's works, the more boldly I dare utter . . . that I believe the Souls of 500 Sir Isaac Newtons would go to the making up of a Shakspere or a Milton . . . Newton was a mere materialist—*Mind* in his system is always passive—a lazy Looker-on on an external World. If the mind be not *passive*, if it be indeed made in God's image, and that too in the sublimest sense—the Image of the *Creator*—there is ground for suspicion, that any system built on the passiveness of the mind must be false, as a system.[2]

Here we have the heart of the matter: Coleridge's inmost nature and deepest craving demanded a mind not passive, as in the Locke tradition, but active and constituent, as in Kant; a Will not frozen in Necessity, as in Hartley, Priestley

[1] *CL*, 387 (to Poole, March 16, 1801).
[2] *CL*, 388 (March 23, 1801).

and Godwin, but free and responsible, as in Kant and Christianity; an Imagination not decorative as in Locke and the neo-classic poets, but creative in the highest sense, as in Wordsworth and his own theory; and we may add by way of anticipation, a God not identified or confused with Nature, as in Spinoza and pantheism, nor 'absentee' as in Deism and Socinianism, but at once transcendent and redemptive, as in Christianity.

I will briefly consider, at this point, which Kantian notions meant most to Coleridge; and then later illustrate their influence upon him at appropriate stages when examining his published works. First and foremost comes the principle just referred to, that the mind is not passive in perception, not a 'lazy looker-on', but active and constituent; that it 'half creates' what it perceives, or in other words that the mind imposes its own forms or 'categories' upon reality, so that we can only approach reality under those guises (time, space, etc.). For Kant himself this chiefly meant that reality, the *Ding an sich*, was not directly approachable by us; for Coleridge its importance was in vindicating the mind's inherent creativeness. Every moment of our lives we are creating, or rather half-creating (because we can only act upon something 'given') the world around us, and so he can claim for the 'primary imagination' the dignity of being the 'prime agent of all human perception'.

Next, the distinction between Reason and Understanding (*Vernunft* and *Verstand*). Coleridge quickly saw the importance of this for his defence of religious truth, and (as we shall see) used the distinction freely in *The Friend*, *The Statesman's Manual* and *Aids to Reflection*. He gave meanings of his own to 'Reason' and 'Understanding' which are not those of everyday speech; I have elsewhere tried to explain them thus:

Reason is the 'organ of the super-sensuous'; Understanding the faculty by which we generalize and arrange the phenomena of perception . . . Reason seeks ultimate ends; Understanding studies means. Reason is 'the source and substance of truths above sense'; Understanding the faculty which judges 'according to sense'. Reason is the eye of the spirit, the faculty whereby spiritual reality is spiritually discerned; Understanding is the mind of the flesh.[1]

Religion and Ethics belong to the sphere of Reason, while Understanding works legitimately on the practical level, in science and in all the affairs of mundane existence. Disaster occurs when either invades the other's province; and Coleridge, with the infidel eighteenth century behind him, was particularly anxious to protect the sphere of Reason and spiritual experience against all attacks from the 'mere' Understanding, the 'mere reflective faculty'.

Thirdly (as we saw), for Kant 'Reality', the *Ding an sich*, the noumenal world, is transcendent, and thus for ever inaccessible to the Understanding. This doctrine was in itself a safeguard against any pantheism which might tend—however unintentionally—to confuse 'God' with 'the World'. But, lastly, this transcendent world is accessible to Reason through our moral experience, through the fact of Conscience. Coleridge came to lean his whole weight upon this doctrine, and to build religious faith firmly upon a moral foundation. According to Kant, Conscience—the category 'ought'—commands us to obey always and only the law we have ourselves evolved, the law of practical reason: that we must act always by maxims which are *universally* applicable. Now this unquestioned authority of conscience, this 'categorical imperative'—what are the postulates necessary to validate it? They are God, Freedom, Immortality: God, the source and sanction of the moral law; Freedom, since without it there can be no moral choice or responsibility; Immortality, to right the wrongs and the imbalances of this imperfect world. These ideas are not rationally demonstrable, but they are 'regulative' ideas, ideas which must be postulated—taken as real—to make sense of our moral experience. Conscience therefore, and not 'reasoning', bids us accept as real those ideas without which it would itself have no meaning and no authority. We shall begin to see, when we come to *The Friend*, what use Coleridge was to make of these principles.

The letters of 1801-2 show a life and mind disordered and

[1] *Nineteenth Century Studies*, p. 29.

drifting; there is illness, opium, irresolution, misery at home ('Sara—alas! we are not suited to each other'), and continual yearnings for escape to some lotus-isle: the Azores, St Nevis—anywhere. On April 4, 1802, he sends Sara Hutchinson the long original draft of what was later *Dejection: an Ode*. On this a great deal has already been written, and it is only to my present purpose to point to one passage —admittedly the best-known and the most discussed:

> O Sara! we receive but what we give,
> And in *our* life alone does Nature live.
> Our's is her Wedding Garment, our's her Shroud—
> And would we aught behold of higher Worth
> Than that inanimate cold World allow'd
> To the poor loveless ever-anxious Crowd,
> Ah! from the Soul itself must issue forth
> A light, a Glory, and a luminous Cloud
>   Enveloping the Earth!
> And from the Soul itself must there be sent
> A sweet and potent Voice, of it's own Birth,
> Of all sweet Sounds the Life and Element.

For our present argument this is important as a stage in the undermining of Coleridge's early pantheism. Nature is no longer felt as

>   a living Thing
> Which acts upon the mind, and with such Hues
> As cloath th'Almighty Spirit, when he makes
> Spirits perceive his presence
>   [*This Lime-Tree Bower*];

nor do we hear of 'the beauty of the inanimate impregnated, as with a living soul, by the presence of Life' [*CL*, 238, March 10, 1798]. Now, Nature is cold and inanimate, dormant or indeed dead, having no inherent life and thus unable to *give* her votary anything. All that Coleridge here claims is that Nature will respond if the soul takes the initiative; there *is* something better to see than the inanimate cold world of everyday prose, but it can only be seen by a soul able to project into Nature its own energy and joy. Of course this is poetry and not a piece of metaphysical reasoning; Coleridge is not trying to 'prove *that*' anything: he is merely reporting how things feel *in the mood of dejection*. Nevertheless, such moods are recurrent, and to most people (the 'poor loveless, ever-anxious crowd') nothing higher is ever vouchsafed than the 'inanimate cold world'. It follows from this that it is not enough to lift up one's eyes to the hills; help will not come thence, but only (if at all) from God. I am sure that the mature Coleridge would have accepted this, the latest scholarly interpretation of Psalm cxxi. All the same, he would have insisted to the end that all things— Nature and Man—live, move and have their being *in* God, and that if we must not look to Nature for what Grace alone can give, Nature can at least be a *means* of Grace.

There was a vital constituent of Coleridge's religion which he did not find in Kant: the 'fact' of Original Sin. This he found in his own experience, his ever-present sense of weakness, failure and defeat; his need of redeeming grace. By 'Original Sin' he did not mean 'man's first disobedience and the fruit of that forbidden tree'; he meant that radical imperfection in human nature itself which led Paul to cry 'the evil that I would not, that I do'. Coleridge knew only too well that Kant's 'sense of duty' was insufficient; indeed, he found it a positive hindrance, since to be obliged to do anything was for him an almost certain guarantee that he would not, could not, do it. In considering the stress he came to lay on Will and Redemption, then, one cannot forget his own weakness of will and his tragic need for deliverance and renewal. None the less, we are all (including St Paul) sinners, and Coleridge's special sins—from which his acutely sensitive moral nature made him suffer a thousand times more than most men—do not diminish the value and truth of his beliefs on this matter. 'Conviction of sin' was with him (as it is with all) a pre-condition of the return to religion.

One of the first clear statements of his return is this, from a letter to George Coleridge (July 1, 1802):

> I . . . have convinced myself, that the Socinian and Arian Hypotheses are utterly untenable; but what to put in their place?

. . . I hold it probable that the Nature of the Being of Christ is left in obscurity—and that it behoves us to think with deep humility on the subject, and when we express ourselves, to be especially careful, on such a subject, to use the very words of Scripture . . . My Faith is simply this—that there is an original corruption in our nature, from which and from the consequences of which, we may be redeemed by Christ—not as the Socinians say, by his pure morals or excellent Example merely—but in a mysterious manner as an effect of his Crucifixion—and this I believe—not because I *understand* it; but because I *feel*, that it is not only suitable to, but needful for, my nature and because I find it clearly revealed.

It will illustrate the unity of Coleridge's total effort, if we set this passage side by side with one from the very next letter (to Sotheby, July 13, 1802, *CL*, 444). In the first he is revitalizing religious belief by bringing it to the test of experience; in the next he is talking about the poetic approach to reality, and making us feel, in a series of brilliant metaphors, how intense, alert and concentrated the poet's absorption in his object must be:

a great Poet must be, implicite if not explicite, a profound Metaphysician. He may not have it in logical coherence, in his Brain and Tongue; but he must have . . . the *ear* of a wild Arab listening in the silent Desert, the eye of a North American Indian tracing the footsteps of an Enemy upon the Leaves that strew the Forest—; the *Touch* of a Blind Man feeling the face of a darling Child. . . .

In both passages (as indeed in all his best work) Coleridge is proving something 'upon the pulses'—first religion, then poetry, by bringing it into immediate contact with life and feeling.

That the doctrine of the *Dejection* Ode was not a permanent creed with Coleridge is proved by a letter of the same year (1802) to Sotheby.[1] Here he is criticizing Bowles for

moralizing every thing—which is very well, occasionally—but never to see or describe any interesting appearance in nature, without connecting it by dim analogies with the moral world, proves

[1] *CL*, 459 (Sept. 10, 1802).

faintness of impression. Nature has her proper interest; and he will know what it is, who believes and feels, that every Thing has a Life of it's own, and that we are all *one Life*. A Poet's *Heart and Intellect* should be *combined*, *intimately* combined and *unified*, with the great appearances of Nature—and not merely held in solution and loose mixture with them, in the shape of formal similies. . . .

This is a germ-passage for the Imagination-Fancy distinction, as is made clear further on where he explicitly contrasts 'Imagination', or the modifying, and co-adunating Faculty' with 'Fancy, or the aggregating Faculty'. His point is here that the Hebrew poets, and second to them the English, show most of this imaginative power. In them,

> each Thing has a Life of it's own, and yet they are all one Life. In God they move and live, and *have* their Being—not *had*, as the cold System of Newtonian Theology represents, but *have*.

In Imagination, then, you have not a projection of the poet's soul into a dead Nature, giving it a semblance of life, but a genuine marriage between two living beings—the poet and Nature—resulting in a new creation which partakes of the life of both. A man quiveringly sensitive to every look on Nature's face, as his Notebooks and letters show Coleridge to have been, and one interested in those changing expressions for their own sake and not for any moral analogies—such a man (save only in moods of dejection) could not long cease to believe in the One Life, within us and without, and could not long think of Nature as cold and inanimate. Did he not at this very time (autumn 1802) write in his Notebook:

> the whole of Newlands full of a shower-mist drunk and dazzling with Sunshine . . .[1]

(to take one random example out of thousands)?

It is not necessarily 'pantheistic' to see thus into 'the life of things', or to believe in the bond between *natura naturans* and the creative spirit of man. As the writer to the Ephesians said, God is not only in all and through all, but also *over* all;

[1] *CN*, I, 1252.

and pantheism is not incurred as long as we are mindful, as Coleridge increasingly became, of this transcendence. Remembering it, Coleridge or any man may enjoy what exhilaration and renewal he can find in the works of God's hands; remembering that help comes ultimately from God, he may without heresy lift up his eyes unto the hills, since God may send his help through them. 'Even the worship of one God', he writes to his Unitarian friend Estlin,

> becomes Idolatry, in my convictions, when instead of the Eternal and Omnipresent, in whom we live, and move, and *have* our Being, we set up a distinct Jehovah tricked out in the *anthropomorphic* Attributes of Time and *Successive* Thoughts—and think of him, as a PERSON, *from* whom we *had* our Being.[1]

In the same month he wrote in his Notebook:

> Every season Nature converts me from some unloving Heresy —and will make a *Catholic* of me at last.... [2]

And a few weeks later he writes to T. Wedgwood, describing a walk over Kirkstone Pass in a fierce winter-storm:

> I never find myself alone within the embracement of rocks and hills . . . but my spirit courses, drives, and eddies, like a Leaf in Autumn: a wild activity, of thoughts, imaginations, feelings, and impulses of motion, rises up from within me—a sort of *bottom-wind*, that blows to no point of the compass, and comes from I know not whence, but agitates the whole of me. . . . The farther I ascend from animated Nature, from men, and cattle, and the common birds of the woods, and fields, the greater becomes in me the Intensity of the feeling of Life; Life seems to me then a universal spirit, that neither has, nor can have, an opposite. God is every where, I have exclaimed, and works every where; and where is there *room* for Death? . . . I do not think it possible, that any bodily pains could eat out the love and joy, that is so substantially part of me, towards hills, and rocks, and steep waters![3]

In June 1803 he outlined in detail the first part of his *opus maximum*, a history and examination of the principles of

---

[1] *CL*, 473 (Dec. 7, 1802).   [2] *CN*, I, 1302 (Dec. 19, 1802).
[3] *CL*, 484 (Jan. 14, 1803).

Logic—'*Organum verè Organum*, or an Instrument of practical Reasoning'—of which he says he can have the first half ready for the press at a fortnight's notice, and from which he hopes the reader may acquire 'not only Knowledge, but likewise *Power*'.[1]

It is interesting to find, as another milestone on the Trinitarian road, the following Notebook entry in March 1803; he summarises thus the teaching of J. Scotus Erigena:

> God is, is wise, and is living. The Essence we call Father, the Wisdom Son, the Life the Holy Spirit—and he positively affirms that these three exist only as distinguishable *Relations* . . . and he states the whole Doctrine as an invention and condescension of Theology to the Intellect of man, which must *define* and conseq. *personify* in order to understand.[2]

At the same time, and throughout the summer of 1803, he is preoccupied with the paradox of his own nature: he has *power*, but not *strength*; he is 'diseased in voluntary power' but disbelieves in 'mechanical necessity'. Yet the struggle to emerge from his eighteenth-century chrysalis goes successfully on, and a letter to Southey, on Aug. 7, shows how introspection had helped to emancipate him from Hartleian 'Associationism':

> I hold, that association depends in a much greater degree on the recurrence of resembling states of Feeling, than on Trains of Idea . . . and if this be true, Hartley's System totters . . . Believe me, Southey! a metaphysical Solution, that does not instantly *tell* for something in the Heart, is grievously to be suspected as apocryphal. I almost think, that Ideas *never* recall Ideas, as far as they are Ideas—any more than Leaves in a forest create each other's motion —The Breeze it is that runs through them; it is the Soul, the state of Feeling—[3]

[1] *CL*, 504-5 (to Godwin, June 4 and 10, 1803).
[2] *CN*, I, 1382.   [3] *CL*, 510.

CHAPTER VIII

SCOTLAND (1803); ILLNESS

ON August 15, 1803, Coleridge set out on a tour in Scotland with William and Dorothy Wordsworth. If I were writing the story of his life I should want to dwell upon this, because it was on that tour that a rift—inconspicuous as yet—first appeared in that formerly perfect triple friendship. Even in the present book, which pretends no further than to narrate the history of his thought, a biographical turning-point so important cannot be passed over.

Coleridge was very reluctant to start on this trip ('I never yet commenced a Journey with such inauspicious Heaviness of Heart . . .'). He put this down to his ill health, and fears of the consequences of driving through rain and wind in an 'Irish-Car'. But there were deeper reasons—buried or unacknowledged resentments towards the friend who had eclipsed him as poet and critic, who had owed him so much but repaid him so scantily; and perhaps deepest of all, pain in comparing his own domestic plight with Wordsworth's well-cushioned home-life. The perfect *rapport* between William and Dorothy, which once he had shared, now seemed to mock his own want of sympathetic support from Sara. After hearing Dorothy (as Kathleen Coburn well guesses) recite *Ruth* at Loch Lomond, he wrote:

> . . . tho' the World praise me, I have no dear Heart that loves my Verses—I never hear them in snatches from a beloved Voice, fitted to some sweet occasion, of natural Prospect, in Winds at Night—[1]

After little more than a fortnight, 'William proposed to me to leave them . . . I eagerly caught at the Proposal: for the *sitting* in an open Carriage in the Rain is Death to me, and somehow or other I had not been quite comfortable.' This

[1] *CN*, I, 1463.

was his explanation to his wife—to whom he also added that Wordsworth's 'Hypochondriacal Feelings keep him silent, and self-centered'.[1] Dorothy in her Journal simply ascribes the separation to Coleridge's state of health and the wet weather; Christopher Wordsworth in his *Memoirs* says that Coleridge was 'too much in love with his own dejection'. Dykes Campbell suggests that he wanted more opium than he dared absorb in front of the others; and quite likely the Wordsworths were keeping a watchful or even suspicious eye upon him. Several Notebook entries indicate that Coleridge at least thought so:

> My words and actions imaged in his mind, distorted and snaky as the Boatman's Oar reflected in the Lake—[2] [A =Coleridge; B =Wordsworth]. A. thought himself unkindly used by B.—he had exerted himself for B. with what warmth! honoring, praising B. beyond himself—etc. etc.—B. selfish—feeling all Fire respecting every Trifle of his own—quite backward to poor A.—The *up*, askance, pig look, in the Boat etc.[3]

Many years later, after the open breach with Wordsworth, and a few weeks after the formal 'reconciliation' of May 1812, Coleridge made the following insertions in his Notebook of the Scottish tour:

> My Friend ⟨O me! what a word to give permanence to the mistake of a Life! . . .⟩
> Here I left W and D ⟨utinam nonq. vidissem!⟩ . . . am to make my way alone to Edingburgh [*sic*]—⟨O Esteesee! that thou hadst from thy 22nd year indeed made *thy own* way and *alone*!⟩[4]

Thus by the autumn of 1803 he had lost much of his old, uncritical adoration of Wordsworth. He thought Wordsworth had neglected him during a two months' illness; he saw him as 'more and more benetted in hypochondriacal Fancies, living wholly among *Devotees*—having every the minutest Thing, almost his very Eating and Drinking, done for him by his Sister, or Wife'; he has dissipated too much of his poetical energy on small pieces, deserting 'his former

[1] *CL*, 514 (Sept. 2, 1803).   [2] *CN*, I, 1473.
[3] *CN*, I, 1606.   [4] *CN*, I, 1471.

98

mountain Track to wander in Lanes and allies' [*sic*].[1] Not only did Coleridge disagree with several of Wordsworth's critical opinions and poetical practices, but found himself at variance with him on weightier issues:

> A most unpleasant Dispute with W. and Hazlitt Wednesday Afternoon, Oct. 26, 1803.—I spoke, I fear too contemptuously— but they spoke so irreverently so malignantly of the Divine Wisdom, that it overset me.[2]

Evidently Wordsworth and Hazlitt had been attacking such writers as Ray, Derham and Paley for their 'pedantic' and unimaginative methods of demonstrating The Wisdom of God in the Creation, especially their quest for universal signs of 'aptitude' and 'contrivance' in Nature. Coleridge thinks this a harmless exercise by good men, and turns the tables by declaring that:

> always to look at the superficies of Objects for the purpose of taking Delight in their Beauty, and sympathy with their real or imagined Life, is as deleterious to the Health and manhood of Intellect, as always to be peering and unravelling Contrivances may be to the simplicity of the affections, the grandeur and unity of the Imagination.[3]

Hazlitt he excuses, because nothing better can be expected of so morose and unloving a temper—'But *thou*, dearest Wordsworth' . . . !

It is odd to find Coleridge taking sides with Paley and the Physico-theologians against Wordsworth; and surely no one took more delight in the beauty of natural appearances than himself. But this Notebook entry—the aftermath of a dispute, and of distaste for Hazlitt—need not be taken too seriously.

More interesting is an entry of the following day (Oct. 27) recording a conversation, while he was sitting to Hazlitt for a portrait, about the Origin of Evil. He 'forced H. to confess', he says,

[1] *CL*, 525.   [2] *CN*, I, 1616.   [3] *CN*, I, 1616.

that the metaphysical argument reduced itself to this: Why did not infinite Power *always* and exclusively produce such Beings as in each moment of their Duration were infinite; why, in short, did not the Almighty create an absolutely infinite number of Almighties?

This (and the rest of the same long entry[1]) is a good example of Coleridge's extraordinary logical insight. He pierces straight to the core of a classic piece of infidelity, and shows why we must not object to moral or physical Evil on principles which would also demand of God such absurdities as those just mentioned. In a succeeding entry (1622) he returns to the question of Evil, and scorns those who brush aside the discussion of 'old' problems like this—preferring something brand-new; the latest chemical or astronomical theory, the latest invention, or up-to-date political moves— 'Something new, something *out* of themselves—for whatever is *in* them, is deep within them, must be *old as* elementary Nature.' This leads him to an utterance which has become familiar (and famous) from its inclusion, almost verbatim, in *The Friend*, the *Biographia Literaria* and *Anima Poetae*:

> To find no contradiction in the union of old and novel—to contemplate the Ancient of Days with Feelings new as if they then sprang forth at his own Fiat—this marks the mind that feels the Riddle of the World, and may help to unravel it.

Then in the very next entry (1623)—also reproduced in *The Friend* (variatim) and *Anima Poetae*—he defends his own use of 'metaphysics', in clear antithesis to the sophisms of Hobbes, Godwin and their kin, and with allusion to the discussions by the fallen angels in *Paradise Lost*:

> What is it, that I employ my Metaphysics on? To perplex our clearest notions, and living Moral Instincts? To extinguish the Light of Love and of Conscience, to put out the Life of Arbitrement—to make myself and others *Worthless, Soul*-less, *God*-less?— No! To expose the Folly and the Legerdemain of those, who have thus abused the blessed Organ of Language, to support all old and venerable Truths, to support, to kindle, to project, to make the

[1] *CN*, I, 1619.

Reason spread Light over our Feelings, to make our Feelings diffuse vital Warmth thro' our Reason—these are my Objects—and these my Subjects. Is this the metaphysics that bad Spirits in Hell delight in?

O for a Coleridge today! For is not this sort of pronouncement exactly what we now need to hear, in these times when clever professors (often of 'Sociology') are continually perplexing our 'clearest notions' and 'moral instincts', and making it appear that individuals are the mere product of environment, having no 'arbitrement' and consequently deserving neither praise nor blame; and teaching that the moral consensus taught and maintained by Christianity for 2000 years has no special authority, but is a mere subjective 'think-so' among many others. The 'little philosopher', as Coleridge says (*CN*, I, 1758), does not 'go down into his own Nature' to refute a System: he merely juggles with it verbally. It is a chief part of Coleridge's greatness that all his best thinking and feeling come from the depths—from that deep sub-conscious well from which his best poetry is also drawn.

The poet was assuredly not dead in him at this time, in spite of his own assertions that it was so. But the poet in him spoke not in verse but in the quality of his 'felt thought', and in some of the most exquisite prose-pictures ever written. To restore 'roundness' to our image of him, and avoid the distortion and impoverishment of regarding him as a mere passage in the 'history of ideas', let me quote the following (it comes next after the above entry on 'metaphysics'):

Sat. Morn. Oct. 29. 1803. Three o'clock. The Moon hangs high over Greta, and the Bridge, on the first step of her Descent, and three hours at least from the Mountain, behind which she is to sink. . . . Yet there is no gleam, much less silver whiteness, on the Lake: simply it is easily seen; and even the Greta stretching strait in an oblique line underneath is not silver-bright, or any where brilliant; but rather the gleam of some baser Composition imitating Silver; it is a grey brightness like the colour of an ash grove in keenest December Moonlight. The Mountains are dark, low, all compact together, quiet, silent, asleep—the white Houses are bright throughout the vale, and the evergreens in the garden. The only Sound is the murmur of the Greta, perpetual Voice of the Vale.[1]

Or this other night-piece:

Wednesday Morning, 20 minutes past 2 °Clock. November 2nd, 1803. The Voice of the Greta, and the Cock-crowing: the Voice seems to grow, like a Flower on or about the water beyond the Bridge, while the Cock crowing is nowhere particular. . . . Now while I have been writing this and gazing between whiles (it is 40 M. past Two) the Break [in the clouds] over the road is swallowed up, and the Stars gone, the Break over the House is narrowed into a rude Circle, and on the edge of its circumference one very bright Star—see! already the white mass thinning at its edge *fights* with its Brilliance—see! it has bedimmed it—and now it is gone—and the Moon is gone. The Cock-crowing too has ceased. The Greta sounds on, for ever. But I hear only the Ticking of my Watch, in the Pen-place of my Writing Desk, and the far lower note of the noise of the Fire—perpetual, yet seeming uncertain—it is the low voice of quiet change, of Destruction doing its work by little and little.[2]

Was ever the moment-by-moment slipping-away of time more truly rendered?

Before the end of 1803 Coleridge had made up his mind that another winter in England would be the death of him. On Nov. 25 he tells Thelwall that he is on the point of departure for Malta or Madeira—'for I dare stay no longer in this climate'. But it was not only his ill health that urged him to flight:

my illness would not materially diminish my Happiness if I were Housemate with Love.[3]

Before he left Keswick he was reading Kant's Ethics; and it is characteristic that he fixes upon the *psychological* weakness of Kant's theory. Kant taught that reverence for the Law of Reason is a feeling generated by the rational concept itself: 'Examine this', says Coleridge, 'for in Psychology

[1] *CN*, I, 1624.   [2] *CN*, I, 1635.   [3] *Ibid.*, 1644.

Kant is but suspicious Authority.'[1] It is not enough to act conformably to the Law of Moral Reason: 'it must not only be our Guide, but likewise our Impulse—like a strong current, it must make a visible Road on the Sea. . . .'[2] In other words, a rational concept will not produce righteousness unless the Will is called into action. Without a breeze the ship is idle and becalmed—or to use a still more powerful *Ancient Mariner* image:

> Under the keel nine fathom deep,
> From the land of mist and snow,
> The spirit slid, and it was he
> That made the ship to go.

It was Coleridge's own self-knowledge that had taught him to distrust Kant here; he knew that, for him, the recognition of a *duty*, so far from generating the impulse to perform it, absolutely paralysed the will. A familiar example occurs on Jan. 9, 1804, while he was staying at Dove Cottage en route for Malta:

> All this evening, indeed all this day . . . I ought to have been reading and filling the Margins of Malthus—I had begun and found it pleasant; why did I neglect it?—Because, I OUGHT not to have done this . . . it is a deep and wide disease in my moral Nature. . . .[3]

It was illness that kept him for nearly a month at Dove Cottage, but the bliss of being nursed by Dorothy and Mary Wordsworth, 'who tended me with Sister's and Mother's Love', also encouraged him to linger on.

> O dear Sir! it does a man's heart good, I will not say, to know such a Family, but even—to know that there is such a Family. In spite of Wordsworth's occasional Fits of Hypochondriacal Uncomfortableness—from which more or less . . . he has never been wholly free from his very Childhood . . . his is the happiest Family,

---

[1] *CN*, I, 1710.   [2] *Ibid.*, 1705.

[3] *Ibid.*, 1832 (see also House, *Coleridge* (Clark Lectures 1951-52), p. 45, and AP, p. 64). Miss Coburn suggests that the 'not' has slipped in by mistake; but I think Coleridge probably meant 'I ought not to have *neglected* this'. The point remains the same either way.

I ever saw. [Wordsworth is] a happy man, not from natural Temperament ... but ... because he is a Philosopher. ...[1]

And this leads Coleridge on to one of his great pre-*Biographia Literaria* utterances about Wordsworth and about Imagination and Fancy:

> Wordsworth is a Poet, a most original Poet ... and I dare affirm, that he will hereafter be admitted as the first and greatest philosophical Poet—the only man who has effected a compleat and constant synthesis of Thought and Feeling and combined them with Poetic Forms ... and with Imagination or the *modifying* Power in that highest sense of the word in which I have ventured to oppose it to Fancy, or the *aggregating* power—in that sense in which it is a dim Analogue of Creation ... and I prophesy immortality to his *Recluse*, as the first and finest philosophical Poem, if only it be (as it undoubtedly will be) a Faithful Transcript of his own most august and innocent Life, of his own habitual Feelings and Modes of seeing and hearing.

On January 14, 1804, Coleridge—in one of those strange and sudden recoveries (like a 'resurrection') which characterized his psychosomatic disorders—rose from his sick-bed and walked the nineteen miles to Kendal through mud and drizzle in four hours and thirty-five minutes. A few days before, however, he had written these ominous words to Southey:

> In bad weather I can not possess Life without opiates ... I must go into a hot climate. ...[2]

[1] *CL*, 535 (to R. Sharp, Jan. 15, 1804).
[2] *CL*, 533.

CHAPTER IX

MALTA

UNHAPPILY the hot climate of Malta was to prove no panacea, and whereas he could tell Southey (in that same letter) that he could not so far 'detect any pernicious Effect' of opium, it was in Malta that, in his loneliness and sick longings, he first fully knew and despised himself as a hopeless addict.

In this book I am not directly concerned with the Malta episode, except in so far as the self-knowledge and remorse he experienced there contributed to his return to full Christianity.

His passion for Sara Hutchinson gnawed continually at his heart, and he felt like a ghost wandering forlornly through the world. Just before landing at Valletta, he made a soul-searing entry in his Notebook, in which, after listing his many bodily tortures, he ends with the following prayer —alas, not answered in the way he hoped:

> O dear God! give me strength of Soul to make one thorough Trial—if I land at Malta, spite of all horrors to go through one month of unstimulated Nature—yielding to nothing but manifest Danger of Life!—O great God! Grant me grace truly to look into myself, and to begin the serious work of Self-amendment— accounting to Conscience for the Hours of every Day. . . . I am loving and kind-hearted and cannot do wrong with impunity, but o! I am very very weak—from my infancy have been so—and I exist for the moment.[1]

Absence from England, for which he had longed so impatiently, now brought the realization—first experienced in Germany five years ago—that England contained all that was dear to him. And the scenery of Malta repelled him: 'O that it were only a more beautiful country!'—'Malta,

[1] *CN*, II, 2091.

alas! it is a barren Rock . . . no rivers, no brooks, no Hedges, no green fields, almost no Trees, and the few that are are unlovely.'[1]

Yet it must not be supposed that in Malta his eye and mind were torpid—far from it. Amidst all the thoughts that brought on 'agony and madness', and the ensuing 'dreadful Smothering upon my chest',[2] his senses were keenly alive to the lizards and the gulls, and the sea and the sky:

> [Lizards] glide across the sunny walk like shooting Stars, green, grey, speckled—exquisite grace of motion—all the delicacy of the Serpent and a certain dignity . . . [a lizard] turns his head and innocent eye sidelong toward me, his side above his forepaw throbbing with a visible pulse. . . .
>
> A brisk Gale, and the spots of foam that peopled the *alive* Sea most interesting combined with numbers of white Sea Gulls: so that repeatedly it seemed, as if the foam-spots had taken Life and Wing and flown up. . . .
>
> O that Sky, that soft blue mighty Arch, resting on the mountains or solid Sea-like plain: what an aweful adorable omneity in unity. . .
>
> One travels along with the Lines of a mountain—I wanted, years ago, to make Wordsworth sensible of this. . . .[3]

Indeed, as E. K. Chambers points out, about one-third of the extracts in *Anima Poetae* come from the Malta Notebooks.

Let me now call attention to some ways in which his thoughts about religion were developing. In November-December (1804) he has this entry, anticipating Tennyson's 'There lies more faith in honest doubt' etc.:

> So far from deeming it . . . criminal to spread doubt of God, immort. and virtue . . . in the *minds* of individuals, I seem to see it as a *duty*—lest men by taking the *words* for granted never attain the feeling or the true *faith*—that is, they only forbear even to suspect that the Idea is erroneous or the communicators deceivers; but do not *believe* the idea itself—whereas to *doubt* has more of faith, nay even to disbelieve—than that blank negation of all such thoughts and

---

[1] *CL*, 606 and 619.　　[2] *CL*, 602.

[3] *CN*, II, 2144, 2345-6-7 (the latter 3 reflecting the scenery of Sicily, where Coleridge spent part of the autumn of 1804).

feelings which is the lot of the Herd of Church and Meeting Trotters.[1]

Here again we see Coleridge, eager as always to supersede Death and Mechanism by Life and Organism, applying this principle to religion, and actually preferring doubt and unbelief, where these imply an active grappling with real difficulties, to the smug acceptance which never looks beyond words at the realities they stand for. Next, in an entry suggested by his reading of H. S. Reimarus, we find Coleridge in possession of an idea familiar to Pascal and to many today, but unacceptable to the deistic nature worshippers of the eighteenth century and Coleridge's own generation:

> Think of all this [i.e. Nature, the Creation] as an absolute Revelation, a real Presence of Deity—and compare it with historical traditionary religion. Two Revelations, the material and moral, and the former not to be seen but by the latter, as St Paul has so well observed—'By worldly wisdom no man ever arrived at God'; but having seen him by the moral Sense then we *understand* the outward World. . . .[2]

Following the same thought-curve is the entry of January 17, 1805, in which he speaks of 'historic faith', and of 'the necessary aid, which this lends to the wavering convictions of the Reason . . ., a Crutch may be an awkward Tool, but still the infirm want Crutches'.[3] And next he is to be seen working his way round to Trinitarian views:

> . . . to shew the unity of Jehovah, Christ, and the Dove admit the adorable Tri-unity of Being, Intellect, and Spiritual Action, as the Father, Son, and co-eternal Procedent, that these are God (i.e. not mere general Terms, or abstract ideas) and that they are one God (i.e. a real, eternal, and necessary Distinction in the divine nature, distinguishable Triplicity in the indivisible Unity).[4]

[1] *CN*, II, 2296.

[2] *CN*, II, 2326. Cf. Pascal: 'La nature a des perfections, pour montrer qu'elle est l'image de Dieu, et des défauts, pour montrer qu'elle n'en est que l'image.' (*Pensées*, ed. A. Espiard, Vol. II, p. 61.)

[3] *CN*, II, 2405.

[4] *CN*, II, 2444. In Miss Coburn's text the fourth word reads 'inanity'—surely an erratum?

In the next entry, still pursuing his approach to the Trinity along the metaphysical route, he refers to the terms used by the 'Platonic Fathers' (as quoted by Bishop Horsley): 'God, Logos and Wisdom' in place of 'Father, Son and Holy Spirit', and proceeds to elaborate on this: God is Being, the 'eternal evermore I am'. Logos is 'Reason', 'communicable Intelligibility', 'the WORD'. Lastly:

> But holy action, a Spirit of holy action . . . is verily the Holy Spirit proceeding at once from Life and Reason, and effecting all good gifts, what more appropriate Term is conceivable than *Wisdom*: which in its best and only proper sense, involves action, application, habits and tendencies of realization.

But why should the Son be both creator and redeemer, as we are taught? Because, as Logos, he is the divine energy, both creative and redemptive:

> the moment we conceive the divine energy, that moment we conceive the Λόγος.

Finally, although this may redeem,

> i.e. procure for us the *possibility* of salvation, it is only the *Spirit* of *holy Action*, manifested in the *habits of Faith and good works*, (the wings of the brooding Dove) that sanctifies us.[1]

Miss Coburn is quite right to say, in her note to this entry, 'It will be seen that Coleridge's return to orthodox Christianity' was made by 'a metaphysical rather than a historical approach'. Yet we must always remember to ask what it was that drove him to return to it at all? and the answer must be, a deepening humility and sense of his own insufficiency. It was no coincidence that his need for redeeming grace became imperative at the time when his self-esteem lay humbled in the dust. In this mood of abasement, all speculations outside orthodoxy seemed again, and more truly than ever, mere 'shapings of the unregenerate mind'.

Even at this stage, however, and for years to come, he found 'historical Christianity' a stumbling-block; Christianity as 'Idea' was more accessible to a mind like his than

[1] *CN*, II, 2445.

Christianity as 'Fact' or 'Event'. This appears clearly in the entry (*CN*, II, 2448) of February 12, 1805, in which he summarizes his escape from Unitarianism. Seven or eight years ago, he says, his mind was

> wavering in its necessary passage from Unitarianism (which as I have often said is the Religion of a man, whose Reason would make him an Atheist but whose Heart and Common sense will not permit him to be so) thro' Spinozism into Plato and St. John.

But now 'it burst upon me at once as an awful Truth. . . . No Christ, no God!'

He now feels this 'with all its needful evidence of the Understanding', and wishes to God that he could feel in his spirit the equal truth of 'No Trinity, no God' (or he may mean that he *does* believe this mentally, but still needs to conform his spirit to it more fully, and live it out). 'Unitarianism in all its Forms is Idolatry'—he can add; and it is a mere trick (of Priestley's) to 'convert' Jews and Mohammedans by simply giving 'the name of Christianity to their present Idolatry'.

> O that this Conviction may work upon me and in me, and that my mind may be made up as to the character of Jesus, and of historical Christianity, as clearly as it is of the Logos and intellectual or spiritual Christianity. . . .[1]

After gazing entranced at a night-sky ('more a Feeling than a Sight'), he breaks out:

> And did I not groan at my unworthiness, and be miserable at my state of Health, its effects, and effect-trebling Causes? O yes!— Me miserable! O yes!—Have Mercy on me, O something *out* of me! For there is no *power*, (and if that *can* be, less *strength*) in aught *within* me! Mercy! Mercy![2]

In many a Malta entry he plumbs the depths of despair, and it is needless (and indeed impertinent) to gloat over them by further quotation. Instead, I will merely glance at a few of his innumerable moments of insight or reflexion.

The difference between knowledge and 'growledge', head-thought and heart-thought, Augustan sunshine and

---

[1] *CN*, II, 2448.　　[2] *CN*, II, 2453.

romantic dimness, eighteenth-century cocksureness and nineteenth-century wonder, is here expressed as the anti-thesis between Paley-Priestley and S. T. C.:

I tell a Paleyan or Priestleyan, he is saying, about

> my *mist*, my delving and difficulty, and he answers me in a set of parrot words, quite satisfied, clear as a pike-staff,—nothing *before* and *nothing* behind—a stupid piece of mock-knowledge, having no *root* for then it would have feelings of dimness from *growth*, having no buds or twigs, for then it would have yearnings and strivings of obscurity from *growing*, but a dry stick of licorish . . . acknowledging no sympathy with this delving, this feeling of a wonder . . .[1]

Here, as so often, there are overtones from his former discipleship to Priestleyan Unitarianism, and his present emancipation therefrom.

The shocking news of John Wordsworth's death by drowning reached him on March 31, 1805. After his first flood of grief has subsided, he seeks relief from 'vain regrets' in John's own reported last words 'I have done my Duty! let her go' [the ship *Abergavenny*, of which he was captain]:

> Let us do our *Duty*: all else is a Dream, Life and Death alike a Dream. This short sentence would comprize, I believe, the sum of all profound Philosophy, of ethics and metaphysics conjointly, from Plato to Fichte (2537).

In a further meditation about Duty, soon after (2556), he makes the Kantian point that in this life, which is a state of probation, 'we are to contemplate and obey *Duty* for its own sake . . . not merely abstracted from, but in direct opposition to the *Wish*, the *Inclination*.' Only Love can so harmonize our nature that 'Duty and Pleasure are absolutely co-incident'.

Writing (in 2598) of the 'character and genius of a nation', he records a further stage in his spiritual journey:

> Let England be Sir P. Sidney, Shakespere, Spenser, Milton, Bacon, Harrington, Swift, Wordsworth, and never let the names of Darwin, Johnson, Hume, *furr* it over!—If these too must be

[1] *CN*, II, 2509.

England, let them be another England—or rather let the first be old England, the spiritual Platonic old England, and the second with Locke at the head of the Philosophers and Pope of the Poets, with the long list of Priestleys, Paleys, Hayleys, Darwins, Mr Pitts, Dundasses, etc. etc. be representative of commercial G. Britain . . .: even so Leibnitz, Lessing, Voss, Kant shall be *Germany* to me . . . and so shall Dante, Ariosto, Giordano Bruno be my Italy, Cervantes my Spain, and o! that I could find a France for my love—but ah! spite of Paschal [*sic*], Madame Guyon, and Moliere France is my Babylon, the Mother of Whoredoms in Morality, Philosophy, Taste—the French themselves feel a foreignness in these Writers— How indeed is it possible at once to *love* Paschal, and Voltaire?

Belonging to the same complex of thought-feeling, on its theological side, is the following attack upon the 'Grotian-Paleyan' type of apologetic, which sought to 'defend' Christianity by legalistic or 'secular' arguments '*ab extra*'— i.e. from outside its living centre. The right way to answer a supposed infidel is not to insist, as they had done, upon the historicity of the miracles, but to address him, thus:

> Well, Brother! but granting these miracles to have been false, or the growth of delusion at the time, and of exaggeration afterward from Reporter to Reporter, yet still all the doctrines remain binding on thee? Still must thou repent, and be regenerated, and be crucified to the flesh, and this not by thy own mere being, but by a mysterious action of the Moral world on thee, of the ordo ordinans. Still will the Trinity, the Redemption, the assumption of Humanity by the Godhead remain Truth, and still will the Faith in these Truths be the living fountain of all true virtue. . . . Believe all these so as thy Faith be not merely *real* but *actual*—Then shalt thou know from God whether or no Christ be of God—It is the importance and *essentiality* attributed to miracles that has tempted men to deny them!—They are extra-essential, tho' not useless or superfluous.[1]

Soon afterwards he is dramatizing a (real or) supposed discussion with William Taylor of Norwich (2643). If you had heard on good authority, he says, of a remedy for a

[1] *CN*, II, 2640. This passage reappears somewhat elaborated in *CL*, 631 (Oct. 4, 1806), to George Fricker.

disease from which you suffered, would you not wish it genuine, and give it a trial? Why then

> do you proceed so differently with the averred remedies of human Sorrows, the Faith in God, Virtue, Immortality! Have not these been recommended to us *probata sunt* by many wise and good men— Why, then this Scorn at the mention of them? This pleasure of Pride in your anticipation of proving them fallacies and impostures? . . . O that you had but once known, how sweet a Thing a deep Conviction is!—the blessedness of Certainty contrasted with the Bubble-bubble of *Positiveness*!

Another cross-link in the Coleridgean complex appears in 2728:

> Modern Poetry characterized by the Poets ANXIETY to be always *striking* . . . I am pleased that when a mere Stripling I had formed the opinion, that true Taste, was Virtue—and that bad writing was bad feeling.

The Malta Notebooks end on a note of despair—even a death-wish. He had come to find health and forgetfulness; he must now return home—and face his wife and loved ones with health worsened, the opium-habit confirmed, and the thought of 'Asra' (Sara Hutchinson) still gnawing his heart. In a thunderstorm he longed to be struck by lightning:

> Flash, like a Love-thought, thro' me, Death
> And take a Life, that wearies me.   (2866)

CHAPTER X

TRINITARIAN DOCTRINE; SARA HUTCHINSON

COLERIDGE was at all times a sturdy 'No Popery' man; on the question of Rome his mind was always made up. Considering the influence later ascribed to him by Newman (who numbered him amongst the awakeners of Church sentiment) his mind showed less 'negative capability' in this direction than one would have expected— less, indeed, than in any other I can think of. And so it is all the more interesting to find him, soon after his return to England,[1] foreshadowing Newman's critique on the Protestant position and the Church of England in particular. Why do we believe Article III of the Thirty-Nine, that Christ descended into Hell? It is not authorized by Scripture; yet Scripture 'containeth all things necessary to salvation' (Art. VI), and 'whatsoever is not read therein is not to be required of any man, that it should be believed as an article of the Faith'. But there is a more searching question: whence the authority of Scripture itself? Who decided which books were to be taken as canonical? Tradition! the Church!—and this, says Coleridge,[2] 'lays open to the Roman Catholics an unarmed place'.

> Strange! they will say, that Books whose authority must rely on Tradition and the decision of Councils should be supposed to preclude and supersede the *necessity* of Tradition and Church-sentence.

The weightiest unanswered question, however, is: where in the Church of England, does the ultimate authority lie in matters of faith? Who decides when there are conflicting interpretations of Scripture within the 'congregation' of the faithful? 'On what or whom', Coleridge asks, 'is the practical authority finally built?'

[1] He landed on August 17, 1806.
[2] *CN*, II, 2888.

This may be considered as one of the two or three main vantage grounds of the R. Catholics, from which their Fire commands the Eng. Church.

Sniping at the Unitarians, on the other hand, becomes so habitual with Coleridge from now on that only an occasional example need be given. A good one (belonging to the same month as the above, Oct. 1806) is the anecdote (2892) of the maid-servant who had been to hear Dr Price preach. On being asked what she thought of him, she replied 'There was neither the Poor nor the Gospel.' Coleridge comments:

> Excellent Hit on the fine *respectable* attendants of Unitarian Chapels, and the moonshine heartless Head-work of the Sermons.

It was in this autumn of 1806 that Coleridge was making up his mind how he could become a full Trinitarian. I have already cited the letter of Oct. 4 to George Fricker (631) where the main topic is miracles, but where faith in the Trinity is assumed to be the living fountain of all true virtue—miracles or no. A few days later,[1] in another letter to Fricker, he gives what amounts to a blue-print for *Aids to Reflection*. What he had said in the previous letter (cf. above, p. 111) was not intended to convey 'the whole of my Christian Faith', but only 'such doctrines, as a clear Head and honest Heart assisted by divine Grace might in part discover by self-examination and the light of natural conscience, and which *efficiently* and *practically* believed would prepare the way for the *peculiar Doctrine* of Christianity, namely, Salvation by the Cross of Christ'. Characteristically, he prays for a more living faith in the 'peculiar doctrine' than he as yet feels—though he has 'a very strong *presentiment*' of its truth. But it is in the next letter[2] that we find as concise a summary as we need of his mature credo.

The argument runs something like this. God's 'Thoughts' are more 'real' than what we call 'things'. He is a self-comprehending Being, i.e. 'he has an Idea of himself'. This Idea from all eternity co-existed with God ('begotten' of

---

[1] Oct. 9, 1806 (*CL*, 633).
[2] Oct. 13 (*CL*, 634), to T. Clarkson.

him), and so is called God's 'Son', who is the Image of God in whom the Father beholds, well-pleased, his whole Being. But, lastly, the interaction of Love between Father and Son is 'intensely real' also—so real as to constitute a Third Person, proceeding 'co-eternally both from the Father and the Son—'

and neither of these Three can be conceived *apart* nor *confusedly*, so that the Idea of God involves that of a Tri-Unity.

This, then, was how Coleridge arrived at 'No Trinity, no God'; there can be no adequate idea of God which has not this threefold structure. The Unitarian God is 'a mere power in darkness': 'no Sun, no Light with vivifying Warmth, but a cold and dull moonshine, or rather starlight, which shews itself but shews nothing else'.

In all this we certainly see Coleridge making his way towards Trinitarian orthodoxy along the high metaphysical road. But the belief was far more to him than a matter of metaphysical speculation—though, being Coleridge, he had to think out the implications of his beliefs to their remotest limits and in their most abstract inter-relationships. The point is, *why* did he undertake this great journey, if intellectual curiosity was not the only reason? The answer—and Coleridge himself repeatedly confirms it—is a deep yearning of his inmost soul for strength, support and forgiveness. He cried out for a Redeemer, and God had heard his cry. He had answered by assuming humanity himself, and laying down his life for sinners. What did this mean, translated back into theological terms? It meant the doctrine of the Trinity.

Coleridge was too great a man ever to suppose that mere head-work could take the place of living faith; he knew the difference between the intellectually 'real' and the morally 'actual'. Even while he is expounding Trinitarian doctrine to George Fricker, he insists upon the 'vital head-and-heart FAITH in these truths'; they must be made true *for you* by living them out in daily life. Ten years before, in spite of his passion for metaphysics, he had known (and he never forgot) how flimsy a support they are in times of suffering:

My philosophical refinements and metaphysical Theories lay by me in the hour of anguish, as toys by the bedside of a child deadly-sick. May God continue his visitations to my soul, bowing it down, till the pride . . . of human Reason be utterly done away.[1]

The final difficulty, that of reconciling historical Christianity with his already-accepted Logos-theology—that of accepting Jesus of Nazareth as the Logos incarnate—he overcame as soon as he had convinced himself that a historical break-through of redeeming love was a necessary climax to the whole scheme of divine administration. Thereafter, the unique fitness of Christianity to meet the spiritual needs of mortal men furnished the final proof of its truth.

The two years (Aug. 1806-Sept. 1808) between the return from Malta and residence at Allan Bank call for no detailed treatment here. But they were years of extreme emotional and physical distress, and with Coleridge, whose heart and head and body were always in close *rapport*, such a period cannot be overlooked.

On arriving in England he felt unable to face a renewal of the old miserable home life; and he knew that his time in Malta, so far from building him up in body and soul, had left him feebler in both. So he kept on postponing the evil hour, and it was not till the end of October (1806) that he at last appeared at Keswick. 'In fact', as Wordsworth wrote to Sir G. Beaumont on Sept. 8,

> he dare not go home, he recoils so much from the thought of domesticating with Mrs Coleridge, with whom, though on many accounts he much respects her, he is so miserable that he dare not encounter it.[2]

The whole story is revealed in Dorothy Wordsworth's horrified impression on meeting him again (at Kendal):

> Never never did I feel such a shock as at first sight of him. We all felt exactly in the same way—as if he were different from what

[1] *CL*, 161 (Dec. 11, 1796).
[2] *Letters of W. & D. Wordsworth* (ed. of 1967, revised by Mary Moorman), II, *The Middle Years*, Part I, No. 43 (No. 275 in de Selincourt's ed.).

we have expected to see. . . . He is utterly changed; and yet sometimes, when he was animated in conversation concerning things
removed from him, I saw something of his former self. But never
when we were alone with him. . . . His fatness has quite changed
him—it is more like the flesh of a person in dropsy than one in
health; his eyes are lost in it. . . . I often thought of Patty Smith's
remark. It showed true feeling of the divine expression of his
countenance. Alas! I never saw it, as it used to be—a shadow, a
gleam there was at times, but how faint and transitory![1]

By the end of the year Coleridge and his wife had agreed
to separate for good and all. This did not mean that they
were never to meet, but that domestic life together was
admitted by both to be impossible. Meanwhile his seven-
years-long passion for Sara Hutchinson, intensified by his
exile in Malta, held him in thrall; and what it gave him in
emotional *élan* it more than took away in frustration and
yearning. Lastly, as a crowning agony, came the jealous
suspicion (culminating on 'that miserable Saturday morning'
of Dec. 27 at Stringston near Coleorton, called by him 'THE
EPOCH')[2] that Sara Hutchinson admired—yes, loved—
Wordsworth more than himself. He knew this to be a mor-
bid fancy, a self-generated maggot in the brain, yet he could
not shake off its obsessive horror. This was the true beginning
of his break with Wordsworth, which did not occur openly
till 1810.

The story of these years is depressing enough. Coleridge
drifted on rather aimlessly, spending most of his time (after
leaving Coleorton) at Stowey and Bristol, and afterwards in
London, where he gave his first course of lectures (Jan.-June
1808, at the Royal Institution). He now recognized the full
extent and ignominy of his enslavement to opium, which
(like many others in those days) he had innocently begun
to take years ago, not as an indulgence but as an analgaesic—
never suspecting the danger of addiction ('my sole sensu-
ality was not to be in pain'). The Notebook entry 3078, for

1 *Op. cit.*, No. 48, to Mrs Clarkson (Nov. 5-6, 1806). 277 in de Selincourt's
edition.
2 *CN*, II, 2975 and 3148, and Miss Coburn's note on 2975.

instance, is a heart-broken cry of remorse at his powerless-
ness to escape from the grim cycle: pain, opium, the withdrawal horrors, then more opium to relieve the latter:

> O who shall deliver me from the Body of this Death? Mean-
> while the habit of inward Brooding daily makes it harder to confess,
> the Thing I am, to any one—least of all to those, whom I most love
> and who most love me—and thereby introduces and fosters a habit
> of negative falsehood, and multiplies the Temptations to positive,
> Insincerity. O God! let me bare my whole Heart to Dr B[eddoes?].[1]

To all this was added the misery of suspicion and jealousy
now clouding, for him, the Wordsworth circle—hitherto
his cherished place of sanctuary.

I have already suggested that the trend of Coleridge's
religious faith towards Trinitarian orthodoxy was a corollary
to his passage through the Valley of Humiliation. Therefore
we must not attach too much weight to the view of his old
Unitarian friend Estlin of Bristol, who saw this trend as a
sad symptom of decline.

> His intellect is all gone, Sir! all his genius is lost, quite lost—he
> is a mere superstitious Calvinist, Sir![2]

This is so wide of the mark as to be truly funny; yet it is
perfectly natural and understandable in one like Estlin, who
had not voyaged with Coleridge through strange seas.

Another Coleridgean trait which appears even in these
dark years is his marvellous resilience—his power to rise
suddenly out of hours of gloom and recapture some lost
pulse of feeling. Of his stay with Poole at Nether Stowey,
for example, he says:

> I have . . . received such manifest benefit from horse exercise,
> a gradual abandonment of fermented and total abstinence from
> spirituous liquors, and by being alone with Poole and the renewal
> of old times by wandering about among my dear old walks, of
> Quantock and Alfoxden, that I have now seriously set about com-
> position [for the R. I. Lectures].[3]

---

[1] Miss Coburn dates this 'before Dec. 1808'.
[2] *CL*, 679 (to Southey, Feb. 5, 1808).
[3] *CL*, 656 (to H. Davy, Sept. 9, 1807).

Similarly, although at one level, or in one mood, his feeling towards Wordsworth had changed, he could still write:

> That there is such a man in the World, as Wordsworth, and that such a man enjoys such a Family, makes both Death and my own inefficient Life a less grievous Thought to me.[1]

And his sense of sheer fun was always liable to break in. A strange gentleman called 'Lanseer' called at his London lodgings one day when he was ill in bed, and left a visiting card. When later he asked his attendant Mrs Brainbridge who this was, she answered:

> I am sure, I don't know ... but from what he said, I guess, he is a sort of a *Methody Preacher* at that Unstintution, where you goes to *spout*, Sir.[2]

[1] *CL*, 670 (to De Quincey, Feb. 2, 1808).
[2] *CL*, 669 (Feb. 1, 1808, to J. J. Morgan).

CHAPTER XI

THE FRIEND
(June 1, 1809-March 15, 1810)

FROM the beginning of September 1808 until the early summer of 1810 Coleridge was living (apart from various absences, longer or shorter) with the Wordsworths at Allan Bank, Grasmere. During that time he produced the twenty-seven numbers of *The Friend*, with Sara Hutchinson acting as his inciter and amanuensis.

The story of that time, already partly known from Coleridge's own letters and those of William and Dorothy Wordsworth, has now been fully told by Barbara Rooke in her excellent edition of *The Friend* (*The Collected Works of S. T. C.*, Routledge & Kegan Paul, 1969). There is therefore no need for me or anyone else to retell it. It is a tale of alternating fits of industry and depressive inactivity, and doubtless without the admonishing presence and watchful care of the Wordsworths and Sara Hutchinson he would not have accomplished what he did. Yet the wonder is rather that he did so much, not only in composition of a high order, but on the practical level in coping with the endless and harassing details of the actual publication: negotiating with printers, struggling to maintain supplies of paper, arranging for postage and subscriptions, etc. etc. The difficulties of producing a periodical from Grasmere in 1809-10—printer cut off by a mountain-range, paper supplies precarious, subscriptions not coming in properly, and all the rest—were more than enough to daunt even a man of robust constitution and inflexible will. And yet Coleridge, despite them all, and despite his ill-health, irregular habits and psychological obstacles, persevered valiantly and surprised his friends by the extent of his achievement. Hazlitt called *The Friend* 'an endless preface to an imaginary work', and its continual eddyings and postponements do still make it rather exasperating to read. It puzzled and disappointed many of its original readers. As Dorothy Wordsworth said, 'everywhere the power of thought and the originality of a great mind are visible, but there is wanting a happiness of manner; and the first number is certainly very obscure'. She goes on:

> I cannot enough admire his resolution in having written at all, or enough pity his sufferings before he began, though no doubt almost wholly proceeding from weakness; an utter want of power to govern his mind, either its wishes or its efforts.[1]

Wordsworth himself despaired of him at the outset, and hoped *The Friend* would never appear at all. Writing to Thomas Poole (about May 30, 1809, only a day or so before the first number came out) he says:

> I am sorry to say that nothing appears to me more desirable than that his periodical essay should never commence. It is in fact *impossible*—utterly impossible—that he should carry it on; and, therefore, better never begin it . . . I give it to you as my deliberate opinion . . . that he neither can nor will execute any thing of important benefit either to himself, his family or mankind. Neither his talents nor his genius, mighty as they are, nor his vast information will avail him anything; they are all frustrated by a derangement in his intellectual and moral constitution—In fact he has no voluntary power of mind whatsoever, nor is he capable of acting under any *constraint* of duty or moral obligation.[2]

Later, however, and for months on end, both William and Dorothy were compelled to admit that he was working hard and regularly, and doing much better than they had expected. But by February 1810, when Sara Hutchinson was about to leave them, Dorothy reports (to Lady Beaumont, Feb. 28) that 'Coleridge's spirits have been irregular of late'; he was disheartened by the 'slow arrival of payments'. Yet he was still disposed to 'fight on', and Dorothy admits that he has been 'very industrious'—in spite of periods of total inaction. 'The fact is he either does a great deal or nothing

[1] *WMY* (ed. Moorman), II, Part I, No. 167 (D. W. to C. Clarkson, June 15, 1809).
[2] *Ibid.*, No. 165.

at all.'[1] When Sara finally left, the work stopped, and (says Dorothy to Mrs Clarkson on April 12):

> I must add the truth that we are all glad she is gone. True it is she was the cause of the continuance of The Friend so long; but I am far from believing that it would have gone on if she had stayed. He was tired, and she had at last no power to drive him on; and now I really believe that *he* also is glad that she is not here, because he has nobody to teize him. . . . We have no hope of him—none that he will ever do anything more than he has already done. If he were not under our Roof, he would be just as much the slave of stimulants as ever, and his whole time and thoughts (except when he is reading and he reads a great deal), are employed in deceiving himself, and seeking to deceive others. He will tell me that he has been writing, that he has written half a Friend; when I *know* that he has not written a single line. . . . He lies in bed, always till after 12 o'clock, sometimes much later; and never walks out—Even the finest spring day does not tempt him to seek the fresh air; and this beautiful valley seems a blank to him.

She adds:

> . . . do not think that it is his love for Sara which has stopped him in his work—do not believe it: his love for her is no more than a fanciful dream—otherwise he would prove it by a desire to make her happy. No! He likes to have her about him as his own, as one devoted to him, but when she stood in the way of other gratifications it was all over.[2]

These are stern and searing words, and coming from so clear-sighted and affectionate a friend as Dorothy they cannot be discounted (as can Mrs Coleridge's shallow and unfeeling judgments—'Lord! how often you are ill', etc.). This must have been, this *was*, how Coleridge appeared as an inmate of Allan Bank, and the Wordsworths showed great love and forbearance in putting up with him for so long. How could they know what he yet had it in him to achieve: that the *Biographia Literaria*, the two *Lay Sermons*, the 1818 *Friend*, *Aids to Reflection*, the *Constitution of Church and State*, *Confessions of an Inquiring Spirit*, a portion of the *Opus*

[1] *Ibid.*, No. 184.   [2] *Ibid.*, No. 188.

maximum, several courses of lectures, and masses of miscellaneous material, were still to come?

The 1818 3-volume edition of *The Friend*, which Coleridge always called a *'rifacciamento'*, was indeed a 'remaking' of the original periodical in that the material was corrected and rearranged. But more important than this for our present purpose was the new section on morality and religion, and the revised version of his essay on *Method* (originally written as an Introduction for the *Encyclopaedia Metropolitana*). This, entitled 'Section the Second, on the Grounds of Morals and Religion and the Discipline of the Mind requisite for a True Understanding of the same', was considered by Coleridge to outweigh, in point of value, 'all my other works, verse or prose'.[1] I shall discuss here only that and other passages which are relevant to my present line of enquiry.[2]

'I do not write in this Work for the *Multitude*', Coleridge told Humphry Davy (Dec. 14, 1808), 'but for those, who by Rank, or Fortune, or official Situation, or Talents and Habits of Reflection, are to influence the Multitude. I write to found true PRINCIPLES, to oppose false PRINCIPLES, in Criticism, Legislation, Philosophy, Morals, and International Law.'[3] (For convenience I shall give references both to the old Bohn edition and to Barbara Rooke's ['*BRF*'].)

The opening sections show Coleridge typically beating about the bush. Paralysed, as ever, by the call of immediate duty, and oppressed by the weight of his own immense reading and thinking, he eddies, and wriggles, and postpones. For the first fourteen sections he might well have taken as motto his own favourite tag: *inopem me copia fecit*; or Donne's

> On a huge hill
> Cragged, and steep, Truth stands, and hee that will
> Reach her, about must, and about must goe;
> And what the hill's suddennes resists, winne so.

---

[1] Pp. 409-524 of Vol. I in B. Rooke's edition.
[2] Reasons for treating *The Friend*, 1809-10 and 1818 together are given on pp. 138-9.
[3] *CL*, 730.

He warns his readers that he will expect from them both thought and attention, and that 'thinking is neither an easy nor an amusing employment'. He will be referring them in all things to principles and fundamental truths. He digresses to condemn arrogance and presumption; he considers how truth can be 'communicated'; he discusses the liberty of the press and denounces censorship; he discusses toleration, and the ways in which the world's evil can best be counteracted. Knowledge of the truth is to be the panacea; the intellect must be habituated to clear conceptions—but the heart must be brought into play as well as the head. Deep feelings must be attached to the great controlling *Ideas*: the ideas of freedom, immortality, God. He hints, by way of anticipation, that religion is to be the ultimate goal: religion whose light is not light without heat, nor its heat warmth without light.

In the XVth essay, the cloud which has for so long been labouring up with stored thunder, begins to discharge its lightning. I am accused, says Coleridge, of 'bewildering myself and readers with metaphysics'—such as Milton's bad spirits delighted to discuss in hell. This gives him his opening; he carries the war straight into the enemy's country with an attack on Godwin ('one of the late followers of Hobbes and Hartley') and on Paley and the utilitarian moralists:

> if I had exerted my subtlety and invention in persuading myself and others that we are but living machines, and that . . . the assassin and his dagger are equally fit objects of moral esteem and abhorrence. . . .

or if (with Paley)

> I had reduced all virtue to a selfish prudence eked out by superstition. . . .

—then indeed I might plead guilty to the charge. 'But what are my metaphysics?'—

> merely the referring of the mind to its own consciousness for truths indispensable to its own happiness! To what purposes do I

or am I about to employ them? To perplex our clearest notions and living moral instincts? To deaden the feelings of will and free power, to extinguish the light of love and of conscience, to make myself and others worthless, soul-less, God-less? No! to expose the folly and the legerdemain of those who have thus abused the blessed gift of language; to support all old and venerable truths; and by them to support, to kindle, to project the spirit, to make the reason spread light over our feelings, to make our feelings, with their vital warmth, actualize our reason:—these are my objects, these are my subjects, and are these the metaphysics which the bad spirits in hell delight in?[1]

He is also scorned by some critics, he says, for his pre-occupation with *old* topics: topics as 'old' as good and evil, necessity and freewill, immortality and 'the ultimate aim'. This leads Coleridge to an eloquent outburst in which the *Lyrical Ballads* principle (renovation of old and familiar objects by the light of imagination) is applied to the whole of life—art, thought and conduct:

to find no contradiction in the union of old and new, to contemplate the Ancient of Days with feelings as fresh as if they then sprang forth at His own fiat, this characterizes the minds that feel the riddle of the world, and may help to unravel it! To carry on the feelings of childhood into the powers of manhood, to combine the child's sense of wonder and novelty with the appearances which every day for perhaps forty years has rendered familiar . . . this is the character and privilege of genius. And so to represent familiar objects as to awaken the minds of others to a like freshness of sensation concerning them. . . . This is the prime merit of genius.

In philosophy, equally as in poetry, genius produces the strongest impressions of novelty, while it rescues the stalest and most admitted truths from the impotence caused by the very circumstances of their universal admission. . . . Truths, of all others the most awful and mysterious . . . are too often considered as so true that they lose all the powers of truth, and lie bedridden in the dormitory of the soul, side by side with the most despised and exploded errors.[2]

[1] Bohn, p. 67; *BRF*, I, pp. 107-8.
[2] Bohn, p. 68; *BRF*, I, pp. 109-10.

Coleridge, a hundred and fifty years ago, was a voice crying in the wilderness; a prophet summoning his fellow-men to depart from evil and seek good, to renounce idols and worship God. The wilderness of his day was much like our own, but nothing like so thick with poisonous snakes and weeds. In denouncing the main corruptions of his time —unbelief, materialism, necessitarianism, utilitarianism, Jacobinism, commercialism—he could still appeal to an accepted body of Christian beliefs and moral standards, which, however often flouted in practice, were still acknowledged as authoritative by almost everyone. Today these beliefs and standards are widely ignored, and a prophet would be derided for appealing to them. Coleridge would have been aghast if he could have seen the 'later sinkings' of our generation. In reading him, therefore, a modern reader (especially one under twenty-five) must make the effort of remembering that 'Christendom' once existed, and existed *then*, so that Coleridge was only exhorting his hearers to become indeed what they already were in theory.

And so he ends this essay with a firm assertion of the belief which is at the base of his whole teaching—a belief then so universally admitted as to be almost unnoticed, a belief both Kantian and Christian—that God, in making man 'in his own image', endowed him with reason, free will, moral responsibility and Conscience. Conscience becomes, not only 'the indwelling word of a holy and omnipotent legislator', but also (as in Kant) the foundation stone of religious faith. Conscience

unconditionally commands us to attribute reality, and actual existence, to those ideas and to those only, without which the conscience itself would be baseless and contradictory, to the ideas of soul, of free-will, of immortality, and of God![1]

In living, conscience is our guide; in thinking, it points to God, 'the Source of all obligation'.

Coleridge became increasingly convinced that religious faith must be founded, not on intellectual demonstration,

[1] Bohn, p. 70; *BRF*, I, p. 112.

but on moral command; that we believe not because we *must* (as in mathematical proof) but because we *ought*.

In the *Biographia Literaria* he tells us that 'there had dawned upon me, even before I had met with the Critique of the Pure Reason, a certain guiding light':

> If the mere intellect could make no certain discovery of a holy and intelligent first cause, it might yet supply a demonstration, that no legitimate argument could be drawn from the intellect *against* its truth. . . . I became convinced that religion, as both the corner-stone and the key-stone of morality, must have a *moral* origin; so far at least, that the evidence of its doctrine could not, like the truths of abstract science, be wholly independent of the will. It were therefore to be expected, that its *fundamental* truth would be such as MIGHT be denied; though only by the fool, and even by the fool from the madness of the heart alone![1]

And one of Coleridge's finest insights was the further perception that belief in God, if it *were* rationally demonstrable, would have no religious value. The existence of God, he says,

> could not be intellectually more evident without becoming morally less effective; without counteracting its own end by sacrificing the *life* of faith to the cold mechanism of a worthless because compulsory assent.[2]

The imagery of Life versus Death predominates in Coleridge's later thinking: Imagination is alive in its struggle to idealize and to unify, while Fancy deals only with objects which are fixed and dead; the Will asserts its life against the 'philosophy of death' which would bind it in chains of determinism; so here, Faith is a living, existential act, a deliberate decision and not a dead mechanical acquiescence. In *The Friend* he defines Faith as 'the personal realization of the reason by its union with the will'; 'it must be an energy . . . a continuous, not a desultory or occasional energy'. God is the 'great I am', the God of the living, not of the dead; and man can claim kinship with the living God

[1] *BL*, I, pp. 134-5.   [2] *Ibid.*, pp. 135-6.

by echoing, however faintly, the same 'I am', in defiance of the philosophies of death.

If, as Coleridge had come to believe, the principles of taste, morals and religion then current were 'false, injurious, and debasing', this could be partly explained by means of a distinction which from now on became increasingly vital to him: the distinction between 'Reason' and 'Understanding', which in his moral philosophy was the counterpart to the Imagination-Fancy antithesis in his literary theory. Having acquired from Kant the terminology for what he already knew and felt, he quickly saw the value of this distinction (Reason—*Vernunft*; Understanding—*Verstand*) for his defence of religious truth, and used it freely in *The Friend*, *The Statesman's Manual* and *Aids to Reflection*. He gives meanings of his own to 'Reason' and 'Understanding' which are not those of ordinary usage: in Essay V of the 'First Landing Place' of *The Friend*, for instance, where the distinction is first clearly defined, he calls Reason 'the organ of the supersensuous', and Understanding 'the faculty by which we generalize and arrange the phaenomena of perception'. I have elsewhere[1] elaborated the distinction thus (using several Coleridgean phrases):

> Reason seeks ultimate ends; Understanding studies means. Reason is the 'source and substance of truths above sense'; Understanding, the faculty which judges 'according to sense'; Reason is the eye of the spirit, the faculty whereby spiritual reality is spiritually discerned; Understanding is the 'mind of the flesh'.

Religion and Morality belong to the sphere of Reason, while Understanding works legitimately on the practical level in the sciences and in all the affairs of mundane existence. Disaster threatens when either invades the other's province. If we allow the head disjoined from the heart, the 'mere reflective faculty', the 'unenlivened generalizing understanding', to invade the sphere of Reason, as happened pre-eminently in the eighteenth century, we get

all the disastrous results seen in the previous century; materialism, determinism, atheism, utilitarianism, the 'godless revolution', 'moral

[1] Cf. my *Nineteenth Century Studies*, p. 29.

science exploded as mystic jargon', 'the mysteries of religion cut and squared for the comprehension of the understanding', 'imagination excluded from poesy'.[1]

In setting up Reason (and Imagination, its aesthetic counterpart) above the Mind of the Flesh, Coleridge was 'seeking to protect the region of spiritual experience against all attacks from the mere Understanding, that is, against the *Zeitgeist*'.[1]

The next division of *The Friend* (called rather confusingly 'Section I') is headed 'On the Principles of Political Knowledge'. It is not my purpose to discuss this here in any detail, though much of it is of great intrinsic interest.

If, as we have just seen, the encroachments of Understanding into the sphere of Reason produce unbelief and all its attendant corruptions of mind and spirit, the opposite kind of aggression—i.e. by Reason into the sphere of Understanding—produces false political philosophies, and above all the Jacobinism which had first attracted and later repelled so many ardent spirits of Coleridge's generation, himself included. Coleridge is anxious here to vindicate his own consistency on two counts: first, in assigning politics to Understanding at all; and secondly in having become an anti-Jacobin after his apparently revolutionary youth. As to this latter, the imputation of personal inconsistency or 'apostasy', which was freely levelled against him (as against Wordsworth) both in his lifetime and later, Coleridge (like Wordsworth) was wont to reply that it was the times that had changed, not he nor his principles. He might indeed, in his youth, have used the current republican jargon and sneered at 'Aristocracy', but he had been a Pantisocrat, not a Jacobin. After allowing for his evident desire and need to 'play down' his early revolutionary ardours, we must concede, I think, that his account of himself is fundamentally just. He had never had in him the stuff of which a full-blown Jacobin is made. And he rightly claimed to have been the first to give a philosophical analysis of Jacobinism and to expose its basic error. As he saw it, this

[1] *Ibid.*, pp. 29-33.

error lay in applying the universal laws of pure Reason within a sphere to which they are not applicable, viz. that of politics. These universal laws are given us for use in self-government, i.e. for morality and the life of the spirit, and not for the ordering of political and social affairs or for legislation. Here, history, experience and 'expediency' must decide; one and the same régime will *not* fit all times and all places. Jacobinism

> confounds the sufficiency of the conscience to make every person a moral and amenable Being, with the sufficiency of judgment and experience requisite to the exercise of *political* Right.[1]

In ancient and complex societies like those of Western Europe, you cannot hope to build government 'on personal and natural rights alone'. 'In a country so various in its soils, so long inhabited and so fully peopled as Great Britain', liberty could not exist 'without difference of ranks and without laws which recognized and protected the privileges of each.'[2] In all this, Coleridge's nearness to Burke is evident; and his only criticism of Burke here is that Burke, while rightly condemning mere 'theory' did not examine with sufficient care the reasons why legislation cannot be based on it alone. Coleridge does not leave this subject without an affectionate backward look at those early days—that dawn when it was bliss to be alive, when he and 'thousands as young and as innocent as myself', had approached 'the shield of human nature from the golden side' (he quotes the famous passage from *The Prelude*). He rejoices that he had once been young and ardent enough to hope so much for mankind, and feels that to those yearnings, and to the Pantisocratic dream, he owes such insight as he now possesses into human nature and the true welfare of nations. Let not the wise conservatism of later years, and of a later historical era, sink into corrupt reaction, or forget, in restraining error or anarchy, the nobler aspiration which had once made Jacobinism attractive to 'lofty and imaginative spirits'!

The only other passage in this section to which I want to draw attention is that (in Essay XV) where, anticipating

---

[1] Bohn, p. 139; *BRF*, I, p. 207.   [2] Bohn, p. 148; *BRF*, I, p. 220.

'Section the Second', he says that the principles of morality he will teach in this work are 'in direct opposition to the system of the late Dr Paley'. Paley, like all utilitarian moralists, takes 'general consequences' to be the 'chief and best criterion of the right or wrong of particular actions'. But, even if the calculation of consequences were possible for mortal men (which it is not), this 'confounds morality with law', drawing attention away from 'the inward motives and impulses which constitute the essence of morality, to the outward act'. It thus reverts to the very 'legality' for which the Gospel substitutes 'faith'. 'Faith' Coleridge here defines very comprehensively as 'a total act of the soul'; it is 'the inward and absolute ground of our actions', and by definition includes them. This is why faith is what 'justifies', rather than the mere doing of good or right things; 'that which God sees, that alone justifies!' 'Good works may exist without saving principles, and therefore cannot contain in themselves the principle of salvation; but saving principles never did, never can, exist without good works'. True, love would be nought without the 'kind offices' it produces, yet

> what noble mind would not be offended, if he were supposed to value the serviceable offices equally with the love that produced them; or if he were thought to value the love for the sake of the services, and not the services for the sake of the love?[1]

To prove that he was not a 'Jacobin' in 1795, he prints here (Essay XVI) one of his Bristol Lectures of that year, in which he urged that we should appeal *for* the oppressed, not *to* them; and that the true friend of 'freedom', uniting 'the zeal of the Methodist with the views of the philosopher', must live personally with the poor and preach to them, not the Rights of Man, but the Gospel. In this lecture, long before he had defined Jacobinism as the misapplication of universal laws to constitution-making and legislation, he had already detected a kind of moral Jacobinism in the teachings of Godwin against the 'irrational' virtues of filial affection, gratitude, love of one's own things, and patriotism. To replace these by 'universal benevolence' and 'cosmopolitanism'

[1] Bohn, p. 220; *BRF*, I, p. 317.

may seem very high-minded and enlightened, but in practice it means the victory of head over heart, and of self over both. And so he warns his hearers against 'that proud philosophy, which affects to inculcate philanthropy while it denounces every home-born feeling by which it is produced and nurtured.'[1]

At last, with 'Section the Second': 'On the Grounds of Morals and Religion, and the Discipline of the Mind requisite for a true Understanding of the Same', we come to the *gravamen* of Coleridge's prophesying—to that part of *The Friend* (pp. 291-364 in Bohn; pp. 409-524 of B. Rooke's Vol. I) which, Coleridge himself thought, outweighed in value 'all my other works, verse or prose'. As usual, the prospect of having to deliver himself, at length, of the most important part of his message to the age, caused him to flinch and postpone the evil hour. We have first to get through a 'Second Landing-Place' full of 'Literary Amusements' of a more than usually otiose kind; and even then the Section itself is preceded by the Letter of Mathetes (John Wilson) and Wordsworth's Reply (fine and important as these intrinsically are). It is not until Essay II that he really comes to grips with his theme.

He begins with an admirable distinction between two schemes of morality: those based respectively on Self-love and on Duty. Supposing, he asks, 'an enlightened self-interest would recommend the same course of outward conduct as the sense of duty would do'; supposing that 'actions diverging from self-love as their centre should be precisely the same as those produced from the Christian principle . . . wherein would the difference be then?' He answers boldly and conclusively, 'in the agents themselves'.

There are nuggets of pure gold to be found in the eddying waters of this essay: the observations, for example, that

no doctrine was ever widely diffused among various nations through successive ages, and under different religions (such, for instance, as the tenets of original sin and of redemption . . .) which is not founded either in the nature of things, or in the necessities of human nature.

[1] Bohn, p. 233; *BRF*, I, p. 336.

Nay, the more strange and irreconcileable such a doctrine may appear to the understanding, the judgments of which are grounded on general rules abstracted from the world of the senses, the stronger is the presumption in its favour.[1]

—that

The feelings will set up their standard against the understanding, whenever the understanding has renounced its allegiance to the reason; and what is faith, but the personal realization of the reason by its union with the will?

—and that we

must not seek to make the mysteries of faith what the world calls rational, by theories of original sin and redemption borrowed analogically from the imperfection of human law-courts and the coarse contrivances of state expedience.

Coleridge developed that line of thought later, in *Aids to Reflection*, when he wrote:

Wherever the forms of reasoning appropriate only to the *natural* world are applied to spiritual realities, it may be truly said, that the more strictly logical the reasoning is in all its parts, the more irrational it is as a whole.[2]

It will be said (and in a sense rightly), that in thus trying to protect the spiritual realities by weaving a magic circle around them, creating 'Reason' their guardian, and forbidding all access to the Understanding, Coleridge (or anyone else who does the like) has taken a dangerous step towards unreason. We may believe whatever we choose, in defiance of logic and common sense, and—like Sir Thomas Browne—silence Satan and the rebellious reason with a *credo quia impossibile*. But Coleridge was far too wise and too acute not to have seen this danger, and knew that—in his own hands at least—his method was not liable to it. No one was ever more alert than he to the faintest hint of the superstitious or the fantastical. The truths 'unknown to feeble

---

[1] Bohn, p. 304; *BFR*, I, p. 430.   [2] *Aids* (Bohn), p. 168.

sense', which he championed, were not the subjective halluci-
nations of the mystical fanatic, or the wishful thinking of the
ordinary man: they were the central affirmations of the
conscience, which Reason sees to be paramount and which
she imposes as obligatory upon the will. They demand not
mere mental acquiescence, but daily realization in living and
doing: 'personal realization of the reason by its union with
the will'.

In the following Essay (III), under the guise of a historical sketch of the rise of Sophistry in Greece, he diagnoses
the intellectual and spiritual malaise of his own times. Here
again he emphasizes the error of

> submitting all positions alike . . . to the criterion of the mere
> understanding, disguising or concealing the fact, that the rules
> which alone they [the Sophists] applied, were abstracted from the
> objects of the senses, and applicable exclusively to things of quantity
> and relation.

Religion, he goes on, signifies

> the act and habit or reverencing THE INVISIBLE, as the highest
> both in ourselves and in nature. . . . If the Invisible be denied, or
> (which is equivalent) considered invisible from the defect of the
> senses and not in its own nature, the sciences even of observation
> and experiment lose their essential copula. . . . Much more then
> must this apply to the moral world disjoined from religion. Instead
> of morality we can at best have only a scheme of prudence. . . .
> *By celestial observations alone can even terrestrial charts be constructed
> scientifically.*

With the 'pure will' regarded as only 'a *means* to an alien
end', 'things are rapidly improved, persons as rapidly
deteriorated'.

> But religion and morals cannot be disjoined without the destruc-
> tion of both.[1]

This essay ends with a promise to follow on with some 'Essays
on the Principle of Method common to all investigations' as
'the basis of my future philosophical and theological writ-

[1] Bohn, pp. 311-14; *BRF*, I, pp. 439-44.

ings'. Accordingly, we get, in Essays IV–XI, what is largely a 'recast' (as Miss Rooke says) 'of the "Preliminary Treatise on Method" topsy-turvied by the editors of *The Encyclopaedia Metropolitana*'—for which Coleridge had originally written it. But first he appends what he calls a 'brief history of the last hundred and thirty years, by a lover of Old England', which he hopes will convey 'what the genius of my philosophy is'. It consists of a set of aphorisms and gnomic phrases, many of them very famous and oft-quoted (more than once by the present writer). Here are some of them, now seen in their proper context:

Mechanical Philosophy . . .

> a system of natural rights instead of social and hereditary privileges . . . the feeling of being an historical people, generation linked to generation by ancestral reputation, by tradition, by heraldry— this noble feeling, I say, openly stormed or perilously undermined.

Imagination excluded from poesy . . .

> the wealth of nations [substituted] for the well-being of nations.

. . .

> Statesmen should know that a learned class is an essential element of a state. . . . But *you* wish for general illumination! You begin with the attempt to *popularize* learning and philosophy, but you will end in the *plebification* of knowledge.[1]

On the Principles of Method

'Method' is the mental initiative whereby the mind organizes its materials from within; it is a principle of life, as opposed to 'mere dead arrangement'. The ordinary, unenlivened mind (for instance) 'kills' time; the superior mind makes time live.

There are two worlds: the world of mind, and the world of nature—the material world. In the first (including pure mathematics and logic) the relation of parts to each other and to the whole is pre-determined by laws originating in the mind itself. But the material world, when investigated by genuine science, is found to obey the same laws as those

[1] Bohn, pp. 315-16; *BRF*, I, p. 447.

deduced independently from the reason. 'Nature' turns out to be 'rational', not by the forcing upon her of alien mental forms (which is what Bacon had censured in the Schoolmen) —but by intrinsic affinity and correspondence. Why should this be so? No 'scientific' answer can of course be given to a question of that sort—only an oracular utterance. And Coleridge's answer is that a 'super-sensual essence', which is itself both rational (Reason in the most exalted sense) and the cause of the material world (Coleridge does not say 'God', but he means it), has pre-established the harmony between the two worlds. Between Nature and Mind he places the Fine Arts, whose function it is 'to make the external internal, the internal external, to make nature thought, and thought nature'.[1]

In any branch of natural history—say, in Botany—where shall we look for a principle of classification which will reduce to unity the manifold phenomena? The 'sense of a principle of connection' is first given by the mind, and afterwards 'sanctioned by the correspondency of nature'.[2] The law first dawns on the mind of a great man, and is then (if true) confirmed by nature. Coleridge insists on this 'mental initiative', which may at first be only an inspired guess or 'hunch', as the true prerequisite of scientific method. Truth must be found within, before it can be reflected back upon the mind from without.

> Man sallies forth into nature . . . to discover the originals of the forms presented to him in his own intellect . . . he . . . discovers . . . that the *reality*, the *objective* truth, of the objects he has been adoring, derives its whole and sole evidence from an obscure sensation . . . which compels him to contemplate as without and independent of himself what yet he could not contemplate at all, were it not a modification of his own being.[3]

But this harmony, this correspondency of outward and inward—what but a divine agency could have pre-established it? 'Religion is therefore the ultimate aim of philosophy.' 'The solution of phaenomena can never be derived

---

[1] From *On Poesy or Art*, *BL*, II, p. 258.
[2] Bohn, p. 332; *BRF*, I, p. 471.   [3] Bohn, p. 358; *BRF*, I, p. 509.

from phaenomena', but from a higher principle of causation; 'Through faith we understand that the worlds were framed by the word of God; so that things which are seen were not made of things which do appear'.

At length, conscious of his prophetic office and anxious to discharge it while his momentum lasts, Coleridge thus solemnly addresses the reader—

Hast thou ever raised thy mind to the consideration of EXIS-TENCE, in and by itself, as the mere act of existing? Hast thou ever said to thyself thoughtfully, IT IS! heedless in that moment, whether it were a man before thee, or a flower, or a grain of sand? . . . If thou hast indeed attained to this, thou wilt have felt the presence of a mystery, which must have fixed thy spirit in awe and wonder. . . .

If thou hast mastered this intuition of absolute existence, thou wilt have learnt likewise, that it was this, and no other, which in the earlier ages seized the nobler minds, the elect among men, with a sort of sacred horror. This it was which first caused them to feel within themselves a something ineffably greater than their own individual nature. It was this which . . . prepared them to become the lights and awakening voices of other men, the founders of law and religion, the educators and foster-gods of mankind.[1]

This great Idea, the idea of Being, is not derived from 'sense', and least of all from the mere 'Understanding'—the faculty which classifies and organizes sense-data. It comes by way of what can only be called 'Revelation'; and the power so revealed—'is it not GOD?' Let us then stop the wastage of so much philosophic energy, by 'removing the opposition without confounding the distinction between philosophy and faith'. Head and heart must not be disjoined, for only both acting in unison can attain to

the glorious vision of that existence which admits of no question out of itself, acknowledges no predicate but the I AM IN THAT I AM!

The concluding passage is splendid, eloquent and true;

[1] Bohn, pp. 361-2; *BRF*, I, p. 514. (The ensuing passages follow soon after.)

and it contains so much of the Coleridgean essence that I must quote it freely:

> The ground-work, therefore, of all true philosophy is the full apprehension of the difference between the contemplation of reason, namely, that intuition of things which arises when we possess ourselves as one with the whole, which is substantial knowledge, and that which presents itself when transferring reality to the negations of reality . . . we think of ourselves as separated beings, and place nature in antithesis to the mind, as object to subject, thing to thought, death to life. This is abstract knowledge, or the science of the mere understanding. By the former, we know that existence is its own predicate, self affirmation. . . . It is an eternal and infinite self-rejoicing, self-loving, with a joy unfathomable, with a love all comprehensive. . . .
>
> On the other hand, the abstract knowledge which belongs to us as finite beings [the text is involved here, so I will paraphrase it]

becomes a source of error and delusion when it sets itself up as the whole of knowledge, instead of being—as in itself it is—'a translation of the living word into a dead language, for the purposes of memory, arrangement, and general communication'.

> Yea (saith an enlightened physician [Sir Thomas Browne]), there is but one principle, which alone reconciles the man with himself, with others and with the world . . . namely, the principle of religion, the living and substantial faith 'which passeth all *understanding*'. . . . This elevation of the spirit above the semblances of custom and the senses to a world of spirit, this life in the idea, even in the supreme and godlike, which alone merits the name of life, and without which our organic life is but a state of somnambulism, this it is which affords the sole sure anchorage in the storm, and at the same time the substantiating principle of all true wisdom, the satisfactory solution of all the contradictions of human nature, of the whole riddle of the world.

I have hesitated long over the question whether to discuss at this point only the 1809-10 version of *The Friend*, leaving the additions of 1818 to be examined in their chronological place. But on the whole, it has seemed best to treat the work

at this point in its final form. If there had been any significant changes in Coleridge's thought between 1809 and
1818—changes, I mean, reflected in the later version—it
would have been important to mark these by separating the
two. The 1818 additions however seen to me no more than
developments or elaborations of ideas already present in the
1809-10 version, or present in his mind at that time.

The only point which seems to be worth noting is that
by 1818 Coleridge had become even more suspicious than
he already was in 1809 of any pantheistic leanings in himself, and more sensitive to the danger of any hostile criticism
on that score. In the early *Friend*, No. 6 (Sept. 21, 1809),
after completing the discussion (left unfinished in No. 5)
on the moral basis of religious belief ('Conscience . . .
commands us to attribute Reality . . . to those [Ideas] without which the Conscience would be baseless . . . namely, to
the Ideas of Soul, the Free Will, Immortality, and God'), he
goes on to say that, *with this faith*, all Nature may be considered not only as the material in which our Duty is to be
realized, but also as

> A Vision of the Most High revealing to us the mode, and time,
> and particular instance of applying and realizing that universal
> Rule, pre-established in the Heart of our Reason: as
> > The lovely shapes and sounds intelligible
> > Of that Eternal Language, which our God
> > Utters: Who from Eternity doth teach
> > Himself in all, and all things in Himself![1]

In 1818, significantly, he omits this pantheistic extract
from *Frost at Midnight* (1798). Yet the long pantheistic
quotation from Bruno, suitably safeguarded as in 1809 by
the phrase 'let the sublime piety of the passage excuse some
intermixture of error, or rather let the words, as they well
may, be interpreted in a safe sense', is retained in 1818:

> *I have thought myself allowed thus to render the less cautious
> expressions of the original* [e.g. 'the infinite power, that creates all
> things, and is the abiding *Being* of all things'], *because the very same*

[1] *BRF*, II, pp. 78-81.

Latin words are to be found in the writings of Joannes Scotus Erigena, who was doubtless a sincere Christian; and equivalent phrases occur in the mystic Theology of one at least, if not more, of the early Greek Fathers. It is most uncharitable to accuse a Writer of pantheism, for a few overcharged sentences: especially as the Writer may have thought himself authorized by certain texts of St. John and St. Paul. [italics Coleridge's].

The 'certain texts' would include 'in him we live, and move, and have our being' (Acts xvii. 28), and 'he that dwelleth in love dwelleth in God, and God in him' (1 John iv. 16).

In 1818, after the publication of the 'rifacciamento', Coleridge composed an extra paragraph which he asked several correspondents to insert in their copies of Sect. II, Essay XI[1] after the phrase 'reunion of the all in one, in that eternal reason whose fulness hath no opacity, whose transparency hath no vacuum'. Writing (for instance) to William Hart Coleridge (Dec. 8, 1818), he explains the need for this insertion:

it's object being to preclude all suspicion of any leaning towards Pantheism, in any of it's forms. I adore the living and personal God, whose Power indeed is the *Ground* of all *Being*, even as his Will is the efficient, his Wisdom the instrumental, and his Love the final, Cause of all *Existence*; but who may not without fearful error be identified with the universe, or the universe be considered to be an *attribute* of his Deity.[2]

Miss Barbara Rooke gives a version of this added passage,[3] taken from the anotated 'Copy D' of *The Friend* (1818). Coleridge here argues that the intellect unaided can indeed lead us to a general affirmation of a Supreme Being, but that there it stops. It cannot account for 'the existence or possibility of the World, as different from Deity'. It has therefore either to identify or confuse the Creator with the Creation, or to deny the reality of 'all finite existence'.

The inevitable result of all consequent Reasoning, in which the Intellect refuses to acknowledge a higher or deeper ground than

[1] *BRF*, I, p. 522. [2] *CL*, 1160 (p. 894). [3] *BRF*, I, p. 522.

it can itself supply . . . is—and from Zeno the Eleatic to Spinoza and from Spinoza to Schelling, Oken, and the adherents of the present day, ever has been—PANTHEISM under one or other of its modes. . . .

This teaches us that in all such speculation the postulates of Conscience, not logic, must be the starting point, and that there will remain a chasm between the One and the Many 'which the Moral Being only, which the Spirit and Religion of Man can alone fill up'.

CHAPTER XII

1810-1816

THIS—as I have already said—is not a biography, so I can excuse myself the painful task of telling the story of the years between *The Friend* and the *Biographia Literaria*. Painful, because during those years Coleridge touched the depths of dereliction and misery. Blow after blow fell upon him: the departure of Sara Hutchinson from Allan Bank, which he interpreted as an act of deliberate deceit and conspiracy; about five months later the breach with Wordsworth, which struck at the very foundations of his life and happiness, and, in spite of formal and outward reconciliation (May 1812), was never really healed; the sudden stopping of Josiah Wedgwood's annuity—and of course all the while the estrangement from his wife and the drifting, loveless, homeless existence to which it led. No one need wonder that with all this to contend against, together with ill health, the agonies of unrequited love and a burning sense of grievance, the opium-habit, already firmly fixed, should have nearly undone him. He did, in fact, nearly succumb to it, especially in the year 1814. The wonder rather is that in spite of all this he achieved so much. He made repeated, desperate and not always wholly vain attempts to conquer the addiction, though constantly relapsing when the horrors of withdrawal overcame him. During these years he gave many courses of lectures; he wrote for *The Courier* newspaper; he saw his tragedy *Osorio*, recast as *Remorse*, run successfully at Drury Lane for twenty-three nights[1]; he began the writing of the *Biographia*. Above all, he was reading and thinking with unabated intensity, and reaching ever-new heights and depths of insight. As always when most

---

[1] *Remorse*, 'the only offspring of his pen which earned pudding as well as praise' (Dykes Campbell), brought him £400; but this was largely offset by debts and the drying up of the Wedgwood annuity.

unhappy and most aware of his own weakness, his meditations were mainly about religion. If, after Malta, any further
purgatorial schooling was needed to make him an orthodox
Christian, those years supplied it.

Dykes Campbell says that after leaving Allan Bank he
went home to Greta Hall (Keswick), and lived there with his
family for five months, apparently happy—but doing nothing.[1] His Notebooks, however, show that his mind was not
lying fallow all that while. In fact it is one of the recurrent
marvels of Coleridge's life that he could so often tranquillize
an emotional crisis by escaping into thought. Opium was for
the relief of physical pain—including the pains of with-
drawal-from-opium; but abstraction, and especially theology,
could best minister to a mind diseas'd. It is significant, for
example, that on the very night before Sara's departure for
Wales (March 4, 1810)—which he records in a parenthesis
—his Notebook entry is about the Law of Association. His
point is that association of ideas does, indeed, *begin* mechanically, by 'common causality'; but in its later stages it comes
under the 'causative power' of the soul itself. The mind
contains clusters of facts, but it is the predominant mood of
the soul that determines which of these shall be called into
life, and in what pattern.

Soon after,[2] he is discussing why it is that nowadays 'a
young man of ingenuous dispositions, warm sensibility and
an enquiring mind' can scarcely avoid Socinianism—and
one must remember that by now he was using that word to
denote not merely Unitarian theology, but the whole ethos
against which he was reacting. Thus the first reason he gives
is the misapplication of categories of the Understanding to
spiritual concerns; whereas in reality the Soul, and Duty,
are not subject to the same logic as 'the phaenomena of the
Senses'. Next comes the inveterate custom of supporting a
religious position by scriptural text-marshalling, 'the con-
sequence of which must necessarily be, that one class of
Texts appearing to contradict the other, the preference will
—and indeed ought to be—given to that sense which is the
most congruous with Reason'. Further, young men are

[1] *Narrative of the Events of his Life* (1894), p. 177.   [2] *CN*, III, 3743.

always apt to idealize and overestimate human nature, 'hence no need is felt of redemption'. The young, too, are often favourable to Necessitarianism (part of the Socinian philosophic hinterland, as we have seen), because 'we least value and think of that which we enjoy in the highest degree'—and the young, not yet under the tyranny of habit, are in that state of enjoyment. Coleridge adds, for final censure, the 'Chillingworthian' notion that the Bible is the Religion of Protestants—i.e. that it contains and proves all that Protestants need and believe, without the help of tradition or the Fathers.

The whole question of the Bible's authority—its status as 'revelation'—was to interest Coleridge increasingly from this time on. This interest, stimulated no doubt by his study of Lessing, Eichhorn and other early German biblical scholars, culminated in the *Confessions of an Inquiring Spirit*, or *Letters on the Inspiration of the Scriptures*, first published posthumously in 1840. I have already referred to this (cf. above, pp. 75-6), and shall return to it later. But meanwhile the Notebooks show him grappling with the central problems, and already vaulting many of the hurdles which were to dismay the faithful for a century to come.

Soon after the entry last quoted, for instance, there is a long meditation on this theme. Orthodoxy today, he says, 'seems confined to an acquiescence in the tenability of all and every proof that has been offered of the *Revelation*, while the Revelation itself is left unthought of'. Let us leave aside 'evidences', including the other parts of Holy Writ and all the accompanying historical facts, and see first 'what are the great component Doctrines contained in Christianity' (he identifies these with 'the old Symbolum Fidei, which was the Conductor of Christianity for so many years'). They are, in his view, the following: First, Natural or Universal Religion, 'that which would have been Religion tho' Adam had retained his perfection'; second, 'the additions that rise of necessity out of the fallen state of the will'; third, 'the completion of this Religion by the system of Redemption'. This 'system' he analyses into its components, beginning with the (Kantian) postulates: God, Freedom, Immortality.

In antithesis we have, on the level of practical experience, Weakness, Sin, Remorse—accompanied by a sense of the *need* of 'Help from above'—a conviction that Repentance without such help will not suffice for Atonement. We are to accept this redemption joyfully, and try to 'realize the *conditions* of it'. All this believed 'from the inmost Heart', and lived out, is Christianity. Whatever opinions may be held, optionally, within this framework, are 'part of the play-ground of Christian Liberty'; and opinions about biblical 'inspiration' are in that class. For instance: is every sentence and word in the Bible 'inspired' in its literal and grammatical sense—or are some parts metaphorical, and if so, which parts, and of what are they metaphors? We should need a new 'inspiration' to determine such points—as, for example, whether the Song of Solomon is 'a spiritual Allegory of Christ and his Church', or 'a mere Epithalamium'. Either of these opinions about Scripture is consistent with basic 'Faith in the Doctrine of Christianity'. Therefore, believe what you like as to the 'Inspiration-system', but hold fast to the Doctrines themselves.[1] Such views as Coleridge here propounds are of course taken for granted now; but if so, it is because he and others after him had the courage to propound them. Let us not forget how far in advance of the times they were in the England of 1810.

Another piece of insight is to be found in an ensuing entry: Space and Time, he says here, are forms of all perception; but perception or intuition is sensuous, i.e. not in God. But, 'except under the forms of Space and Time we can predicate nothing'; it follows, therefore, that 'concerning God we can neither talk sense or nonsense'; we can only legitimately talk 'piously or impiously'—in other words, only the language of reverence, only *religious* language is appropriate in speaking of God.

All through the spring and summer of 1810, when Coleridge was 'doing nothing', his Notebooks show an increasing preoccupation with religion, especially with the problems of miracles, the proper interpretation of Scripture, and the reconciliation of philosophy with Christianity.

[1] *CN*, III, 3754.

In his reflexions upon the Christian miracles, Coleridge is struggling, not to write them off, but to demote them from their traditional place of honour as 'evidences'. The real basis of the Christian faith (as we have seen) is its fitness to meet our condition as sinners needing redemption. How *can* miracles 'prove' the very grounds for our belief, viz. the need for redemption from a fallen state? The Gospel miracles may help to support the belief that Jesus *was* the Christ, the Redeemer; but the belief in the Christ-Redeemer must have been produced already by other means. Christ himself 'demanded Faith as the condition of working the miracle', and it is for us likewise to have Faith before we appeal to miracle in confirmation of it. Coleridge's characteristic position on miracles is that we do not believe in Christ because of them, but that we are at liberty to believe in miracles because it was Christ who worked them; which means, I think, both that we cannot set limits to the powers of such a being as we believe Christ to have been, and also that, as the works of that being, the miracles have value in confirming or symbolizing his religious teachings.

A striking illustration of this way of thinking occurs in entries No. 3848 and No. 3849, where the topic is the miraculous feeding of the five thousand as related in John vi. What exercises Coleridge here is the apparent conflict between Christ's actual exertions of miraculous power and his reluctance to base his claims upon them. Here, he has fed the hungry crowd, but when afterwards they ask him for a 'sign', such as manna in the desert (as if Jesus had not just done the like for them), he replies, *not* by referring them to the miracle of yesterday, but by explaining that miracle as a 'symbolical analogy' to the doctrine he wishes to teach them, viz. that he is the 'Bread of Life'. What matters is not that Moses gave them manna, or that Jesus himself gave them literal bread to eat, but that the real 'bread', the life-giving bread, is what 'comes down from heaven' in the spiritual sense—is, indeed, himself as sent by God. It is not certain whether Coleridge understood this as the interpretative method of the writer of St John's Gospel; what is certain, I think, is that he himself longed to approach the 'miracles' in that way. Whether they 'occurred' historically or not (and Coleridge is not the man to question it) the importance of them is the spiritual truth they symbolize. Later, he argues that although Christ did several times 'refer to his miracles as proofs of his divine Mission', there are no cases (as far as he can remember) in which this was 'his avowed primary aim for working a miracle'. Coleridge is very much aware of the contrast between this attitude of Jesus himself towards his miracles and that of modern apologists who lean heavily upon them as 'evidence' or 'demonstration' of the 'truth' of Christianity.

It is interesting to find Coleridge criticizing the Socinians for inconsistency: they rely on miracles as evidence for Christ's credibility, yet offer nothing 'to make us believe the miracles which [they] gave us no reason to anticipate' (No. 3892). There are, in true believers, certain 'a priori determinations of the Conscience to anticipate and expect' miracles; and many Socinians believe in miracles only because they have been brought up 'in the common world of Christianity' and imbibed its ethos. 'Yea, I say, the Socinians themselves would not attach the belief they do to these miracles, were it not that they share feelings which Socinianism itself could never inspire!' Observe the third-generation Socinians of Germany, who have long been cut off from orthodoxy: 'they have now almost to a man rejected the miracles—and yet retained what they deem the religion'.

In all this Coleridge seems to me to be in a cleft stick; one side of him, the 'rational' side which had once led him to Socinianism, is still trying to play down miracles, or at least to 'understand' them as allegories of what really matters; the other side, the believing, marvelling side towards which he is more and more leaning, sees religion as psychologically inseparable from expectation of the miraculous and readiness to accept it. Providence, he says,

has plac'd for the wisest purposes a religious instinct in our nature, which leads us to be ever credulous where *religious feelings* (i.e. the stern precepts and sublime hopes and fears of Morality) are the declared moral of the miracle, but yet as a check to this, has at the same time so constructed our minds, that a miracle as a miracle, *as a work of power without any adequate Object of Doctrine* [italics mine], excites *horror* . . . and *hatred*—(No. 3894).

If Conscience, or the Practical Reason, is made the basis for a predisposition to expect miracles, so too (as we have already partly seen) it authorizes—even necessitates—belief in the Trinity. Plato had deduced the Triad: The One, the Logos and the Spirit, both essentially and '*existentially*' (was Coleridge the inventor of this word—as of so many others adopted from him?). But it is an old mistake to suppose that the Triad is 'an hypothesis to enable us to *conceive* Deity':

> Whereas this as well as all other positions concerning God are authorized by the Practical Reason exclusively—but the practical Reason never does more than command the admission of a Postulate, as far as the existence of any thing is necessary to the truth of some other which is practically necessary—The doctrine of Sin and Redemption first authorized by practically necessitating the doctrine of the Trinity—before that time it was a pure Philosopheme, tho' most beautiful and accurate (No. 3814).

It is evident, then, that in the spring of 1810 Coleridge was still approaching the Trinity by the congenial (to him) metaphysical route, though powerfully urged by practical needs—his sense of sin and insufficiency. The Incarnation, the historical side of Christianity, is not uppermost in his thinking.

The Socinians, he reflects, place too much weight on the miracles as evidence for their one strictly 'religious' belief, viz. that in the resurrection of the body and a future state of rewards and punishments. But this doctrine, as the Socinians held it (i.e. in disconnection from the main body of orthodoxy), 'is equally unimaginable . . . as the Trinity, original Sin and Redemption, and far more incomprehensible'. To the orthodox, the miracles are only 'auxiliary evidence' for a religion 'whose Truth and Necessity is proved *a priori*'.

Though trying—as a religious philosopher aware of the

moral foundation of all theological speculation—to keep his faith within what he beautifully calls 'the modesty of the Gospel', he yet reverts wistfully to the Platonic shapings of his youth. 'It would not be amiss', he says, if our young intellectuals 'had made part of their intellectual voyages in the groves and enchanted Islands of Plato, Plotin, and even Proclus—rendering the mind lofty and generous and *abile* by splendid Imaginations. . . .' (No. 3820.)

Entry No. 3879 shows Coleridge using all the freedom of the modern commentator in tackling the problem of 'variety-in-concurrence' in the Gospel narratives. He finds the accounts of the Resurrection in Matthew and John so discrepant as to exclude the possibility of their both being eye-witness reports. He would prefer to regard the fourth Gospel, rather than the first, as the work of its alleged author, and mentions 'that unlucky anachronism of Zachariah the son of Barachiah' (Matt. xxiii. 35) as adding to his unease about 'Matthew'.

In one of the few *dated* entries of this time (No. 3900, June 17, 1810), his recent reading of 'Nightingale's portraiture of Methodism' produces some thoughts on that society, and on contemporary religion in general. He finds the Methodist preachers largely lacking in intellectual grasp of their own doctrines, and only kept faithful to them by the force of adhesion: 'Limpets on the Rock of Salvation'. Nowadays a minister should be learned enough in both Roman and Socinian doctrines to be forearmed against either extreme. Further, in a passage which anticipates Matthew Arnold's well-known contrast between the Puritan ethos and 'Culture's' idea of perfection, he comments wryly on the type of physiognomy everywhere and at all times produced by 'Pietism', whether in its Moravian, Quaker or Methodistical form. We recognize an ideal of perfection in the countenances of Raphael's saints, or in the Apollos of the ancients—'but contemplate the phiz of a Puritan!' A more serious complaint, against the Methodists in particular, is their equivocal position as 'Dissenters and pretended non-Dissenters', and (doctrinally) their stress on *my* salvation rather than *ours*.

Coleridge's lack of inhibition as a biblical critic is well illustrated in Nos. 3903-5, where St Paul is shown to be anything but a 'clear Reasoner' or 'luminous Logician'. For instance, the apostle uses the word 'law' to mean now the Moral Law and now the Mosaic Law—and it is not always clear which he intends. And if Coleridge is not afraid to criticize St Paul, still less does he shrink from pointing out the lack, in modern Quakers, of any adequate intellectual grasp of their own principles. Such a grasp is not essential to the piety of any individual Quaker or other sectarian, but it is essential for the permanence of the sects themselves that they should contain at least some members who possess it.

In a meditation on the life of St Teresa, written in the same month (June) as the above strictures on Methodism etc., Coleridge writes glowingly of a spiritual state which of course (like everyone else) he knew, but which too often, alas, eluded him: the state of 'the *moral* Being'

> after difficult Conquest, the total State of the Spirit after the victorious Struggle, in which and by which *the* WILL has preserved its perfect Freedom by a deep and vehement Energy of perfect Obedience to the pure, practical Reason, or Conscience! Thence flows in upon and fills the Soul that Peace, which passeth Understanding! (No. 3911)

The most painful struggles are not too costly if they bring, to the victorious, such unspeakable reward; this Coleridge knew well, though the weakness of the flesh seldom allowed him to taste it. This moral victory, won for the sake of conscience and not for the reward it brings (though not without knowing it will come), seemed to him so much the aim and *raison d'être* of religion, that it is no wonder he grounds Christianity itself on morality. The 'Pagan-plotinic Religion', he writes (No. 3918) differs from the Christian,

> to the infinite advantage of the latter, in proceeding from the Intellect as from the Apex, downward to the *moral* Being—from the speculative to the practical Reason.

Whereas Christianity, 'in all its disguises, excepting Socinianism', begins with the moral will, and ends with it, and regards the intellect altogether as *means*. . . .

On the other hand, 'the Plotino-platonic Philosophy' has this great merit: that it never allows its followers to lose *themselves* in the multitude of scattered *objects*; on the contrary, it rouses the Soul to 'acts and energies of creative Thought'. To this remark he adds the (biographically interesting) comment that it was not Taylor's translations which first led him to the study of this philosophy, but *vice versa*. Still, he urges that no one can read the extracts in Taylor—those relating to our moral nature—without an inkling that here is 'a system congruous with his nature, and thence attracting it' (No. 3934).

No. 3955 well illustrates Coleridge's effort to base religious faith on something firmer than (what were always alien to him) historical 'facts' or probabilities:

> to *be a christian* is *not* to do *this or that* because on the whole this or that historical fact appears to us better supported than the assertion of the contrary—that Xst really did rise than that he did not—or that he was really dead than that it was a state of suspended animation . . . in short, Religion *cannot* be *Prudence*.

The story of the rift between Coleridge and Wordsworth has been told and re-told, and there is no need to repeat it in detail here. All that is asked of readers of this book is that, in considering Coleridge's life and work between 1810 and 1816 (i.e. between Allan Bank and Highgate), they should constantly remember the state of mind into which it threw him. To meet with harshness and contempt from the man and poet whom he had loved and served so devotedly, and with whom there had been a marriage of minds unique in English literary story, was a blow that struck at his vitals.

It will be remembered that in October 1810 Coleridge left the Lakes in the company of the Basil Montagus, who had invited him to their London house to undergo medical treatment. Before they departed, Wordsworth warned Montagu in confidence that he would find Coleridge a difficult and troublesome lodger. No one can blame Wordsworth

for doing his; his warning was well-meant, and justi-
fied by the sad experience of Coleridge's long sojourn in
his household. If blame is due to anyone it is to Montagu,
who shortly after their arrival in London, told Coleridge
(after a quarrel) what Wordsworth had said, adding some
fictitious heightenings of his own. E. L. Griggs summarizes
(from Crabb Robinson and other sources) what Montagu
seems to have said to Coleridge:

'Wordsworth *has commissioned* me to tell you, first, that he has no
Hope of you'; that 'for years past [you] had been an ABSOLUTE
NUISANCE in the Family'; and that you were '*in the habit* of
running into debt at little Pot-Houses for Gin'. Likewise, Wordsworth was reported to have spoken of Coleridge as a '*rotten drunk-
ard*' who was 'rotting out his entrails by intemperance'.[1]

However true, and however deserved, these remarks may
mainly have been, they threw Coleridge (coming from his
dearest friend and idol) into a state of horror and stupe-
faction from which he withdrew for a year and a half into
proud and tragic silence. He later thought he had done
wrong in not writing; and Wordsworth on his side claimed
that he had never 'commissioned' Montagu to pass on such
wounding remarks to Coleridge. On this sort of footing a
formal 'reconciliation' was brought about in May 1812, but
ever after

They stood aloof, the scars remaining,
Like cliffs which had been rent asunder.

A rift of some sort, though not necessarily such a painful
one, might very likely have occurred sooner or later; indeed,
the old intimacy had already been blighted by the jealousies
over Sara Hutchinson, by Coleridge's habits, and by his
increasing awareness of the egocentric strain in Wordsworth and his family circle. Wordsworth may have been
nearer the truth than Coleridge would ever have admitted—
nearer, I mean, to what may have been latent below the
conscious level—when he said he believed that Coleridge
was actually 'glad of a pretext to break with him'. Not

[1] *CL*, III, p. 296.

consciously 'glad', of course; but using justifiable dudgeon as an escape from a relationship which had become strained and different. Before passing on, I will just illustrate Coleridge's state of mind from some Notebook entries made soon after the blow fell:

> How perceptibly has ———'s love for poor C lessened since he has procured other enthusiastic admirers!—As long as C., almost all dissenting, was the *sole* Admirer and Lover, *so long* he was loved. ... W. authorized M. to tell me, he had no Hope of me! O God! What good reason for saying this? The very belief takes away all excuse, because all kind purpose for the declaration (3991).

> How our very virtues, the consciousness of them, I mean, make us unhappy. What a deadly pang do I not feel from the deep sense, how truly and with what an eagerness and prodigal readiness of self-sacrifice I have loved (3993).

> Sunday Night. No Hope of me! absol. Nuisance! God's mercy—is it a Dream? (3997).

> a compressing and strangling Anguish, made up of Love, and Resentment, and Sorrow ... (4001).

It is, to my mind, both revealing and touching that, soon after all this (to be exact, on Nov. 3, 1810) Coleridge made two long entries in his Notebook: one about religion, the other about love and friendship. Written as they are in a calm, judicial style, they show Coleridge's extraordinary powers of detachment and self-conquest.

The entry about religion[1] is headed 'Confessio Fidei of S. T. Coleridge'. It is an important statement, and may be taken as a summary of his thinking over the past few years—since Malta, let us say. There are two sections and two 'Corollaries': the first section lays down the principles of 'Natural' Religion; the second, of 'Revealed'. The final Corollary applies the foregoing to the establishment of Trinitarian doctrine.

First, then, he affirms that he is a Free Agent, possessing Will and Reason, and is therefore a morally responsible being—a being with a Conscience. 'Hence it becomes my absolute Duty to believe, and I do believe, that there is a

---

[1] *CN*, III, 4005.

God, that is, a Being in whom Supreme Reason and a most holy Will are one with an infinite Power. . . .' (We saw how, in *The Friend*, he had made belief in God a command of Conscience—Conscience, which commands us to attribute reality and existence to those ideas without which Conscience itself would have no meaning.) Nature, 'the wonderful works of God in the sensible world', is a 'perpetual Discourse, reminding me of his Existence, and Shadowing out to me his perfections.' But Nature is only an auxiliary support to faith; to be effective, it must presuppose the belief in God which conscience has already called into being.

> It is therefore evident to my Reason, that the existence of God is absolutely and necessarily insusceptible of a scientific Demonstration. . . .

Scripture has by implication taught this, by *commanding* us to believe in one God—that is to say, its method is apodeictic and not demonstrative. A command relates to the will, whereas a scientific demonstration is 'compulsory on the mind' and independent of the will.

Further, Conscience forbids us to regard the Pleasures and Pains of this life as moral motives or ends; it refers us instead to a 'spiritual state of being'—

> and I believe in the Life to come, not through arguments acquired by my Understanding or discursive Faculty, but chiefly and effectively because so to believe is my Duty, and in obedience to the Command of my Conscience.

All this, says Coleridge, 'would have been my Creed, had I been born with Adam'; it may therefore be called 'Natural Religion'. Next we come to 'Revealed Religion', and 'my Belief as a Christian':

1. First, it is 'the fundamental article of Christianity, that I am a fallen creature', 'a child of Wrath':

> This fearful Mystery I pretend not to understand—I cannot even conceive the possibility of it—but I know, that it is so!

Conscience—again—'the sole fountain of certainty, commands me to believe it, and would itself be a contradiction, were it not so—and *what is real, must be possible* [my italics].

2. Incarnation and Redemption:

> I receive with full and grateful Faith the assurance of Revelation, that the Word which is from all eternity with God and is God, assumed our human nature in order to redeem me and all mankind from this our connate Corruption.

Reason convinces me that no other mode of redemption was conceivable; and, without revelation, I would have yearned for a Redeemer—though not expecting any such extreme manifestation of divine love.

3. This incarnation was made manifest and real to us in Christ Jesus, and I believe

> that his miraculous Birth, his agony, his Crucifixion, Death, Resurrection, and Ascension, were all both Symbols of our Redemption . . . and necessary parts of the aweful process.

4. I believe in the 'descent and sending of the Holy Spirit', by whom alone I can be sanctified, delivered from my inheritance of sin and become an inheritor of God's Kingdom.

The final Corollary, as I have said, enlarges upon the doctrine of the Trinity in the light of the foregoing. The Trinity, says Coleridge (cf. above, pp. 114-15), would in any case (i.e. without the Christian revelation) have been a necessary Idea of speculative reason; that is, once admit the postulate of an intelligent Creator, and you must also admit that he must have had co-eternally an adequate Idea of Himself, in and through which he created all things. But God's 'ideas' are more real than our 'things', thus his idea of himself was also more real than our 'realities', i.e. it *existed*, it was a Person, the Logos. But this is still only a speculative idea, and to such ideas we are not bound to attribute real existence. What transforms the Trinity from a speculation into a doctrine enjoined upon us by conscience, is the Redemption. To Christians, therefore, the belief in the Trinity (the necessary theological counterpart of the redemption: there must be a Redeemer, and he must be divine) is obligatory, commanded by conscience. It is 'false candour' for a Christian believing in Original Sin and Redemption to concede the name of 'Christian' to anyone who denies the divinity of Christ. To the Socinian or 'Psilanthropist' ('mere-man-ist'), the Crucifixion presents merely the image of a good man 'dying in attestation of the Truth of his Preaching'; to the Christian, it represents 'God incarnate taking upon himself the Sins of the World, and himself thereby redeeming us and giving us Life everlasting —not merely teaching it.'

How will all this strike a believer of our own time?— one who, following the lead of Coleridge and later rejuvenators of Christian doctrine, tries always to *realize* his beliefs and live them into day-to-day truth, and not merely *acquiesce* in formulae offered from outside, swallowing them untasted like pills? One must remember of course that in this Confession of Faith Coleridge is avowedly summarizing and codifying beliefs he has fought to attain; he is not now engaged in the fight itself. It were to be expected, then, that his tone would be comparatively formal and emotionless, as in the clauses of any creed. In reading Coleridge on religion I always try, not merely to understand *what* he says, but also *why* he says it, and *how* he came to say it. And it is remarkable how often I find it possible to go with him all, or nearly all, the way. This is why it is worth while to study him and to try to interpret him. But I confess that here I can only go with him part of the way; after that, I seem to lose sight of the living teacher in a mist of orthodox phrases. In all the first part of the Confession, the part about 'Natural Religion', he carries me along with him. I can share (in some sense, perhaps not the same as his own) his belief in a 'future life', and—passing on to the section on Revealed Religion—I can even assent to the general proposition that man is a 'fallen' and sinful creature, provided that (as Coleridge himself says elsewhere) 'The Fall' is taken to symbolize the radical imperfection of human nature at all times, and is not regarded as a historical event in Eden. My hesitation begins when he says—as indeed orthodoxy has always said—that the Word 'assumed our human nature

in order to redeem me and all mankind from this our con-
nate Corruption' . . . 'taking upon himself the Sins of the
World, and himself thereby redeeming us' . . . etc. Why
take Coleridge to task for merely stating what every Christian has always believed, or said he believed? Simply for that
very reason! Simply because we have come to expect from
him something much better than the clichés of orthodoxy—
namely, the essence and inward *meaning* of orthodox belief.
We are getting this from him when he plants belief firmly
on a moral foundation, and makes it the subject of a command and not a demonstration. We are not getting it when
he falls back upon the old phrases about incarnation and
redemption. *What these strange notions mean* is what we are
entitled to be told by a Coleridge, but he does not tell us.
So the nagging question remains unanswered—not the
paradox of Incarnation, God and Man united, for Church
history has sufficiently shown that no solution need be
expected of that conundrum—but the question why and
how this Incarnation, supposing it to have occurred, *redeems*
us. By 'paying back' the debt of Adam, the 'price of sin'?
—but that presupposes the fierce old tyrant deity whose
wrath could only be assuaged by the blood of his own son,
and who enters into cosmic bonds and covenants—primitive
notions which one would have expected Coleridge either to
reject, or to infuse with new meaning. By the extreme pathos
of the situation, whereby God himself condescends to suffer
the worst that flesh can endure, in order to show the infinity
of his love for us? We are to be overwhelmed, shamed into
salvation, by the spectacle of such love? But that begs the
whole question; if we are to be moved by this sacrifice, we
must first believe in God, believe in his infinite love, believe
that he can show this by becoming man and suffering
death upon the Cross. Without these presuppositions, what
is the crucifixion?—no more than it was to Pilate and the
pagan world: an obscure trouble-maker (even though a 'just'
one) being executed according to accepted procedure. Then
perhaps Jesus redeems us by his teaching and his shining
example? Oh no! this is 'Socinianism'; Christ *gives* us
eternal life, not *teaches* us how to attain it (as Coleridge here

expressly says). We know, of course, that Christianity has always tried to keep the Redemption alive by insisting that we must *appropriate* it by faith—*making* it our own, *making* it apply to us, by prayers for grace and by hearty repentance. But too often the Redemption is presented as a *fait accompli*, a divine transaction once-for-all completed, signed and sealed. Or, in another metaphor, the wand has waved, the magic has worked, and we have been saved, whether we know it or not. Anything further than all this from Coleridge's best insights cannot be imagined; his phrases in this Credo are just the sort of dead objects for which he wanted to substitute living organisms. I think we know enough about his later thought to be sure that he did not become an addict to theological formulae as formerly to opium. But I believe that he did at times—perhaps at times of great emotional stress like this autumn of 1810—use religion as a drug; and if he did, and when he did, so much 'the less Coleridge he!'

The entry about love and friendship, dated the same day as the above, is headed 'Ego-ana'. It contains reflexions on the loss of his two dearest friendships, and although the tone is calm and the style (at first) impersonal, the references to William and Sara become more and more explicit as he goes on. It is one thing to be loved by a friend, and quite another to have a friend who is pleased to be loved and admired by me. One human being 'entirely loving me (this, of course, must have been a Woman)'—'in short, a WIFE, in the purest, holiest sense of the word', even without physical union and without parenthood, would have sufficed. I am conscious, he continues, of having for the fourteen best years of my life felt 'the most consummate Friendship . . . for a man whose welfare never ceased to be far dearer to me than my own, and for whose Fame I have been enthusiastically watchful.' Also, for ten years 'I have LOVED so as I should feel no shame to describe to an Angel'. Yet I am now forced to admit that 'No one on earth has ever LOVED me'.

He writes this without any of the embarrassing signs of self-pity, yet when any man—even Coleridge—says 'nobody loves me', it is likely that he is trying to shift on to others the blame for his own shortcomings. If nobody loves me, the chances are that it is because I am an unlovable person, though I may have loved others in my own way. Coleridge was too great a man not to see this, and he immediately adds, 'Doubtless, the fault must have been partly, perhaps chiefly, in myself. The want of reliability in little things, the infliction of little pains, the trifling with hope . . .' etc. One gives him due credit for this admission, though he does seem here to be viewing his own defects through a diminishing glass. Who that had not (like the Wordsworths) had Coleridge as an inmate for eight months could know how truly he was 'gey ill to live wi' '?

Coleridge, however, finds in himself another kind of explanation: his 'voluntary self-humiliation', the 'habitual abasement of myself and talents in comparison with the merits of my Friend'. Men, and still more women, take us at *our* own evaluation; if we are modest and self-effacing they think us poor-spirited. This accounts for 'Asra's' 'wavering and lukewarmness' towards him; women, he says, prefer those who 'are preferred by those around them'.[1]

In his *letters* of the succeeding months, on the other hand, he often writes much less collectedly about the treatment he has received from Wordsworth; he speaks of the wound that 'Wordsworth has wantonly and without the slightest provocation inflicted',[2] and we get phrases like 'unprovoked sufferings', 'thunder-clap', 'anguish', 'derangement of the brain', and so forth.[3] Sometimes in bitterness he speaks truth, as when he tells Crabb Robinson that 'Wordsworth is by nature incapable of being in Love, tho' no man more tenderly attached—'[4] And of himself he can write with equal insight:

moral obligation is to me so very strong a Stimulant, that in 9 cases out of ten it acts as a Narcotic. The Blow that should rouse, *stuns* me. . . . But I have never had any one, in whose Heart and

---

[1] *CN*, III, 4006.   [2] *CL*, 821 (April 28, 1811, to D. Stuart).
[3] *CL*, 823 (*c.* May 1, 1811, to Mrs Coleridge).
[4] *CL*, 814 (March 12, 1811).

House I could be an Inmate, who loved me enough to take pride and joy in the efforts of my power. . . . And I am too weak to do my Duty for the Duty's Sake [*ibid.*].

In accord with this thought is a Notebook entry made some months earlier:

Mere knowledge of the right, we find by experience, does not suffice to ensure the performance of the Right—for mankind in general.

It is the character and essence only of a perfect soul that knowledge of the Right is its sole motive of action; it alone, unlike most of us sinners, does its duty for duty's sake. Is there a medium to bridge the gap between 'mere conviction' and the appropriate action? Yes!—

This medium is found in Prayer, and religious Intercommunion between Man and his Maker.

What, he asks soon after, is the real difference between the best Theists and Atheists? Both understand that the Known is not enough to account for itself, and therefore that an Unknown must exist. The difference is that the Theist dedicates his 'noblest feelings of Love and Awe' to that Unknown, and connects it with his conscience and actions; whereas the Atheist 'leaves it a blank in the Heart, because it is a Blank in his Understanding'. Of course, for Coleridge, the Understanding had in such matters no say which was not subject to veto by the heart and the conscience. He goes on to develop the doctrine of *The Friend* concerning belief in God. He distinguishes between the *cause* of our having the '*Idea*' of God, and the *reason* for our believing in his *existence*. The 'Idea' of God is an assumption of the intellect, necessary to give intelligibility and wholeness to the mighty sum of things; so far, it is like a mathematical idea (e.g. that of a perfect circle), not realized in any one instance of its kind, but 'regulative' of them all. But whereas we do not attribute actual existence to (e.g.) the Idea of a Circle, we do attribute it to the Idea of God—or at least, he characteristically adds, 'those who do, know that all men ought to'. It is *a living God* that we believe in, not a speculative idea.

From the time when he left the Montagus, Coleridge was mostly domiciled (though not continuously) with John Morgan and his family. From November 1811 to January 1812 he gave a course of seventeen lectures on Shakespeare at Crane Court, Fleet Street. Directly these lectures were over, he went back to Greta Hall, picking up his boys at Ambleside en route, but studiously avoiding the Rectory at Grasmere[1]—although Dorothy wrote to Mrs Coleridge imploring her not to let him leave the north without seeing them:

> I passed through Grasmere; but did not call on Wordsworth. I hear from Mrs C. that he treats the affair as a trifle and only wonders at my resenting it—and that Dorothy Wordsworth before my arrival expressed her confident hope, that I should come to them at once!!—I, who 'for years past had been an ABSOLUTE NUISANCE in the Family'.[2]

Two days before leaving Keswick for London (via Penrith, not Grasmere) he wrote again to Morgan (March 24):

> the Grasmere Business has kept me in a fever of agitation—and it will end in compleat alienation—I have refused to go over, and Wordsworth has refused to apologize . . .

By the end of March (1812) he was back in London with the Morgans, never to return to the Lakes again. Another course of lectures (on Drama) followed in May–June, and yet another (on mixed topics) in the winter of 1812-13. I have already mentioned the formal 'reconciliation' with Wordsworth in London (mid-May, 1812), brought about by Crabb Robinson. This at least made it possible for them to meet again; by May 19, Wordsworth had seen Coleridge several times, walked with him to Hampstead, and attended at least one of his lectures. The last words that need be said on the affair in this book may as well be Coleridge's own, from a letter to his old friend Poole on February 13, 1813:

---

[1] Where the Wordsworths had moved from Allan Bank.
[2] *CL*, 856 (Feb. 23, 1812, to Morgan).

A Reconciliation has taken place—but the *Feeling* which I had previous to that moment, when the¾ths Calumny burst like a Thunderstorm from a blue Sky on my Soul—after 15 years of such religious, almost superstitious, Idolatry and Self-sacrifice—O no! no! that I fear, can never return. All outward actions, all inward Wishes, all Thoughts and Admirations, will be the same—*are* the same—but—aye there remains an immedicable *But*.[1]

From about the middle of 1811, no doubt in preparation for his lectures, *Biographia Literaria* material begins to appear in the Notebooks—sometimes in a form afterwards used verbatim in that work. For instance in No. 4066 there is an interesting version of the Fancy-Imagination distinction. Here he calls Fancy 'the imagination in its passive sense', presenting our conceptions as dead, fixed forms (like 'the Gorgon Head, which *looked* death into every thing'). Whereas Imagination is 'the fusing power, that fixing unfixes, and while it melts and bedims the Image, still leaves in the Soul its living meaning—'

Similarly, in 4112, we find him experimenting with, and finally reaching, the definition of A Poem which he afterwards used in the *Biographia*, beginning (in this version) with:

A Poem is that species of composition which being . . . opposed to Science, as having for its immediate object the communication of Pleasure, not of Truth . . . etc.

Who but Coleridge, however, would have inserted, between these two passages of literary theory an entry (4109) in which the Lamarckian theory of evolution is philosophically stated:

Instincts, or the germinal Anticipations in the Swell of nascent evolution, the dark yet pregnant prophecies of the Future in the Present bud or blossom forth in the Organs, and the Volitions beget the instruments of Action—

The entry defining Poetry ends with an almost verbatim draft for one of the most celebrated passages in the *Bio-*

[1] *Ibid.*, 888

graphia, that in which poetic genius is described as revealing itself in 'the balancing and reconciling of opposite or discordant qualities . : . more than usual State of Emotion with more than usual Order . . .' etc. So, too, in 4115 we find 'the sense of musical delight', and the power to 'modify a series of Thoughts by some one predominant Thought or Feeling', and much more of the familiar material (and often the very words), applied to the Shakespearean imagination.

Coleridge never ceased to feel and to declare, in various terms and guises, the difference between head-knowledge and heart-knowledge—the knowledge which is made up of intellectual abstractions from sense-data, and that which springs from involvement with our whole being. The fancy-imagination antithesis is one way of expressing this, and so is his distinction between popularly-diffused, 'useful' knowledge and wisdom through symbol and myth. 'Enlightenment' may explode many a 'superstition', but too often at the cost of the truth which was latent in the superstition:

> That thin and meagre Knowledge, which spreads over the People at large, in taking away their errors takes away too those feelings, those magnificent Truths implied in those errors . . . which are the offspring of the human Heart (No. 4154).

So 'rationalism', the unenlivened Understanding, has given us Socinianism in place of the divine non-sense of Christianity.

By the latter part of October, 1813, Coleridge was in Bristol, where he remained, for the most part staying with Josiah Wade, till the summer of 1814. Here he gave several courses of lectures, but they were truncated and interrupted by illness and above all by opium and spirits, which at this time reached the height of their malign influence over him. Some time in the spring of 1814, Cottle noticed that Coleridge's hand trembled when lifting a glass of wine. 'This good-natured and simple-minded fellow', says Chambers, 'must have been the only one of Coleridge's friends who did not by this time know what was the matter with him'.

He now learned what it was, and wrote Coleridge a reproving letter. Coleridge replied tragically, admitting all, and offering to put himself under voluntary restraint if the money could be raised. Cottle told Southey all this, and proposed subscriptions to raise an annuity for Coleridge. Southey's reply was truly characteristic; he strongly opposed the idea, referred to Coleridge's 'most culpable habits of sloth and self-indulgence', and declared that all his woes and embarrassments were 'owing to one accursed cause—excess in opium'. All that he needed to do was to 'leave off opium', come back to Greta Hall, and do some honest work for his family at last. Coleridge replied (to Cottle) that it was precisely will-power that he *could not* exert; after abstinence his pulse weakens and he fears death.

It is yet another example—none more striking—of Coleridge's amazing spiritual resilience, that during the April of 1814, when he was in the depths of addiction and remorse, and talking of voluntary restraint in Dr Fox's 'private mad-house', he should have been able to write Cottle a series of letters on religious themes: letters, too, more than usually impersonal in tone, and full of sustained and close reasoning. The first of these (*CL*, 913, early April?) is mostly about Eternal Punishment, but it begins (in its present fragmentary form) with a very interesting reply to what was evidently someone's (Cottle's own?) criticism of a phrase in *Religious Musings* (line 56).

> The declaration that the Deity is 'the sole Operant' is indeed far too bold; may easily be misconstrued into Spinosism; and therefore, though it is susceptible of a pious and justifiable interpretation [cf. the remarks quoted above, p. 139, on Bruno's 'pantheism'], I should by no means now use such a phrase. I was very young when I wrote that poem, and my religious feelings were more settled than my theological notions.

Of the rest of the letter, which is full of sense and insight, I will only quote this sentence:

> To him who but for a moment felt the influence of God's presence, the thought of eternal exclusion from that presence would be the worst hell his imagination could conceive.

The second (No. 921, dated by Griggs *c.* April 27) is about Prayer. Christians, he says, expect no miraculous or outward results from prayer; its 'effects and it's fruitions' are spiritual, and accompanied (as Archbishop Leighton has said) 'by an inexpressible Kind of Evidence, which they only know who have it'. To this he adds that even those who (like himself) cannot claim to have it, can *presume* it—

> 1. because Reason itself . . . feels the *necessity* of Religion; 2. but if this be not true, there is no Religion, no *Religation* or Binding over again, nothing added to Reason—and therefore Socinianism is not only not Christianity, it is not even *Religion*—it doth not *religate*, doth not bind anew.

The first outward result of prayer is 'a penitent Resolution, joined with a consciousness of weakness in effecting it'—and he adds, remembering his own many broken vows and fruitless prayers, a dread 'lest by breaking and falsifying it the soul should add guilt to guilt by the very means it has taken to escape from Guilt'.

This letter is noteworthy for containing the first reference to Leighton (1611-84), of whom Coleridge afterwards made such use in *Aids to Reflection*. For Leighton he had a great reverence, speaking of his works (in a note to this same letter) as occupying a midway space 'between inspired and uninspired Writings'—'something that must be felt even as the Scriptures must be felt'.

The third letter (late April, 1814) is a reply to Cottle's request for his views on the Trinity. It begins, as might be expected, with a refutation of the Socinian view that this doctrine is not to be found in Scripture. Coleridge chooses here to take 'the clear revelation of Scripture' as the basis of his belief, though he admits that it can also be supported by reason, or 'moral demonstration'. In this context, he is not concerned to argue the case for or against scriptural 'inspiration'; we may (he says) 'assume inspiration as admitted'. This granted, he can hurl Scripture back at the Socinians who refuse to see the Trinity there. He well knows their 'shifts and quibbles', and was once 'beguiled' by them; but now, 'escaped from their sophistries', he can declare that 'Socinians would lose all character for honesty, if they were to explain their neighbour's will with the same latitude of interpretation as they do the Scriptures'. Of course the doctrine is difficult and mysterious: 'it would be strange if otherwise'. But what is 'Revelation' for, if it 'reveals' nothing beyond our human grasp? It is an easier task, in any case, to overcome these difficulties than to surmount the obstacles confronting those (the Socinians) who admit the divine authority of Scripture, and yet try to force it into teaching Christ's mere humanity. Whereas in reality, 'not in an insulated passage, but through the whole breadth of its pages', the New Testament *does* declare the doctrine.

The 'moral demonstration' which Coleridge then sketches is ingenious, but to my mind less interesting than the more metaphysical approach described above (cf. pp. 114-15). It is based on the assumption that mind and matter are distinct, and that mind controls matter. We can conceive that one mind could control any number of limbs, or even separate bodies, and that these would still constitute one 'person' so long as the one mind ruled them. On this imperfect analogy he asks us to conceive of the One Mind of the Universe as operating in Three Persons. Still, we are not to accept this 'divine doctrine' as something which is 'clear to finite apprehension', but because Scripture teaches it. It is 'a doctrine of faith, not of demonstration' (Leighton).

There is one other important thing in this letter: 'I have in my head some floating ideas on the *Logos*, which I hope hereafter to mould into a consistent form. . . .' This is the first announcement of a theme which was to become the *leit-motiv* of Coleridge's later life and thought.

Letter 923 (dated by Griggs May 3-4, 1814) is of interest because, though written in humble repentance before God for wasted talents, he can yet be proud enough, before man, to

challenge the proudest of my literary contemporaries to compare proofs with me, of usefulness in the excitement of reflection, and the diffusion of original or forgotten, yet necessary and important truths and knowledge; and this is not the less true, because I have suffered others to reap all the advantages.

By September 12 (letter No. 951, to Daniel Stuart), Coleridge was settled as 'joint tenant with Mr Morgan of a sweet little Cottage at Ashley, half a mile from Box, on the Bath Road'. He reports that in mental and bodily health he is now 'on the whole better than I have been for at least 12 years'. After a few pages in which (as in 923, but much more explicitly) he sets forth his positive claims to distinction, as a counterpoise to his admitted failures and self-reproaches:

> I dare assert, that the science of reasoning and judging concerning the productions of Literature, the characters and measures of public men, and the events of nations by a systematic Subsumption of them under PRINCIPLES deduced from the Nature of MAN; and that of prophecying concerning the Future . . . was as good as unknown in the Public Prints before 1795-96. . . .

—after this, and after describing what sounds like an ideally ordered daily routine, he elaborates upon the theme of the Logos (announced in April, as aforesaid). His book on this subject, which was to crown his life's work, and which—if one could have credited his own statement in *Farley's Bristol Journal* August 27, 1814[1]—he was 'about to put to the press', was to be entitled 'Christianity the one true Philosophy'—or '5 Treatises on the Logos', or 'communicative Intelligence, Natural, Human, and Divine . . . illustrated by fragments of *Auto*-biography' (the germ of *Biographia Literaria*). The third Treatise, on the Divine Logos Incarnate, was to be a Commentary on St John's Gospel; the fourth on Spinoza and Spinozism; and the last, on modern Unitarianism, its causes and effects. The purpose of the whole, he says, is 'a philosophical Defence of the Articles of the Church, as far as they respect Doctrine, or points of Faith'.

By March 1815 he is at Calne in Wiltshire, staying (with the Morgans) at the house of a Dr Page; here he remained for about a year. It was the beginning of a period of exceptional activity; Coleridge was making a spurt to atone for lost time. During the next two years he collected his Poems

[1] See *BL*, II, 230.

for the volume called *Sibylline Leaves*, and wrote the *Biographia Literaria* (both these were published in 1817), the two *Lay Sermons* (1816-17), *Zapolya* (1817), the *Treatise on Method* (1818) and the 'rifacciamento' of *The Friend* (1818). And all the while the *opus maximum*, now called the 'Logosophia', was fermenting in his mind.

A typical illustration of Coleridge's habitual effort to connect and to unify is seen in letter No. 956 (March 7, 1815, to Cottle), where he dilates an aesthetic theory, within a few rapid lines, into cosmic proportions. One can watch and feel his mind taking sudden wing for an Icarus-flight—but a flight, not now into heady pantheism, but into *orthodox* speculation. Commenting on Cottle's poem 'Messiah', with evident desire to speak truth without hurting the author's feelings, he remarks that

> The common end of all *narrative*, nay, of *all*, Poems is to convert a *series* into a *Whole*: to make those events, which in real or imagined History move on in a *strait* Line, assume to our Understandings a *circular* motion—the snake with it's Tail in it's Mouth.

Then at once he shoots off into infinity: to the eye of God all past and future are one eternal present, all straight lines part of 'the great Cycle'—and 'such is a poem to that Image of God, which we were created into, and which still seeks that Unity, or Revelation of the *One* in and by the *Many*'. The One in the Many? Ha! is there here a whiff of the pantheistic opium? No, not if we remember the great paradox that

> tho' in order to be an individual Being it [i.e. man, the Image of God] must go forth *from* God, yet as the receding from *him* is to proceed towards Nothingness and Privation, it must still at every step turn back towards him in order to be at all—

He is now alert to resist every Spinosistic tendency, while never losing his reverence for Spinoza himself. A few days later (March 10, 1815) he is acknowledging to Dr R. H. Brabant of Devizes the loan of two books by Dr Edward Williams. On one of these, *A Defence of Modern Calvinism* (1812), he remarks that if modern Calvinism is really like this he has taken his last farewell of it:

It is in it's inevitable consequences Spinosism, not that which Spinosism, i.e. the doctrine of the Immanence of the World in God, might be improved into, but Spinosism with all it's Skeleton unfleshed, bare Bones and Eye-holes, as presented by Spinoza himself.

It differs only in lacking that 'noble honesty, that majesty of openness, so delightful in Spinoza',

which made him scorn all attempts to varnish over fair consequences, or to deny in words what was affirmed in the reasoning.

But no—it differs in more than that:

O I did injustice to thee, Spinoza!—Righteous and gentle Spirit, where should I find that iron Chain of Logic, which neither man or angel could *break*, but which falls of itself by dissolving the rock of Ice, to which it is stapled—and which thou with all thy contemporaries didst mistake for a rock of Adamant?

And what was this rock of ice? Coleridge explains in a footnote that it was the concept of God 'as an Object', 'a' God. Spinoza should have known that every 'object' presupposes a 'subject'; he should have started from either *natura naturata* as the objective pole, or '*I per se I*' as the subjective, and found at the 'equator' 'The living God', the identity of subject and object, who not only has within himself the ground of his own existence, but also the 'originating Principle of all dependent Existence in his Will and Word'. We are here in the presence of a great mystery, nothing less than the central paradox of existence, which only Faith can overleap: how can there be Many as well as One? How can the Immanence of God in the Creation, and the Immanence of the World in God, be reconciled with the existence of human beings, each with free wills and each thus morally responsible—beings at once dependent and independent? Coleridge could now solve this riddle by means of his distinction between Reason and Understanding. Understanding can only rivet upon us the iron chain of logic, and bind us fast in fate; but Reason, which is allied to the Will, knows by spiritual discernment, and by practical experience, that we are free. There is contradiction here?

Yes, of course! but is it not just what we should expect? Should we not expect the riddle of the painful earth to pass all understanding? Where the Understanding thus distorts the very basis of our moral lives, its conclusions *must* be wrong; this is a case where we must listen only to Reason, which tells us that the most 'pious' conclusion is the true one.

Perhaps all this helps to explain how it was that the famous 'One Life' passage in *The Eolian Harp* appeared *for the first time* in 1817, in the errata to *Sibylline Leaves,* and was not finally incorporated in the poem until the edition of 1828. One would have supposed that at these dates Coleridge would have been blue-pencilling pantheistic phrases in his earlier work, not putting in new ones. But we have seen that he had *accepted* the paradox and was no longer afraid of it; there *is* 'one Life within us and abroad', and we *are* part of it; yet as moral beings we rise superior to it, we are not its puppets. Similarly, God *is* in all things; in him we live and move and *have* our being (not *had*), and all nature *does* speak to us of its Maker; but this is a safe belief only so long as we do not allow the understanding, 'the mere reflective faculty', to paralyse us with a logic which is false to the spiritual facts.

I think, too, that stirrings of pantheistic sentiment ('and what if ——?'), and glimpses into the one life ('the life of things'), were among the most important sources of romantic poetry. If you felt inspired, the chances were that you felt 'pantheistic'—in some sense or other of that protean word. And this meant, let us remember, that if your intellect, or your conscience, or your theology (or all three) taught you later on that pantheism was a wicked heresy, you were more than likely to check your poetic impulses as 'shapings of the unregenerate mind'. I pass this over to the literary critics, for what it is worth, as yet another possible clue to the poetic 'decline' of Coleridge and Wordsworth (and others) in their maturer years.

The summer of 1815 was the gestation-time of the *Biographia Literaria,* Morgan holding a watching-and-writing brief as Sara Hutchinson had done for *The Friend.* The story of its birth has often been told, and I need not repeat it here in any detail. Originally designed as a 'general Preface' to the new edition of his Poems (*Sibylline Leaves*) it grew on his hands into a separate work. He had been reading *The Excursion* and the 1815 Poems and Preface, and by July he tells Brabant that he has felt

> the necessity of extending, what I first intended as a preface, to an Autobiographia literaria, or Sketches of my literary life and opinions, as far as Poetry and *poetical* Criticism are concerned . . . I have given a full account (raisonné) of the Controversy concerning Wordsworth's Poems and Theory . . . (as I believe) compleatly subverting the Theory and . . . proving that the Poet himself has never acted on it except in particular Stanzas which are the Blots of his Compositions.—One long passage—a disquisition on the powers of association, with the History of the Opinions on this subject from Aristotle to Hartley, and on the generic difference between the faculties of Fancy and Imagination—I did not altogether insert, but I certainly extended and elaborated, with a view to your perusal—as laying the foundation Stones of the Constructive or Dynamic Philosophy in opposition to the merely mechanic.[1]

Nothing could better illustrate Coleridge's mental habit than this quick conversion of a literary distinction into a philosophical one—or, putting it another way, his instant perception that the difference between two kinds of poetry bore a strict analogy to the difference between two world-views, and could therefore supply ammunition for his campaign against the 'philosophy of death'.

By September 17 (when the work was finished) he can tell Gutch (letter No. 974) that

> The Autobiography I regard as the *main* work . . . both because I think that my *Life* etc. will be more generally interesting [i.e. than the Poems], and because it will be an important Pioneer to the great Work on the *Logos*, Divine and Human, on which I have set my heart and hope to ground my ultimate reputation. . . .

The philosophical part, originally 'meant to comprize . . . a few pages', 'has now become . . . a sizeable Proportion of the whole'.

[1] *CL*, 972 (July 29, 1815).

Coleridge had not only been reading Wordsworth this summer: he had been brooding over his image of Wordsworth the man. The faults he now finds in his friend's character (as well as opinions) are seen in clearer relief after the estrangement, and are subconsciously felt as a sort of bitter compensation for his own defects. He

> would rather groan under his manifold sins and sorrows, all either contained in, or symbolized by, [Opium] than cherish that self-concentration [of Wordsworth's] which renders the dearest beings *means* to him, never really *ends* . . . [Wordsworth] has more than once gravely preached to [me] as a new discovery, what [I] had been years before attempting but in vain to persuade [W.] of, not only in conversation but by long letters—but who can re-articulate the pulses of the Air? And as to the Letters, they not being those of [W.], η αδελφηαδελφολατρα [the sister brother-worshipper] had made threadpapers of them![1]

His thoughts about *The Excursion* are measured and just, and I think quite free from any personal animus. The 'Ruined Cottage' he has 'ever thought the finest Poem in our Language' (of comparable length); and as to the rest, 'one half the number of it's Beauties would make all the beauties of all his Contemporary Poets collectively mount to the balance'. And yet, he did not feel it to be 'equal to the Work on the Growth of his own spirit'. Who would dispute this? Proofs abound in *The Excursion*, he goes on, that Wordsworth's genius 'has not flagged'; what makes him uneasy is that the poet seems to have

> convinced *himself* of Truths, which the generality of persons have either taken for granted from their Infancy, or at least adopted in early life, and attached all the weight of his own experiences and thought to doctrines and words, which come almost as Truisms or Commonplace to others.[2]

But Coleridge's finest comment on *The Excursion* (to be read in conjunction with chapters XXI-XXII of the *Biographia*) is in his letter to Wordsworth himself, of May 30, 1815.[3]

---

[1] *CN*, III, 4243.   [2] *CL*, 964 (to Lady Beaumont, April 8, 1815).
[3] *CL*, 969.

Lady Beaumont had 'most reprehensibly' (as E. L. Griggs rightly says) shown Wordsworth Coleridge's letter to her, and Wordsworth—in a stiff little letter oddly compounded of resentment and an affected willingness to be corrected— had asked for concrete examples of the faults imputed. Coleridge's reply is, in effect, that he is disappointed with *The Excursion* because, in spite of its many and high excellences, it was not *The Recluse*—not the great philosophical poem he had hoped for and waited for.

CHAPTER XIII

HIGHGATE; THE LAY SERMONS

ON April 10, 1816, Coleridge informed Byron that, in order to conquer the opium habit, he was about to lodge with 'a respectable Surgeon and Naturalist at Highgate' (Gillman). To Gillman himself he wrote on the 13th, announcing his approaching arrival, and warning him to be firm and strict, as 'unless watched carefully, I dare not promise that I should not with regard to this detested Poison be capable of *acting* a Lie', and using every kind of subterfuge: 'the cunning of a specific madness'. He arrived on April 15, 1816, 'to pass a month'—but he stayed for the rest of his life (i.e. eighteen years). Although there is evidence that he occasionally smuggled opium into the house, and although the opium-taking never ceased entirely, Coleridge did in this final period master the addiction, and did what was possible to make up for lost time. Those were years not only of production, but of inward poise, recovered self-respect, and unremitting mental and spiritual activity.

He had in fact written the *Biographia* and the first *Lay Sermon*, with Morgan as amanuensis, before the Gillman régime began. The latter work, known as *The Statesman's Manual*, bears the date 1816, so before discussing the relevant parts of the *Biographia* I propose now to consider it and the second *Lay Sermon* (1817) together.

Both *Sermons* are by-products of the resurgent energy which led to the remaking of *The Friend*, and they are as it were outliers of the same stratum. Their aim, in broadest terms, is the same: the prophetic recall to first principles, the denunciation of Mammon-worship, the substitution of the 'vital' for the 'mechanic' philosophy, the advocacy of true Christianity—in a word, a heroic challenge to the almost irresistible because unquestioned assumptions of the past 50 years.

The first *Lay Sermon* is titled 'The Statesman's Manual; or, The Bible the Best Guide to Political Skill and Foresight', and it is addressed, so the title-page reads, to 'the Higher Classes of Society'. No one knowing Coleridge would be misled for a moment into supposing that he was to use the Bible in any 'fundamentalist' or illiberal way. Nor would they impute to him any snobbery in the reference to the 'higher classes'; in those days the class-structure was still natural and functional, and anyone wishing to reverse certain cultural and ethical trends would have to do it by convincing, or winning over, those who did in fact set the tone and determine the direction of society. Coleridge was writing in the period of exhaustion, confusion and transition following the end of the Napoleonic wars, when the country's whole economy was shifting uneasily from a war to a peace footing, and when agriculture's historically privileged position was threatened both by the peace and by the Industrial Revolution. Although he does not here pretend to offer any 'practical' solution to these problems, he shows (as one would expect) a remarkable awareness of the way things work in political economy.

But Coleridge was a prophet and a soul-doctor, not an economist or politician. It was not for him to offer nostrums for the day, or any short-term expedients—no cure, indeed,

> That flatters us, because it asks not thought:
> The deeper malady is better hid;
> The world is poisoned at the heart.
> (*The Borderers*, 1034)

It is this deeper malady, this heart-poison, that Coleridge diagnoses, and it is in this, the true prophetic office, that he feels a kinship with Isaiah and Jeremiah. The Bible, the foundation-stone of Western civilization, is still for him (however 'enlightened' his views of its 'inspiration' were or became) the most potent symbol of that ancient wisdom from which the modern world was in apostasy.

The sufficiency of the Bible as an authoritative guide in all matters of personal Christian duty is generally admitted. But its authority extends beyond this; it is applicable also to all the great mutations of the world. Revolutions are explainable, not 'by anecdotes', but by the 'rise and fall of metaphysical systems'. World views are the real historical determinants. Coleridge was far from sharing the 'Marxian' view that social-economic causes are at the bottom of all historical change, and that 'ideas' are only mirages of the former. So far, indeed, that, according to him, the most important changes (even in commerce) 'had their origin in the closets or lonely walks of uninterested theorists'. The crimes and failures of 'the late dread [French] revolution' were all due to the neglect of maxims clearly enunciated by sages from Thucydides to Harrington—maxims which, however, had already been set forth far more cogently in the Bible. The Hebrew writers had this great advantage over all others, that their maxims flowed from the universal principles of reason, and these maxims 'are understood in exact proportion as they are believed and felt'. There is no attempt in the Bible to persuade by philosophic demonstration; its truths are of the kind which must be spiritually discerned, intuited by the Reason—not acquiesced in by the Understanding. Hence 'the imperative and oracular form of the inspired Scripture ["Thou Shalt", "Thus saith the Lord"] is the form of reason itself in all things purely rational and moral'. 'Knowledge' in the Bible is supremely rational; it is of the kind which is 'antecedent to the things known', whereas that of the understanding (the 'creaturely mind') is 'posterior to the things it records and arranges'; it follows that biblical 'knowledge' is likewise 'a spring and principle of action'. The understanding may suggest motives and guess at consequences, but the knowledge of God which is Faith 'produces the motives, involves the consequences'.

In appealing thus to the Bible, then, Coleridge is really reversing the procedure of the soap-box evangelical who proclaims 'the Bible is true from cover to cover! Believe it, and do what it says, or be damned!' What he asserts is that the saving principles were always acknowledged until their eclipse by Mr Locke and his worse disciples, and that they are found most authoritatively stated in the Bible—hence its supremacy amongst holy books. One can say, however, I think, that Coleridge is trying to enlist on behalf of his own system of beliefs the unquestioning respect for the Bible which in his day was still almost universal—however superstitious or nominal much of it may have been. It is as if he were saying to the worldly-wise men of his time 'You think I am mad to set myself against the Zeitgeist like this? Well, if so, the biblical writers were mad too, and surely you don't believe that, do you?'

Coleridge knew very well, as Mill said later, that universal acceptance of a belief may amount to much the same as ignoring it altogether; in reference to the Bible, there had descended upon us 'the deep slumber of a decided opinion'. He notes, as one of the gravest obstacles to taking the Bible seriously, 'the notion that you are already acquainted with its contents':

> Truths of all others the most awful and mysterious . . . are considered as so true as to lose all the powers of truth, and lie bedridden in the dormitory of the soul. . . .

You want something *new*, something not already latent within you? But 'to find no contradiction in the union of old and new' [and here he repeats the well-known passage from *The Friend*]—to contemplate the old and permanent with fresh feelings and to realize it anew, is precisely the mark of a lively mind.

If you ask for specific examples of biblical relevance to the present age, where—in the historical and prophetic books—will you *not* find them? And the great merit of biblical history, distinguishing it sharply from that of today, is its 'freedom from the hollowness of abstractions'. This sets Coleridge off on one of his diatribes against the philosophy of death. The history and political economy of the past 150 years

> partake in the general contagion of its mechanic philosophy, and are the product of an unenlivened generalizing understanding. In the Scriptures they are the living educts of the imagination. . . .

—of that reconciling power which, combining reason with sense-images, produces symbols 'consubstantial with the truths' they convey. History and prophecy, facts and persons, all have in Scripture a two-fold significance, 'a temporary and a perpetual, a particular and a universal application'.

Do not make the common mistake of confusing symbol with allegory or metaphor! The present age, alas! 'recognises no medium between literal and metaphorical', and so we are expected to identify faith either with a blind, literal fundamentalism, or with the counterfeit interpretations of the allegorizing understanding:

> Now an allegory is but a translation of abstract notions into a picture-language, which is itself nothing but an abstraction from the objects of the senses. . . . On the other hand a symbol . . . is characterized by a translucence of the special in the individual, or of the general in the special [the reference is to 'genus' and 'species'] . . . Above all by the translucence of the eternal through and in the temporal. It always partakes of the reality which it renders intelligible; and while it enunciates the whole, abides itself as a living part in that unity, of which it is the representative.

Similarly, the Bible differs from Greek philosophy in affirming, not a Divine Nature merely, but 'the living God'. In short, the Bible not only puts God at the centre of all political and moral issues, but it is concrete and imaginative in its style, and so fights alongside Plato, Shakespeare and Wordsworth in the struggle against the principalities and powers.

We have now, forsooth! a popular press, circulating libraries and a new 'reading public'. But Coleridge wants no part or lot in the 'plebification' of knowledge; he reiterates that he is now writing *ad clerum*, that is, to men of sound clerkly learning. And he thinks he has seen among such (where exactly, one wonders?) one hopeful sign:

> The notion of our measureless superiority in good sense to our ancestors, so general at the commencement of the French Revolution and for some years before it, is out of fashion. We hear, at least, less of the jargon of this enlightened age.

This, however, must not be allowed to produce despondency. We must not withhold education from 'the people' just because they have followed false lights; we must make it more thorough, make it universal. And the re-education of the élite itself is the first and essential step. But the task will be formidable:

> . . . alas! the halls of old philosophy have been so long deserted, that we circle them at a shy distance as the haunt of phantoms and chimeras.

Glancing back, before summing up, at what he has written, Coleridge offers for its defects an apologia in both senses of the word: apology, and justification. He knows he has rambled, and that his essay resembles 'the overflow of an earnest mind rather than an orderly premeditated composition':

> Yet this imperfection of form will not be altogether uncompensated, if it should be the means of presenting with greater liveliness the feelings and impressions under which they were written.

Here we have the true philosophy and vindication of Coleridge's methods or lack of methods in composition; to be at his best his mind must be in action and growth, and his feelings ardent as he composes. Thus he shines most of all in conversation, where he can range freely and follow the scent wherever it leads; next best, in marginal annotations, in notebooks and in letters, where formal arrangement is not expected. Least of all in set composition, where the requirements of order and strict progression freeze the genial current, and often inhibit him altogether. Thus the very nature of Coleridge's philosophy and religion, which required the soul and all its faculties to be continually alert and growing, and never to set rigidly in any mould, told against his effectiveness as an expounder of his own 'system'. There is much to be said for communication by hints and glimpses, and many of Coleridge's subtlest aperçus are far more suggestive, reverberate more, as fragments than they could in formal completion. On the other hand it can be said that a sound argument or exhortation can be conducted in orderly fashion, without loss of inner life, by a mind in command of itself and its materials. Some may even think that Coleridge's philosophy was itself the rationalization, rather than the *rationale*, of his basically immethodical tendencies. But the methodical we have always with us; a Coleridge we have not always—and who would wish him other than he is?

In conclusion, Coleridge urges that there are two wrong approaches to the Scriptures: the blindly literal, which accepts the words without enquiring into their meaning—or, if baffled, says 'it is a mystery'; and the reductive, which says 'Oh, it *only* means so-and-so', and reduces all the poetry, grandeur and symbolic richness of the Bible to the level of trite morality and the forms of the mere Understanding. What Coleridge (supported by St Paul) demands, is a 'spiritual intuition, or positive inward knowledge by experience of the mystery of God'. The 'mere acquiescence in truth, uncomprehended and unfathomed' is not enough; the Christian must know and possess the truth by living acts of faith ever renewed.

Appendix C of *The Statesman's Manual* is important as a summing-up of Coleridge's whole prophetic message to his times. It revolves round his great habitual antitheses: The One and The All, Reason and Religion, Reason and Understanding. Reason strives after 'knowledge of the laws of the whole considered as one'; Understanding, the 'science of phenomena', is concerned exclusively with 'particulars in time and space'. Reason seeks the One and the All, but in its search—if alone and without counterpoise—it is always in danger of falling into either atheism or anthropomorphism. But religion rights that unbalance, and, mediating between Reason and Understanding, maintains the proper balance between the Universal and the Particular. What this means, I think (or one of its meanings), is that religion is always about the immediate situation—my duty now, my relationship to somebody or something today, etc., and therefore pulls us continually back from abstraction to actuality; but, in doing so, it hallows each duty, person and choice by relating it to God. For the like reason, Religion has always fostered the Fine Arts, 'the common essence of which consists in a similar union of the Universal and the Individual'.

These reflexions lead Coleridge to give another of his analyses of 'Jacobinism'. Reason unbalanced leads straight to the impostures of the Jacobin philosophy, which is a hybrid between despotism and 'abstract reason misapplied to objects that belong entirely to experience and the understanding'. It gives us Cosmopolitanism without love of one's own country, and philanthropy without kindness; and it builds society on 'natural rights instead of social privileges, on the universals of abstract reason instead of positive institutions'. It follows, then, that reason

> must be interpenetrated by a power, that represents the concentration of all in each—a power that acts by contraction of universal truths into individual duties, as the only form in which those truths can attain life and reality. Now this is religion. . . .

Coleridge has not finished until he has delivered himself further on the Understanding, and the evil legacy of its uncorrected use: the 'philosophy of death':

> The eye is not more inappropriate to sound, than the mere understanding to the modes and laws of spiritual existence.

Its characteristic is 'clearness without depth'; its knowledge is of 'superficies without substance' and Coleridge cannot refrain from adding here that

> The completing power which unites clearness with depth, the plenitude of the sense with the comprehensibility of the understanding, is the imagination. . . .

Since the end of the seventeenth century, with the ascendency of the scientific and commercial spirits, the Understanding has renounced its allegiance to reason and religion, and set up alone as 'a harlot by the wayside'. The consequent debasement of all values culminated in the French Encyclopaedists and in the antichristian excesses of the Revolution.

> Prurient, bustling, and revolutionary, this French wisdom has never more than grazed the surfaces of Knowledge . . . and most assuredly it has purchased a few brilliant inventions at the loss of all communion with life and the spirit of nature. As . . . the result! . . .

an ignorant contempt of antiquity—a neglect of moral self-discipline—a deadening of the religious sense. . . .

Thank heaven! in spite of 'Thomas Payne' and his compeers, things have never been so bad in England. Open infidelity is no longer fashionable—indeed, it has even become 'a mark of original thinking to defend the Belief and the Ten Commandments: so the strong minds veered round, and religion came again into fashion'.[1]

The main differences between the 'mechanic' and the 'vital' philosophies are summed up in this: that the mechanical demands for every mode of existence 'real or possible visibility', and so knows of nothing but relations of 'unproductive particles' in space. 'This is the philosophy of death, and only of a dead nature can it hold good.' In life, and in a living and spiritual philosophy, reason and understanding interpenetrate, and generate a *tertium quid* including themselves but higher than each: religion. Religion is a 'total act of the soul'—'a life within life, evermore organizing the soul anew.'

In Appendix E Coleridge analyses with great subtlety the grounds on which we hold anything to be credible or incredible, and shows that such judgments rest upon (often unconsciously held) metaphysical presuppositions. Coming to the immediate issue, he asks point-blank:

> Is it likely that the faith of our ancestors will be retained when their philosophy is rejected?

And rejected it has been, ever since the Revolution of 1688, and the associated triumph of Locke and his philosophy—

> that system of disguised and decorous Epicureanism, which has been the only orthodox philosophy of the last hundred years. . . .

Locke managed to please all parties, and exploit all the unexamined assumptions, by 'threading on the dried and shrivelled, yet still wholesome and nutritious fruits, plucked

[1] A phenomenon familiar in our own times through the writings of Chesterton, C. S. Lewis and many professional theologians. No doubt S. T. C. was thinking of *le christianisme* as revived by Chateaubriand etc., but in the England of his time what other example is there save Coleridge himself?

from the rich grafts of ancient wisdom, to the barren and worse than barren fig-tree of the mechanic philosophy'. Thus 'sensible' (i.e. Laodicean) Christians,

> delighted with the discovery that they could purchase the decencies and the creditableness of religion at so small an expenditure of faith, extolled the work [Locke's *Essay*] for its pious conclusions:

while the infidels praised it for its basic principles, from which, if rigorously applied, only their own kind of conclusions could legitimately be deduced.

In conclusion Coleridge declares once again his conviction that

> the principles both of taste, morals, and religion, taught in our most popular compendia of moral and political philosophy, natural theology, evidences of Christianity, etc., are false, injurious and debasing.

What is more, the present-day 'defences' of orthodoxy, of the Church articles and of the 'true principles of government and social order', will never be effective so long as their authors—as is too often the case—share the same presuppositions as their antagonists ('worship the same Baal with their enemies'). The orthodox champion will appeal in vain to the language of Scripture, and the Socinian will expose the incongruity of orthodox belief with the Lockean principles that both sides accept, as long as 'all alike preassume, with Mr Locke, that the mind contains only the relics of the senses'.

The Second *Lay Sermon* (1817), 'addressed to the Higher and Middle Classes, on the existing Distresses and Discontents', starts as an enquiry into the causes of the post-war malaise. 'Peace has come without the advantages expected of peace.' In the late transition from war to peace the national economy has reeled. During the war 'we almost monopolized the commerce of the world', and with the artificial stimulus of war, trade and agriculture enjoyed 'unprecedented prosperity'. Now that this is all over, what next? Coleridge shows considerable political and economic insight in analysing the causes of poverty, unemployment, the agricultural depression, etc.; but my concern is with that later part of his argument where he returns to first principles and seeks for the 'deeper malady' hidden in the spirit of the age. He finds it in

> the over-balance of the commercial spirit in consequence of the absence or weakness of the counter-weights. . . .

What are these 'counter-weights'?

The first, which Coleridge—unlike writers of today—can refer to as a natural law, and which therefore causes him no embarrassment or feeling of guilt, is

> the ancient feeling of rank and ancestry.

Admittedly there were evils as well as benefits flowing from this old social system, but 'still it acted as a counterpoise to the grosser superstition for wealth'.

The second deficiency (of which we have heard before) is caused by

> the long and ominous eclipse of philosophy; the usurpation of that venerable name by physical and psychological empiricism; and the non-existence of a learned and philosophical public . . . neither philosophy nor theology, in the strictest sense of the words, can be said to have even a public existence among us.

Gone are the days when Lorenzo the Magnificent used to discuss metaphysical problems with Pico della Mirandola, Ficino and Politian—as topics most germane to the arts of government. Today, our public men despise all metaphysical speculations—even those recent works which are supposed to be 'so many triumphs of modern good sense over the schools of ancient philosophy'. Yet, Coleridge insists,

> an excess in our attachment to temporal and personal objects can be counteracted only by a pre-occupation of the intellect and the affections with permanent, universal, and eternal truths.

The third and most important counterpoise or corrective to the commercial spirit is Religion: religion in the true and proper sense—that full faith which expands the intellect while it purifies the heart, and which is sovereign over the whole man, his outward acts as well as his mind and his affections. Mere 'warmth without light' will not do; neither will mere 'acquiescence without insight'.

Here Coleridge breaks off to explain once again why the true Light, the Light of Life, is not the Socinian moonlight (light without warmth). The self-styled 'Unitarians' should rather be called 'Psilanthropists', or 'assertors of the mere humanity of Christ'. These people conceive Christianity to consist in 'a few plain doctrines', confirmed indeed by the miraculous events recorded in Scripture, but really needing no New Testament to confirm them—since they have always been known. Indeed these men, though professing reverence for the Scriptures, only 'pick and choose' from them 'morsels, and fragments for the support of doctrines which they had learned beforehand from the higher oracle of their own natural common sense'. Of course many Socinians are in fact very good men, but their goodness is not the natural produce of their system: 'the fruit is from the grafts, not from the tree'. The natural fruit would be an 'overbearing, scornful, and worldly disposition'; and it is a fact that this is 'the only scheme of religion that inspires in its adherents a contempt for the understandings of all who differ from them'.

Most men do not trouble themselves at all about religion; they just leave such matters to the parson, or—if they care about maintaining a respectable public image—go through the customary Sunday motions. But Coleridge has also in mind a much more interesting class of men, for whom he invents the inspired title 'Christian Mammonists'. We in our time, since Max Weber published *The Protestant Ethic and the Spirit of Capitalism*, have been familiarized with the links between religious profession and economic practice—especially with the ways in which Protestantism (with Puritanism as its most distinctive manifestation) either encouraged, or at least did not check, worldly accumulation. But who before Coleridge was acute enough to apply this sort of analysis to a Protestant sect, the Quakers, whom he selects here as his most striking example? As in so many other fields, so here—in the sociology or economics of religion—he is far ahead of his time. The only forerunner I can think of was John Wesley who, when deploring the decline of evangelical fervour among the more prosperous Methodists, observed that the very morality their religion enjoined—frugality, thrift, prudence, restraint etc.—led straight to wealth, and that in turn to worldliness. The Quakers are the best representatives of a class whose religion has preserved them from 'all the gayer and tinsel vanities of the world'; the English character owes to their example 'some part of its manly plainness in externals'.

> Here then, if anywhere . . . we may expect to find Christianity tempering commercial avidity and sprinkling its holy damps on the passion of accumulation.

But do we find this? The Quakers are godly people, practising a 'pure household religion', with family prayers and Bible readings twice a day; they believe 'the threats and promises of Revelation', and their lives—personal, domestic and social—are disciplined and unexceptionable. Yet their faith is not of the kind which overcomes the spirit of the world. Admirable as are their industry and sobriety, these very virtues advance their worldly interests and win the approval of society. Unless there is some 'adequate counterpoise', their way of life will lead them to consider all things in the light of utility, prudence and market value. And in fact we do not find that the unworldly feelings of such people lead them to moderation in their worldly pursuits. There are all too many righteous men: honest in their dealings, 'scriptural in their language, alms-givers, and patrons of Sunday schools', men who pray daily not to be led into temptation, who yet daily pursue with all their might the very temptation from which omnipotence alone could deliver them. The fact is that the Quakers, though shrewd in business, have neglected *learning*, and especially theology: they have moreover no trained ministers. Their Christianity has been poured upon them, once and for all, 'as from a shower-bath', and there is nothing left for the reason or understanding to do. Their Christianity relates purely to such matters as grace, justification, redemption and atonement; it is an *opus operatum*, a *fait accompli*, and exists in splendid isolation from all worldly concerns. Therefore it embodies no necessary critique of such concerns; it leaves its devotees with the world 'all before them', free to exploit it to the utmost. So, while gluttony, drunkenness, unlawful sex, war and dishonesty are sinful, the pursuit of wealth is not—particularly if you do not *enjoy* what it can buy. Or rather, this pursuit is pictured as hungering and thirsting after righteousness alone, but not forgetting meanwhile that righteousness brings its due rewards to the good man. Thus, 'habitually taking for granted all truths of spiritual import', this kind of religion

> leaves the understanding vacant, and at leisure for a thorough insight into present and temporal interests, which, doubtless, is the true reason why its followers are in general such shrewd, knowing, wary, well-informed, thrifty, and thriving men of business. But this is likewise the reason why it neither does nor can check or circumscribe the spirit of barter. . . .

To be efficacious, religion must be 'the poetry and philosophy of all mankind'; it must reign over both heart and head; nothing less will provide the requisite 'countercharm to the sorcery of wealth'.

CHAPTER XIV

BIOGRAPHIA LITERARIA (*1817*)

IT does not fall within my present purpose to discuss this celebrated book in any detail. Its most widely read section, the critique on Wordsworth, has long been thoroughly absorbed into the bloodstream of literary criticism—and moreover, I am concerned here mainly with Coleridge's religious thinking. The *Biographia* is not, except by implication, a direct contribution to this; and to such passages as are relevant I have already alluded above.

It is difficult to find any concise phrase describing what the book is really 'about', or to what main conclusions it was meant to lead up. If it were indeed only, as the title page of 1817 reads, 'Biographical Sketches of my Literary Life and Opinions', one could readily accept its digressive and fragmented shape and be thankful for the many flashes of insight—sometimes prolonged into sustained illumination—which occur throughout. But the guns it carries are too heavy for us to treat it as a pinnace. To drop the metaphor, the philosophic sections—the refutation of Hartleian Associationism, and the Subject-Object discussion—are so closely reasoned and so formidable that we are led to expect what we never get: a full *exposé* of the metaphysics of the Imagination, and a full vindication of Christianity as the only true philosophy. It is tantalizing to be forced to think so hard with Coleridge about the foundations of poetry and religion, and then never to be given the superstructure: or rather, never to be shown how the completed structure is linked with the bedrock. One might say, indeed, that the book is 'about' what Coleridge himself was 'about'; its central purpose is that to which he himself was dedicated, and all his other prose writings, viz. to exalt Imagination and Reason over Fancy and Understanding, to expose the insufficiency of the mechanical philosophy, to assert Life and Liberty against Death and Necessity, and to vindicate religion against infidelity—more particularly, Orthodox Christianity against Socinianism. But the book is Coleridge himself in another sense; it is Coleridge discoursing on Highgate Hill, veering and eddying between anecdote, literary criticism of the finest order, and metaphysics of the most austere. All the way through, he is excusing himself from the final plunge by remembering his great work, his *opus maximum*, in which his entire thought will at last be displayed with due subordination of parts to whole. So, although he will sometimes allow himself to enlarge further upon the philosophic sub-structure than any English critic had yet done, he will not go *all* the way. Not yet! Wait for my treatise on the Logos or Communicative Intelligence, and my commentary on St John, and all will be made plain. The classic instance is of course the end of Chapter XIII, so exasperating to many, where just as the game is in sight and the hounds are in full cry (we have emerged bruised and lacerated from the thicket of abstractions), he breaks off with a 'letter' to himself from an imaginary friend urging him to leave all that for a more fitting occasion. Good advice in a sense, no doubt, and certainly welcome to the kind of literary reader who finds all he needs in Chapters XIV-XXII. But annoying to those who know that Coleridge could, if he would, have established the Imagination quite firmly on his metaphysical foundations, and who innocently and excusably thought that at this very point he was going to do it.

So one is thrown back, as in spelling out theological doctrines from scriptural hints, upon piecing together such oracles as Coleridge has uttered, and interpreting them in the light of what we know of his main drift and ends.

The subject of the poetic Imagination, as Coleridge regards it, is by no means remote from his religious preoccupation; on the contrary, it is an essential part of it. With Coleridge, as we well know, no main study or topic was remote from the others or from the whole, and to establish the autonomy and validity of imaginative experience was an important step in establishing the same for religious experience. And so we must take his encounter with

Wordsworth's poetry, as described in Chapter IV here, as a stage in his religious progress. There was, he felt immediately, something new here, something rich and strange, which had been absent from poetry (as far as he knew) since Milton. What was it? It was the something he afterwards called Imagination, but in 1796 it presented itself as (to quote the oft-quoted once more):

> the union of deep feeling with profound thought; the fine balance of truth in observing, with the imaginative faculty in modifying the objects observed; and above all the original gift of spreading the tone, the *atmosphere*, and with it the depth and height of the ideal world around forms, incidents, and situations, of which, for the common view, custom had bedimmed all the lustre, had dried up the sparkle and the dew drops.[1]

Fired by this thought, of the revitalization of the commonplace, Coleridge quotes from *The Friend* a passage I have already discussed (above p. 125), in which genius is said to be shown typically in this power to be amazed at the obvious:

> to contemplate the ANCIENT of days and all his works with feelings as fresh, as if all had then sprung forth at the first creative fiat. . . . To carry on the feelings of childhood into the powers of manhood; to combine the child's sense of wonder and novelty with the appearances, which every day for perhaps forty years had rendered familiar . . . this is the character and privilege of genius. . . .

This power, which in Chapter XIV he describes simply as that of giving 'the charm of novelty to things of every day', he felt to be predominant in Wordsworth, and 'I no sooner felt'—he says in a phrase that epitomises his whole life, mind and character—'I no sooner felt, than I sought to understand'. Repeated meditations on this poetic experience convinced him that it was the work of a power higher than any manifested in Augustan or eighteenth-century poetry as a whole, a power which he came to distinguish as Imagination in opposition to Fancy. Like scores of others, I have said my piece (years ago) about Coleridge's Imagination-

---

[1] *BL*, I, 59.

Fancy distinction, and I do not wish to discuss it again in the present context. My concern now is simply to emphasize that the distinction is not merely, in Coleridge, a distinction between two kinds of poetry, but an aspect of the antithesis between two world-views: the mechanical and the 'dynamic', the dead and the living. He needed 'imagination', just as he needed Reason, Freewill, and moral responsibility, to support him in his campaign against the Philosophy of Death. For in Imagination, as in Willing, man is free, self-determining and creative. In Imagining, man is repeating, on a finite scale, the eternal creativity of God. How can this be substantiated, shown to be more than a 'what if?' or a 'dare I add?'? It cannot, of course. All that can be done is to write suasively in support of such a view, and I must content myself with pointing to some of Coleridge's ways of doing this.

Coleridge takes pains first, in Chapters V-VIII, to demolish the doctrine of Association as taught from Hobbes to Hartley. Not that he denies that we do in fact associate ideas and images, and that long trains of such images can be followed up by anyone relaxed enough to yield to the stream. But what concerns him is not the linkages but the stream that carries them in a particular direction; not the rustling of the leaves but the breeze that agitates them. In other words, association is not effected mechanically, but by the spiritual breeze, the state of mind or soul, which summons from the vast storehouse of images just those which it needs. What he resists is the doctrine that the mind is compounded out of sense-impressions, that it is built up and constituted out of them, that its motions are mechanically produced by impulses from without. For him, will, reason and life are the pre-conditions, not the outcome, of organization. Hartley's system leads logically (or would, if his heart had not been wiser than his head) to blind mechanism: 'the whole universe', Coleridge reflects as he writes, 'co-operates to produce the minutest stroke of every letter, save only that I myself, and I alone, have nothing to do with it.' Whereas in reality the Will, and acts of thought and attention, are distinct powers whose function it is to 'controul, determine, and modify the phantasmal chaos of association'.[1] Similarly Hume's degradation of 'cause and effect' into a mere succession of ideas linked by 'association' leads to a corresponding degradation of every fundamental idea in ethics and theology. The great fault of all materialist explanations of mental phenomena is that, presupposing material particles moving in space as the basic reality underlying all things, they try to visualize these phenomena in terms of matter and motion, whereas they are really independent of both. Hartley's vibrating 'tubes' and mental 'hooks', used by him to explain association of ideas, are prime examples of this attempt 'to render *that* an object of the sight which has no relation to sight'. This is the 'despotism of the eye', from which mechanical materialism suffers, and which leads it to 'mistake distinct images for clear conceptions'. Real thinking must keep clear, as Aristotle did, of 'fictions'—fictions such as the attempt to 'picture' the mind as a mass of interlocked particles and configurations.

But the mystery remains: there is the external world, and there is myself, 'Object' and 'Subject'. How can these come into contact?—how can there be 'knowledge'?—and what is it 'knowledge of'? Coleridge summarizes (Chapter VIII) the history of philosophers' attempts to bridge the gap created by the Cartesian dualism: Matter as mere 'extension' in space, and Thought, non-material and spaceless. In the materialist explanation, which reduces mind to matter-in-motion, perception is not accounted for; motion can only generate more motion. A looking-glass, as the Cambridge Platonists had seen, reflects objects but is not *conscious* of them. And the materialist's mind is no more than a mirror, a 'lazy looker-on'. Priestley, to defend materialism, stripped matter of all its accepted properties and left only 'spiritual' powers or energies (cf. p. 35 above).

Coleridge, in his retreat from materialism, does not fall into solipsism or subjective idealism. He is just as certain of the world's existence as of his own. The 'Object' is there, and whatever it may be it has the power to excite in me, the 'Subject, a representation of itself. We have know-

[1] *BL*, I, 81-82.

ledge, we have 'truth', when the representation corresponds to the object. If we ask, how do we *know* when or if it does so correspond?—what validates that 'knowledge'? Coleridge could only have replied (and I do not know that he ever did, clearly): experience, faith, and perhaps Theological speculation. I do not see that he could have found much fault with Descartes's reply: 'because God is not a deceiver'.

I do not propose to try to summarize Chapters XII-XIII, in which, with the well-known importations from Schelling (duly noted by Sara in 1847, and by Shawcross), he sets forth some of his metaphysical presuppositions. I do not pretend, even after many readings during more than fifty years, fully to understand them. I am content, following Coleridge's own maxim, to 'presume myself ignorant of his understanding'. I will merely try to suggest in what way he might have hoped that his metaphysics, and his theory of knowledge, might have given support to his faith in Imagination, in the soul of man, and in God. And let me just remark first on what to anyone unfamiliar with Coleridge might seem odd, namely, that in a work which to a degree un-exampled in English literary criticism uses metaphysics as the groundwork of literary theory, and which elsewhere defends metaphysical thought as needful and religious, he should yet condemn it in Chapter I. He says there that even before the age of 15 he had 'bewildered' himself 'in metaphysicks, and in theological controversy' beside which even poetry and romances had seemed insipid. From this state he was delivered by the 'genial influence' of Mr Bowles's Sonnets. But, he goes on,

> Well were it for me, perhaps, had I never relapsed into the same mental disease: if I had continued to pluck the flower and reap the harvest from the cultivated surface, instead of delving in the *unwholesome quicksilver mines of metaphysic depths* [my italics]. But if in after time I have sought a refuge from bodily pain and mismanaged sensibility in *abstruse researches* [do.], which exercised the strength and subtlety of the understanding without awakening the feelings of the heart; still there was a long a blessed interval, during which my natural faculties were allowed to expand, and my original

tendencies to develop themselves: my fancy, and the love of nature, and the sense of beauty in form and sounds.[1]

This must have been written in one of those moods, at one time frequent but later rare, in which he would let himself guess that he had once been a poet indeed. His more habitual pose in maturity was to deny that he had ever really been one—*Wordsworth* was the poet—and to embrace 'abstruse research' as an anodyne, or an escape from domestic misery and the pangs of hopeless love. To judge from the above and other remarks, and especially from the famous passage in *Dejection*, he would wish to be regarded as a poet *manqué*, who had plunged into metaphysics in the spirit of 'evil, be thou my good'. No doubt he often used introspection and abstract thought as he used opium. But he was so greatly gifted in just that kind of analysis that he cannot have really regarded it as vicious—even though he knew that it was stealing from him 'all the natural man' and becoming, in a derogatory sense, the 'habit of his soul'. For the most part, he accepted the toil of thought as his allotted portion; and, after all, the main burden of his prophetic message was the recall from the false philosophies of the age, and a plea for return to the older ways of metaphysical thinking. We have in Coleridge a most complex nature, and must not be surprised by these fluxes and refluxes of thought and passion. 'Nor useless do I deem' it to follow him, as I am trying to do in this book, mainly on the level of thought. Having accepted the atrophy of his poetic powers, he staked everything upon his intellect, and intended his final and greatest work to be philosophical. That it was never completed is no argument; neither was *Christabel*.

To return, then: there is 'Object', or Nature; and there is 'Subject', or Intelligence. But—and this is Coleridge's point—we must not dwell upon either side exclusively, or think of either as more 'real' than the other. We must rather dwell upon their fusion or coalescence. For it is the fact, transcending all Cartesian and other dualisms, and perhaps truly to be called miraculous (though S. T. C. does not

[1] *BL*, I, 10.

call it so), that these 'antagonists' are always and unremittingly locked in embrace. Subject and Object are one in the act of knowledge. The two polar opposites at the heart of things: the universe of objects, and the 'supervening' intelligence, interpenetrate, to beget a *tertium aliquid*, partaking of both. Now the starting point of the 'dynamic' (Coleridge's) philosophy is the affirmation of self-consciousness: 'I AM'. We should start here, with self-knowledge, not with the 'IT IS' affirmation of materialism. Fichte (says Coleridge) 'by commencing with an *act*, instead of a *thing* or *substance*', dealt a mortal blow to Spinozism.[1] In introspection we already have the first and basic instance of the coalescence of subject and object, for in becoming conscious of self I am making the subject, I, its own object. But consciousness of self is inseparable from consciousness of the not-self; we cannot choose but be, not only conscious, but conscious *of*. What is happening when we are aware of 'tree', 'table', etc.? We are registering these things as modifications of our self-consciousness; we are knowing ourselves in them. Not that the things are 'unreal' for that reason; they are most real, and the only 'things' we can know by sensation. 'Things', as we know them (and we can only so know them) are the product of the fusion of the I and the not I. There is that without us (what I. A. Richards called 'x') which, when it acts upon and with the I, produces 'things', the world. No other world is given or will be given, so let us not call it 'subjective' or 'unreal'—even though we 'half-perceive and half-create' it. Why should we not? Is it not better to be partners with Nature (God?) in constituting our world, than to be passive receivers of something alien to us?

We are edging nearer and nearer to the central point. It is the affirmation, dogma or intuition—call it what you will, for it is certainly not 'demonstrable', any more than religious faith is—that a bond exists, an affinity, between Nature and Man whereby these interchanges and fusions ('ennobling interchange Of action from without and from within')[2]

[1] *BL*, I, 101.
[2] *Prelude*, XIII, 375 (1850 text); XII, 376 (1805).

are not only possible (what is real must be possible) but truth-bearing.

Perhaps we are now in a position to reconsider the celebrated definition of 'Imagination' at the end of Chapter XIII of the *Biographia*:

> The IMAGINATION then, I consider either as primary, or secondary. The primary IMAGINATION I hold to be the living Power and prime Agent of all human Perception, and as a repetition in the finite mind of the eternal act of creation in the infinite I AM.[1]

The I and Not I, subject and object, are coalescing all the time to give the world of everyday experience. We are participants and collaborators in this process, not passive beholders of an *opus operatum*. This is why Coleridge assigns 'perception' to the faculty he calls 'Imagination', rather than to some purely intellectual faculty; he wants to stress the *creativeness* (albeit unconscious at this primary level) of our mere perceptions themselves. When you or I have apprehended 'tree' or 'table' we have already exercised the (primary) Imagination. To call perception itself 'imaginative' is to hint as broadly as possible at the universality and central importance of the imaginative function. But that is not all: there is Coleridge's theological addendum:

> the repetition in the finite mind of the eternal act of creation in the infinite I AM.

This is sometimes dismissed as pious cliché or 'mental bombast', and is certainly ignored by some even of Coleridge's most sympathetic interpreters. But in fact, to him, it was not only a sober truth but also one on which everything depended. He did not flourish it as a piece of fine-sounding rhetoric; it summarized the results of years of hard thinking. The Primary Imagination gives us The World through the interaction of Object and Subject, the Not-Ourselves with Ourselves; but how then did the Not-Ourselves come to exist? Because of the necessary creativeness of God: that is to say, God's self-consciousness, which is his word or the

[1] *BL*, I, 202.

Logos, creates the world, since in him thought and act are one. In giving existence to all things possible, he made man 'in his own image'. Our minds are thus reproductions in miniature, and on a finite level, of the mind of God—and specifically of God as Creator. In him we have (not *had*) our being, so we are miniature creators every minute of our waking lives. The mixture of sheer dogma and 'revelation' with psychological experience in all this is very remarkable. It may be distasteful to many today, but it must be grasped if we want to understand Coleridge.

'Miniature creators' perhaps—at least let us grant it provisionally, for the sake of peace. But not *poets*: for that, we need something more—the Secondary Imagination:

> The secondary Imagination I consider as an echo of the former, co-existing with the conscious will, yet still as identical with the primary in the *kind* of its agency, and differing only in *degree*, and in the *mode* of its operation. It dissolves, diffuses, dissipates, in order to re-create; or where this process is rendered impossible, yet still at all events it struggles to idealise and to unify. It is essentially *vital*, even as all objects (as objects) are essentially fixed and dead.

Here we meet with some new principles, principles necessary to explain why the work of the primary imagination—wonderful as it is, and repeating in miniature the divine creativity itself—is yet not enough. It does not satisfy the deep craving of the human heart for

> something loftier, more adorned
> Than is the common aspect, daily garb,
> Of human life.[1]

'The world', being part-constituted by us, is not necessarily 'fixed and dead'—though it can all too easily become so. Its quality varies with the quality (imaginative or moral) of the beholder. Most of us belong to the 'poor loveless ever-anxious crowd' who can see only an 'inanimate cold world'.

And 'would we aught behold of higher worth'—? Presumably we should answer 'yes! but how is this possible?

[1] *Prelude*, V, 575 (1850); 599 (1805).

And if it were, would it be *true*?' Coleridge's answer is, first:

> we *receive* but what we *give*
> And in *our* life alone does nature live.
>
> .   .   .   .
>
> Ah, from the soul itself must issue forth
> A light, a glory, a fair luminous cloud
> Enveloping the earth!

We see what we deserve to see, what our eye brings means of seeing.

It may be objected that it is unfair to quote from the poem *Dejection* (1802) in trying to explain what Coleridge wrote nearly fifteen years later. I agree that in general this sort of procedure would be hazardous and unscholarly—rather like using *Religious Musings* as a commentary on *Aids to Reflection*. Coleridge's mind, as I have often said, was continually growing and flowing, and without strict precautions one ought never to say 'his view *was that* . . .' etc. Moreover, *Dejection*, as its title proclaims, was the expression of one particular mood, however settled that mood seemed likely to become. But Coleridge quoted this poem himself, in 1814, to illustrate the views he then held about 'The Beautiful',[1] and I know of no repudiation, in the later writings, of the poem's teaching. When he said 'in our life alone does nature live', and when he spoke of an 'inanimate cold world', he did not mean that nature was inwardly and essentially 'dead', or the world in itself really cold and inanimate. He meant that they *appear* so to the eye and soul of dejection. But even in this poem he makes it clear that the world need never appear cold or dead; only give him *Joy*, and it will soon come to life again. It never had been dead; but it could not respond to him as long as, without Joy and without the shaping spirit of imagination, he failed to give it the kiss of life.

Most people spend their whole lives (except perhaps for 'moments ah! too rare') in the uncreative and unawakened state. Their world is the everyday world of prosaic routine,

---

[1] *Principles of Genial Criticism*, in *BL*, II, 240-41.

cold and inanimate, full of objects fixed and dead, the world
of the Primary Imagination. Well! if this is the *donnée* of
the primary imagination, which imitates in small the creativeness of God, must it not be a 'true' representation? And must
not all attempts to heighten or embellish it lead simply to
misrepresentation and falsity (Bentham said 'all poetry is
misrepresentation')? Coleridge would answer 'Yes, if the
modifications are fanciful; no, if they are imaginative'. He
knew that there was a way—Shakespeare's way, Wordsworth's way—of heightening and 'intensifying' (S. T. C.
coined this word) nature *without* distorting it. It was to express
this that he invented the symbol of 'moonlight on a known
and familiar landscape', and the image of polishing a piece
of marble to bring out the veins already there. Wordsworth's
poetry, above all, abounded in example of imaginative
power—the 'auxiliar light' from within, which 'on the setting
sun Bestowed new splendour'—power exerted to modify
nature, yes, but 'working but in alliance with the works
Which it beholds'. If it be asked: who *wants* all this?—why
struggle to see a 'light that never was on sea or land'? Why
not be content with the daily ration of cold porridge, eaten
by the light of common day?—the answer, or one answer,
could be 'Divine discontent! We are made that way, made
with a craving for something "loftier" than the "common
garb of human life"'. Some seek this through the various
escape-routes (sexual, chemical, etc.); the wiser sort seek it
in art, which works the miracle for you. You may not be
able to work it yourself, but wouldn't you *like* to see the world
transformed like this if you could? Well, if you can't *live*
poetry in your own life, attain it through the eyes of others!

Let us return to the text of Chapter XIII. I have been
glossing Coleridge rather freely, but it was in the hope of
disclosing some of the missing links and unstated assumptions, in and beneath his argument. The Secondary Imagination, then (let us think of it as the poet's imagination),
carries on one step further the work of the Primary. It
consciously ('co-existing with the conscious will') sets about
the business of 'subjecting the shows of things to the desires
of the mind' (Bacon's phrase), that is to say, giving new life,

shape and unity to the flux of everyday images. It 'dissolves, diffuses and dissipates, in order to re-create'; dissolves *what*? The ice-crust of the commonplace, which hems us in (*Was uns alle bändigt, das Gemeine*); the dead inanimate world of the Primary Imagination, which will not start into life without our initiative. 'It struggles to idealize and to unify': to 'idealize' here does not mean to give a *couleur de rose*, and therefore false, picture of anything; it means to pick out the essential 'idea' of a thing, person or action, and present it free from accidental trappings. It also means to steep it in the life and thought of the poet, making it not just a casual fact but a living symbol of his emotion. Coleridge tells us, elsewhere in the book, and much more memorably than when he is trying to be formal and scholastic, how this imagination works. It gives 'the charm of novelty to things of every day'; it modifies objects by 'reducing multitude to unity, or succession to an instant', and by transferring to them a 'human and intellectual life . . . from the poet's own spirit', shaping them into a symbol of 'a predominant passion'. It reconciles a whole series of opposites:

> sameness, with difference; . . . the general, with the concrete; the idea, with the image; the individual, with the representative; the sense of novelty and freshness, with old and familiar objects; a more than usual state of emotion, with more than usual order; judgment ever awake and steady self-possession, with enthusiasm and feeling profound or vehement. . . .[1]

'It is essentially vital, even as all objects (as objects) are essentially fixed and dead.' I think what I have already said and quoted explains that.

> A primrose by the river's brim
> A yellow primrose was to him,
> And it was nothing more.

The regular action of the world tends to make Peter Bells of us all. If a primrose, or anything else whatever, is a mere 'object' to us, and if the whole world is just an aggregate of such objects, then we are responding to it on the level of

[1] All these phrases from *BL*, XIV.

the mere understanding. Directly the poetic imagination is evoked, the whole spectacle takes on a new and exciting aspect, and depth on depth of meaning is suggested. Consequently poetry, if truly imaginative, is life-bearing and life-enhancing; consequently too, it is akin to religion and necessary for Coleridge's prophetic message. Fancy merely toys with the wooden jigsaw pieces supplied by memory and association; it tries to enliven and rejuvenate, but only succeeds in decking out the lifeless.

But there are still some gaps in the argument, of which some readers may well be uneasily conscious. Granted that imaginative work gives us pleasure, enhances life, satisfies human cravings and so forth—what relation have its products to 'Truth'? Why do poets and critics claim that an imaginative interpretation is 'truer' than a factual or scientific account?—why 'forms more real than living man'? On the level of empirical psychology one could say, I suppose, that a poetic image (say a description of a flower or an animal) is 'truer' to human experience of these things because it sees them in their emotional setting, and not just as objects for dissection and analysis. But this would not be enough for Coleridge, nor would it satisfy those who even today feel that art is somehow bringing them nearer to reality than 'real' life does—giving them glimpses into 'the life of things'. Coleridge does not set forth the whole position connectedly, but there are oracles from which we may fill in the gaps if we want to.

Some of the clearest of these are to be found in the essay *On Poesy or Art* (1818?), printed at the end of Vol. II of Shawcross's edition of the *Biographia*. He has been discussing the meaning of 'imitation' in aesthetic theory, and showing how this differs from 'copying'. A 'mere' copy, such as a waxwork, is universally allowed not to be 'art', whatever accidental interest it may have. No, a true 'imitation' is something that humanizes nature; it exists somewhere midway between a thought and a thing. There must be, in an artist's 'imitation', an unlikeness in the likeness, a difference in the sameness. And what is the 'nature' which is being imitated? Here we come to the very heart of the mystery, and find—in the centre of the labyrinth—one of Coleridge's most exciting formulae, one which always sets him a-quiver with speculative animation: the distinction between *natura naturata* and *natura naturans*. *Natura naturata* ('nature natured') is the fixed and dead world of the primary imagination; it is the *fait accompli*, the *opus operatum*. Don't imitate *that!*—if you do, you can produce nothing but Mme Tussaud effigies or photographs. *Natura naturans* ('nature naturing') is the world still alive and at work, straining and yearning after fuller realization of itself. How do we know that there is such a world? The answer is of course that we don't, in the sense of being able to prove it or verify it scientifically. The most we can say is that this is a metaphysical way of signifying (or signalling) what the world feels like to an awakened sensibility. To understand Coleridge—and this is all I am trying to do: not to 'prove' any proposition—one must simply realize that such an intuition (or intimation) excited him with a sense of approach to a glimpse of 'Truth'. And what if—? *Dare* I say—? Let us have the passage, then:

> If the artist copies the mere nature, the *natura naturata*, what idle rivalry! . . . Believe me, you must master the essence, the *natura naturans*, which presupposes a bond between nature in the higher sense and the soul of man.[1]

There is then this 'bond'; 'the life which is in us is in them [the things outside us] likewise'. O the one life within us and without! It is in virtue of this shared life that the imagination, when dealing boldly with substantial things and not merely decorating surfaces ('fancy'), can mould things in the direction of their own unfolding.

There is only one other thing to add—a wild surmise: the artist, he has been saying, must 'make the external internal, the internal external', must 'make nature thought, and thought nature'—then

> Dare I add that the genius must act on the feeling, that body is but a striving to become mind—that it is mind in its essence.[2]

[1] *BL*, II, 257.   [2] *Ibid.*, 258.

We may perhaps sum up the drift of all this, and show its relevance to our present purpose, with these phrases from Chapter XIII:

> We begin with the I KNOW MYSELF, in order to end with the absolute I AM. We proceed from the SELF, in order to lose and find all self in GOD.
>
> . . . true metaphysics are nothing else but true divinity.[1]

A few scattered references to religion must be noticed, or noticed again (cf. above, p. 127) before leaving the *Biographia*. There is, in Chapter IX, the important acknowledgment of his debt to Plato, Plotinus, Ficino and Bruno, who all (he says) contributed to prepare his mind for 'the welcoming of the "Cogito quia sum, et sum quia Cogito" '. Further, 'how dare I be ashamed of the Teutonic theosophist, Jacob Behmen [with whom Schelling himself had so much affinity]'? Or of Fox, or of Law? All these, mystics some of them, shared a sense of the 'indwelling and living ground of all things'. They helped

> to prevent my mind from being imprisoned within the outline of any single dogmatic system. They contributed to keep alive the *heart* in the *head*; gave me an indistinct yet stirring and working presentiment, that all the products of the mere *reflective* faculty partook of DEATH . . . and enabled me to skirt, without crossing, the sandy deserts of utter unbelief.[2]

True, this style of thought, *may* be 'converted into an irreligious PANTHEISM'. Spinoza had beckoned, and never wholly lost his spell over Coleridge. But he could at no time believe that Spinoza's *Ethics* were 'incompatible with religion, natural or revealed', and now—at the time of writing the *Biographia*, he is 'thoroughly persuaded of the contrary'.

Chapter X is called 'A Chapter of Digressions . . .' and it is so. But *what* digressions some of them are!—many of them much to my purpose, and some already glanced at. One of the best is the Quantock meditation on the Supreme Being. The *idea* of such a Being seemed inescapable, a

[1] *BL*, I, 186 and 191.   [2] *Ibid.*, 94-98.

logical necessity, though his 'existence' could not be 'demonstrated'—any more than that of even any external *object* can. Nor could this Being's mere existence, however credible, be taken as evidence for his *moral* attributes as creator.

> For a very long time, indeed, I could not reconcile personality with infinity; and my head was with Spinoza, though my whole heart remained with Paul and John.[1]

Then follows the most important passage of all (cf. above, p. 127), in which Coleridge avows that, even before he read Kant, there had dawned upon him 'a certain guiding light' (I will repeat it here: it can hardly be too much stressed):

> If the mere intellect could make no certain discovery of a holy and intelligent first cause, it might yet supply a demonstration, that no legitimate argument could be drawn from the intellect *against* its truth. And what is this more than St Paul's assertion, that by wisdom, (more properly translated by the powers of reasoning) no man ever arrived at the knowledge of God? . . .
>
> I became convinced, that religion, as both the corner-stone and the key-stone of morality, must have a *moral* origin; so far at least, that the evidence of its doctrines could not, like the truths of abstract science, be wholly independent of the will. It were therefore to be expected, that its *fundamental* truth would be such as MIGHT be denied; though only by the fool, and even by the fool from the madness of the *heart* alone. . . .

And there is an even bolder affirmation, pointing still more directly to an 'existentialist' type of decision:

> It could not be intellectually more evident without becoming morally less effective; without counteracting its own end by sacrificing the *life* of faith to the cold mechanism of a worthless because compulsory assent.[2]

If 'God exists' were a statement of the same order as 'Twice 2 are 4', it would have no *religious* value; nobody could deny it. But a religious affirmation is a statement of faith, not of fact; and its religious value consists precisely in its committing the believer to a certain kind of living. 'Conscience

[1] *BL*, I, 134.   [2] *BL*, I, 134-6.

peremptorily commands it', says Coleridge; and in adopting
it we are not just assenting to a demonstration, but obeying
a vision. The words used by Coleridge of the Imagination
are applicable to Faith, and may legitimately be adapted
thus:

> Could a rule be given from *without*, [faith] would cease to be
> [faith], and sink into a mechanical [assent]. . . . The *rules* of
> [religious believing] are themselves the very powers of growth and
> production.[1]

Finally, there is in the last Chapter (XXIV) a summarized
statement of faith which anticipates in brief much of *Aids
to Reflection* (see below, Ch. XVI). He has been com-
plaining bitterly of unfair treatment by reviewers, particularly of the suggestion that he had shown 'potential infidelity'
in the first *Lay Sermon*. An egregious accusation indeed!
and one very difficult for a modern mind to take seriously;
he had said that where Reason and Religion 'are their own
evidence', miracles are superfluous. Miracles may be *pillars*
of the Church, but they are not its *foundation*. He then lists
what he thinks the true evidences of Christianity: (1) its
'consistency with right Reason'; (2) the miracles through
which it was first revealed; (3) the sense in us of the desir-
ableness, the need, of Redemption; (4) the experience of
actually living out the faith, the 'Trial of it'. Of these (3)
and (4) are now the most operative. You must *be* a Christian
in order to have faith in it—this is the circular argument
'incident to all spiritual truths'. ' "Do the will of my Father,
and ye shall KNOW whether I am of God".'

He ends with a final slap at the Unitarians. He has been
accused of denying them the name of Christians. Well, how
can I *tell* whether or no a man is a 'Christian'? A man may
have so much divine love in his heart that his speculative
opinions don't signify, however erroneous they may be. All
that can be said is that if the doctrines I believe in are
Christianity, then Unitarian*ism* is not.

[1] *BL*, II, 65.

CHAPTER XV

THE PHILOSOPHICAL LECTURES
(1818-19)

BETWEEN the *Biographia Literaria* and *Aids to Reflection* (1825) Coleridge 'sat upon Highgate Hill'— thinking, writing and above all talking; and in the regular weekly 'at homes' receiving and influencing an increasing number of eager young listeners. Here at last he had found his most congenial mode of communicating with a public, and disseminating his ideas. As he said, he could do nothing with *effort*: thus, he felt more at ease writing letters than essays, and most of all, in conversation (chiefly monologue). 'My eloquence', he said himself, 'was most commonly excited by the desire of running away and hiding myself from my personal and inward feelings, and not for the expression of them.'[1] Not many 'great talkers' have been so frank about their motives or impulses, and one's own experience confirms the truth of his self-analysis. Much 'brilliant' talk is undoubtedly a smoke-screen put up for defence and evasion. But Coleridge was also capable, in congenial company, of being genuinely excited and fired by ideas, and would mount up on wings like an eagle. Or he would run—and not faint—even when his pursuers lost the scent, and gave up the chase ('Did you understand what C. was saying?' 'Not a word.' 'Neither did I.'). What he could not do with pen in hand and a deadline to meet, he could do with joy and triumph, in monologue, given sympathetic and responsive listeners. He also gave, in 1818, two more courses of Lectures, one literary and one philosophical. Before discussing *Aids*, then, I will glance at a few important passages in the Letters, Notebooks and Lectures of this period. Many of the best of these, naturally, appear in his published books—and these I shall pass over.

In a Notebook entry of 1818 (4408) he speaks of the

[1] Quoted (from Allsop's ed. of *Letters*, 1836) by Shawcross, *BL*, I, 208.

enormity of 'leaving out God' in philosophy. No doubt it happens because in Science the introduction of a 'Will' destroys the first postulate of this discipline. But—'if God be', how wretched must be the system which uses Him merely as a starting point! Shortly after this, he lists a few observations on the nature of religion:

(1) It is not a system of speculative propositions, or dogmas; it is wholly *practical* in its aim, and therefore *imperative* in its tone.

(2) Miracles are not *proofs* of religion, but they may well be necessary *results* of revelation.

(3) Belief founded entirely on *historical* evidence is insecure.

(4) Christ is to be thought of not primarily as a *'teacher'*, but as a *'doer'*.

(5) Socinianism is not a religion but a theory. It skirts and evades the true depths, and sets up a Deity who is merely a 'good-natured pleasure-giver'. It coaxes us with 'if you will only be good!—yes, I know all that, but my will is weak.

(6) Stop weakening Scripture by glib explainings-away, and by *allegorizing*. This is a slippery slope.

(7) The great object of Religion is the subjugation of the outward senses to Faith—or putting it another way, of the *passive* kind of Belief to the active and self-created kind.[1]

In the late summer of 1817, writing to Frere, he doubts if by 'Natural Light' alone man could have learnt any of the *moral* attributes of God—an observation of immemorial orthodoxy, and certainly older than Bacon, who had said the same. The following month, he sends C. A. Tulk (a Swedenborgian) a long summary of his metaphysical 'system', which was formed (he says) from the study of Plato, the school of Ammonius, Scotus Erigena, Bruno, Behmen and Spinoza, 'long before Schelling had published his first and imperfect view'. In December 1817 (13th, to J. H. Green) he explains that although he reverences Kant as the only philosopher for thinking men, he rejects his moral teaching as Stoical and loveless. Fichte's great contribution to the Dynamic Philosophy was the substitution of 'Act' for 'Thing' as the first step (cf. above, p. 195). As for the

[1] *CN*, III, 3581 (my own summary).

Natur-philosophen, Schelling and Steffens: since his own opinions were formed long before he knew them, or Fichte, he almost feels he might have been more useful if left to his own devices without ever having been aware of their co-existence. Schelling was too ambitious, too anxious to figure as the 'Grand Seignior of the *allein-seligmachende Philosophie*'—but a great and stimulating genius all the same. (A year later he calls Schelling's ideas 'Behmenism, translated from visions into Logic' (To Tulk, Nov. 24, 1818)). It is interesting, and pleasing, to find him ('early May' 1818) defending legislation on behalf of the 'poor Cotton Factory Children'. Anticipating the Ruskinian line, and that of all later humanitarians, he denounces standard 'Political Economy' as a pseudo-science based on mistaking certain abstractions for the whole of human nature.

Coleridge's 'Philosophical Lectures' (1818-19), one of the last courses he delivered, are rich indeed in matter—nothing in the least like them had ever been given before in England—but most of the material has already been before us in other contexts. Coleridge hated lecturing, seldom commanding in the lecture-room the spontaneity and fire which came readily in a drawing-room. He lamented to Collins that *he* must lecture to live, whereas Scott, Southey and Byron had captured their own age and posterity too. Poetry, for him, was out of the question; it would only revive the feelings from which 'abstruse research' gave asylum. There were thirteen of these lectures, and in Miss Coburn's edition (pieced together from newspaper notices and Frere's jottings), they make a sizeable volume.

All the possible philosophies were worked out, Coleridge insists, long before Christ. All we have since seen have been various re-appearances, bound up with the manners and politics of each period, but not in themselves new. So it is not surprising to find that he attributes to Pythagoras his own latest views (recently set forth in the *Biographia*) on the Subject-Object relation. There is a homogeneity between subject and object; the power that contemplates is in essence one with that in nature which produces the object contemplated. The soul is not a 'passive receiver'; the mind is itself an 'act', and the outward object is partly the product of mind. All the main ways of thinking followed fast: subjectivism (Zeno), scepticism (Eleatics), materialism (Democritus), etc.

There are but two philosophies in the final analysis: the Platonic and the Aristotelian. Obviously Coleridge belongs to Plato, but he gives Aristotle his due as the inventor, or rather discoverer, of logic—the laws of thought. Plato begins with the thinking *power*, and teaches us to look, not at phenomena, but at the essential *powers* behind them. 'Objects' themselves can only be seen by 'seeing powers', and that which could *make them be seen* must be an agent with powers like the beholder's. What seems passively a 'seen object' must owe its existence to an active power. For Aristotle, on the other hand, the mind *is* a 'blank or empty receiver', which nevertheless can and must generalize sense-data as 'reality'.

Throughout these lectures Coleridge (as the Cambridge Platonists had done before him) censures the false and upholds the true doctrines of his own age under the guise of a historical survey. All this has been said and thought before! The same errors have been exploded again and again, yet they recur in unabated vigour. For instance, in Lecture VI (on Sceptics, Stoics, Epicureans and Christians) he uses Epicureanism to expose that kind of modern amorality which strikes 'ought' and 'should 'out of its vocabulary, and admits no universal criterion of duty or virtue. Then there is 'Theodore the Atheist', prototype of the modern honest agnostic, whose position proves the truth of St Paul's 'no man by power of reasoning ever arrived at God' (cf. above, p. 204). Self-knowledge (Stoicism) teaches the moral imperative, but Christianity supplies the *aid* to the obeying of it. In a fine sermon-passage he shows how philosophy can only point to a Good which by philosophy alone is unattainable. Light *and* warmth together are essential—not moonlight *or* stove! Plotinus *begins* with the beatific vision instead of—like Christianity—leading up to it. Religion is the 'final cause' of philosophy, but there can be no true religion without philosophy. Religion meets the hopes, not proofs, 'derived from the sum total of our human nature'; and man can become like his Maker in one way only—the moral way, by imitating His goodness.

On the Schoolmen (Lecture IX) Coleridge is very interesting. He begins by protesting against the notion of their 'uselessness'—even though in the earliest stages they sometimes mistook logical truths for 'existential [one of S. T. C.'s most remarkable coinings] realities'. Show me (he says) one single opinion formulated since the fifteenth century which had not been propounded by some schoolman during the Realist-Nominalist disputes!—the disputes, that is, between those who held that the forms of the human mind, by which man is compelled to think, are *existential realities*, and those like Locke who held that they were mere 'reflexes' from the senses. He sees Occam on Faith as an anticipator of knowledge through and by the moral Will; and alchemy as the precursor of true chemistry. The Schoolmen at least deserve our respect for trying to re-unite reason and religion, with due subordination of reason to religion (Lecture XI).

From the Middle Ages to the Restoration, you had metaphysics without experimental physics and (C.'s own phrase) 'experimental psychology'; from the Restoration on we have had the two last without metaphysics. Bruno taught that every being, however apparently inanimate, has a *life* to be elicited; he also taught the law of 'polarity': Being manifests itself as a tension of opposites, but opposites which have a ground of identity and unite to form a *tertium quid* (cf, above, p. 195). Behmen, 'my own friend', taught the 'indwelling and living ground of all things' (above, p. 203). Bacon showed that the *prudens quaestio dimidium est scientiae*, and did *not* recommend mere sterile accumulation of observed facts. He trusted that the laws of reason would be found to correspond to the laws of nature, and, like Plato, understood that the link between them is the One Great Being whose eternal reason is the ground both of the mind's ideas *and* of the corresponding external realities.

Dogmatic Materialism (Lecture XII) is founded upon 'fictions' (i.e. corpuscular configurations imagined as 'visible') and other unsupported assertions—'atoms' of various alleged sizes, shapes and 'powers'. It represents Life as the *product* of 'organization'—which is literally preposterous or hind-foremost. It is as if one should call building the product of the house; whereas all organization presupposes an organizing power. Mind is reduced by this teaching to sensation, which is 'explained' as the property of specific kinds of atoms in motion. All processes of perception are represented as purely passive, and so all our actions are mechanically determined. But motion can only propagate motion, so consciousness is not accounted for.

Kant has undermined the foundations of this vile heresy by showing that the mind is not a mere 'passive recorder' but is active in perception and half-creates ('constitutes') its own objects. Of equal significance is Kant's teaching about Reason, Conscience and Religion: it is not Reason that assures us of God, but Conscience; yet Reason can *assent* to what Conscience requires.

The final Lecture (XIII, March 22, 1819) is supposed to be about German philosophy approached through Locke; but preliminaries occupy two-thirds of it. It ends with an echo of *Biographia*, which is thus rendered by the reporter:

> Having first shown that though the reason could bring nothing positively coercive in proof of religious truths, which if could it would cease to be religious and become mathematical, yet he demonstrated that nothing could be said with reason against them.

CHAPTER XVI

AIDS TO REFLECTION (1825)

'IT would indeed be more correct to say that the present volume owed its accidental origin to the intention of compiling one of a different description than to speak of it as the same work.' So wrote Coleridge in the 'Advertisement' to the first edition of *Aids* (1825). The original intention had been to compile an anthology from Leighton's works, with brief notes and biography, to be called 'The Beauties of Archbishop Leighton'. As he proceeded, his mind and spirit caught fire; commentary soon outgrew the texts, and Coleridge found himself writing a book on the process of reaching belief in Christianity—beginning with Need and ending with Trial.

I think the success of *Aids* (for to me it is his best prose work) is largely due to this 'accidental origin'. Coleridge could never work well by sheer effort, or under a sense of compulsion; as he said, he could not write mechanically like Southey. 'I converse better than I compose, and write better letters than essays'—and he might have added 'better marginalia'. *Aids* is in a sense a volume of marginalia on Leighton. By adopting the method of quotation and comment Coleridge shuffled off the constraints of formal treatise-making, and attained, quasi-undesignedly, the freedom to be himself, and to do an important thing *tanquam aliud agendo*. Because he was supposed to be commenting on Leighton, he could produce, as it were incidentally or as a side-issue, an introduction to Christianity far more effective than anything he could have done by direct attack.

Aids to Reflection is still, *mutatis mutandis*, a book one could and should put into the hands of the very class of readers for whom it was originally intended: 'the studious Young at the close of their education or on their first entrance into the duties of manhood and the rights of self-government'. Considering the immense changes that have come about since 1825, it is startling how often Coleridge speaks straight home to our condition. He belonged to that rare class of minds which are prepared to set themselves against the master-currents of their time, and to go on fighting the *zeitgeist*, alone if need be, with unremitting courage and determination. He knew that his opinions ran directly counter to most of the teachings and presuppositions prevalent for the past 150 years: and as we can now see, it is for that very reason that his message is so often pertinent to our own age—an age which has inherited the same valuations and acted upon them still more heedlessly and unquestioningly. Christianity certainly seemed at a very low ebb in 1825, consisting as it did too much of 'acquiescence without insight, warmth without light—the adherence of limpet to rock'; confronted too, from without by much open infidelity, the overspill of the French Revolution, and corroded within by what Coleridge called the 'dry rot' of Socinianism. In those days the popular mind associated intellectual enlightenment with unbelief, and assumed all believers to be feeble-minded or fanatical. It was therefore with amazement that they found Coleridge, admittedly the profoundest and subtlest thinker and most learned man of his generation, taking sides with the angels and offering to prove that 'the Christian Faith is the perfection of human intelligence'. Today, when established Christianity has dwindled to a degree which would have shocked the men of 1825, such a proposition may seem still more, much more, 'unacceptable' and incredible. Yet we are not unfamiliar with the spectacle of the intellectual turned (or remaining) Christian; we have the literary line leading from Chesterton to C. S. Lewis, T. S. Eliot and W. H. Auden; we have the Christian thinkers in apostolical succession from Kierkegaard to Jaspers, Bultmann, Tillich and Bonhöffer. Voices crying in a much worse wilderness than Coleridge's, no doubt; and some of them making a faith out of what he would have thought atheism itself. Still, in so far as they have tried to rejuvenate Christianity by making it a matter of doing and willing, a matter of existential decision, they are to be thought of as his successors. There is a passage in the 'Author's Preface' to *Aids* which—style apart—might have been written by Maritain or some other neo-Thomist of the 1930s:

> Whatever is achievable by the Understanding for the purposes of worldly interest, private or public, has in the present age been pursued with an activity and a success beyond all former experience, and to an extent which equally demands my admiration and excites my wonder. But likewise it is, and long has been, my conviction, that in no age since the first dawning of Science and Philosophy in this island have the truths, interests, and studies that especially belong to the Reason, contemplative and practical, sunk into such utter neglect, not to say contempt, as during the last century. It is therefore one main object of the present volume to establish the position, that whoever transfers to the Understanding the primacy due to the Reason, loses the one and spoils the other.

So he announces, in the 'Introductory Aphorisms' of *Aids*, that he aims to rescue vital truths from the neglect caused by their universal acceptance (cf. Mill's 'deep slumber of a decided opinion'); to bring truth to life in his readers by teaching them to *reflect* upon it in relation to conduct and being, and to turn their minds inward upon themselves.

The general plan of *Aids*—a plan elastic enough to allow Coleridge plenty of enlivening digression, and so to keep him spontaneous—is to lead his disciple through the preliminary stages of Prudence and Morality to Religion; that is, to show how religion is the crown and fulfilment of maxims admitted even by worldly wisdom to be expedient or binding. Prudence is shown to exist at various levels, from the basest self-regard up to more enlightened kinds of self-love, and upwards still to fusion with real morality.

It may surprise some readers today to find Coleridge opening his section 'Reflections, introductory to Moral and Religious Aphorisms', with an attack upon the ethics (or non-ethics) of 'Sensibility'. This does not seem at first sight to have much relevance to us today. Dean Inge spoke

of the 'poisonous legacy of Rousseau'; this is a denunciation
of the poisonous legacy of Sterne—and who is now in
danger from that quarter? Yet this is the passionate strain
in which Coleridge writes:

> All the evil achieved by Hobbes, and the whole School of Material-
> ists, will appear inconsiderable if it be compared with the mischief
> effected and occasioned by the sentimental philosophy of STERNE,
> and his numerous imitators. The vilest appetites, and the most
> remorseless inconstancy towards their objects, acquired the titles
> of *the Heart, the irresistible Feelings, the too tender sensibility*; and
> if the Frosts of Prudence, the icy chains of Human Law thawed
> and vanished at the genial warmth of Human *Nature, who could
> help it?*

Leaving Sterne out of account, and the special forms of
sentimentalism associated with his name, we have something
here which applies more startlingly to the present time than
to Coleridge's—for the pleas of 'irresistible feelings',
'nature' and 'who could help it?' are now urged in excuse
for complete moral anarchy and abdication of responsibility,
without even the hypocritical assumption of 'sensibility' to
cover them. What Coleridge opposed with all the force of
his nature, and would have opposed now, was any doctrine
tending to impair the dignity and prerogatives of Man by
substituting impulse for responsible decision and plunging
the Will back into Nature and the chain of physical causation.
'Do you in good earnest aim at Dignity of Character?'—he
asks his (supposed) youthful reader. He takes for granted
the answer yes (could he today?), and goes on: then eschew
the twilight realm between Vice and Virtue!

> Are not Reason, Discrimination, Law, and deliberate Choice,
> the distinguishing Characters of Humanity? Can aught, then,
> worthy of a human Being, proceed from a Habit of Soul, which
> would exclude all these . . . ? Can anything *manly*, I say, proceed
> from those, who for Law and Light would substitute shapeless
> feelings, sentiments, impulses, which as far as they differ from the
> vital workings in the brute animals, owe the difference to their
> former connexion with the proper Virtues of Humanity . . .?

In our own time the notions of human dignity, responsible will and self-government (formerly known as 'character', a word now disappearing from use), have been watered down by psycho-analysis, and by the determinisms (economic or biochemical) which teach that our conscious motives are all suspect, all epiphenomena—rationalizations of the 'real' motive-forces and drives which are subconscious. Moreover, the individual has not much chance of respect, or claim to dignity, in a planet which is already overstocked with people (all very much alike and mostly rather low-grade), and will very soon be suffocated with them. It is significant, I think, that the visual arts have largely renounced the human and other natural forms in favour of abstractions and distortions; and that music has renounced the expression of natural emotions in favour of mathematical and other patterning. The artists of the pictures in *Punch* (other than advertisements and political cartoons) no longer—as they did up to twenty years ago—show men and women as they are; they prefer to represent them (often very amusingly) as gnomes, insects, moon-calves or goblins. This is not a Coleridgean digression: it is meant to show that this present age has more to learn from him, if it would but listen, than his own times had.

In the 'Prudential Aphorisms' he makes some characteristic points and distinctions. For instance, though the dictates of virtue may coincide with those of self-interest, they do not proceed from the same point. Happiness may indeed be the reward of virtue, but virtue is not to be pursued for the *sake* of this reward—or it loses its quality as disinterested goodness. In other words *consequences* must not be made *motives*:

> Wherein, if not in this, differs the friendship of worldlings from true friendship? Without kind offices and useful services, wherever the power and opportunity occur, love would be a hollow pretence. Yet what noble mind would not be offended, if he were thought to value the love for the sake of the services, and not rather the services for the sake of the love?

Bearing in mind the stages in the spiritual pilgrimage of

his readers, he offers in 'Moral and Religious Aphorisms'
much wise preliminary advice. Thus, in tackling the works
of theologians, begin by habitually translating 'the theological terms into their *moral* equivalents', saying to yourself

> This may not be *all* that is meant, but this *is* meant, and it is that
> portion of the meaning, which belongs to *me* in the present stage
> of my progress. For example, render the words, sanctification of the
> Spirit, or the sanctifying influences of the Spirit, by Purity in Life
> and Action from a pure Principle.

While we are still at the stage of contemplating religion
'under the form of morality', we are to be reminded that
there is more to come; there are spiritual truths which can
only spiritually be discerned. But, remembering how antecedent unity is everywhere manifest or deducible in the
physical and the moral worlds, it will not be hard to admit
the unity of morality and religion—even though, at first,
only as something conceivable. While admitting, too, that
the Divine Spirit aids us at a level 'deeper than our Consciousness can reach (Coleridge was a century ahead of his
time in realizing the reach of the subconscious depths), we
must yet guard above all against those who would destroy
the freedom of Will. The Will is *not* comprehended in time
and space; it is not 'included in the Mechanism of Cause
and Effect'. It is in the strict sense supernatural, which
means simply 'above nature', without implying anything
miraculous or mystical. The acknowledgment of 'an infinite
omnipresent Mind as the Ground of the Universe' is for all
purposes the starting point. This acknowledgment, or
'Reconcilement with God' (Leighton, Aph. VII) brings
with it an ineffable peace of mind, which Leighton calls a
'sense' of the reconcilement.

In succeeding sections Coleridge speaks a good deal
about the right understanding and interpretation of Scripture—but his views on this topic can best be set forth when
we come to discuss the *Confessions of an Inquiring Spirit*. It
will be enough to notice, here, that he is always anxious to
persuade us that the Old Testament *does* teach the hope of
a future life—despite its lack of emphasis on this point

and the many texts of contrary sense. He cites Proverbs xiv. 32, 'the righteous man hath hope in his death'—but the N.E.B. translates this 'the upright man is secure in his own honesty'; and it is to be feared that most of the texts on which S. T. C. and others relied have crumbled in like manner. It is therefore reassuring to find that Coleridge, as we should expect of such a sage, had a firm grasp of the least assailable of all doctrines of immortality: that 'as we truly *are*, only as far as God is with us, so neither can we *possess* (that is, enjoy) our Being or any other real Good, but by living in the sense of his holy presence'.

Still on the borderline between morality and religion, Coleridge distinguishes acutely between Christianity and Stoicism. He recognizes that of all the ancient sects the Stoic came nearest to Christianity, but he sees it as vitiated, like Kant's ethics, by its effort to extinguish the 'feelings', or to give the highest honour to acting virtuously *against* inclination. Christianity, on the contrary, teaches us the better art of bringing the feelings into conformity with conscience, and so enlisting their powerful support to 'our struggling, task'd morality'. 'Its especial aim, its characteristic operation, is to moralize the affections.'

There is an intermediate state, a state of transition, between mere morality and 'spiritual religion'—and it is to be expected that it should be so, since 'every state, which is not progressive, is dead, or retrograde'. More important, belief itself, like imagination, is essentially progressive, active and alive, not fixed and dead like a mere *opus operatum*. Coleridge quotes Leighton's phrase about 'that senseless deadness which most take for believing', and agrees that true belief follows and in a sense includes unbelief. Faith which is not a continually renewed victory over doubt has already lost some of its sinew. The thought of being rigidly fixed in sectarian conformity inspires one of Coleridge's best Aphorisms (No. XXV):

He, who begins by loving Christianity better than Truth, will proceed by loving his own Sect or Church better than Christianity, and end in loving himself better than all.

In the section headed 'Elements of Religious Philosophy preliminary to the Aphorisms on Spiritual Religion', we meet with most of the main Coleridgean positions, many of which I have discussed already, but which ought, I think, to be seen again in their present context.

First, 'that there is more in man than can be rationally referred to the life of Nature and the mechanism of Organization; that he has a will not included in this mechanism; and that the Will is in an especial and pre-eminent sense the spiritual part of our Humanity'. Coleridge feels (as not so many could now) that he can take for granted his readers' assent to these propositions He then distinguishes the postulates of religion and ethics from those of geometry:

> 'the difference being, that the postulates of Geometry *no* man *can* deny', while 'those of Moral Science are such as no *good* man *will* deny.'[1]

It is, and in the nature of things must be, possible to deny the postulates of religion and morality, to 'disclaim our nature as moral beings'; 'were it otherwise, the Creed would stand in the same relation to Morality as the multiplication table'. 'I cannot', he says in another place, 'as I could in the case of an arithmetical or geometrical proposition, render it *impossible* for you to suppose it [viz. that free will is a delusion]. . . . Were it not [in your power to suppose this], the belief of the contrary would be no subject of a *command*, no part of a moral or religious *duty*'.[2] Coleridge repeatedly insisted, here as in *The Friend*, the *Biographia*, etc., that religious belief is an act of faith, made in response to the imperative of conscience or 'Practical Reason'. To make it logically demonstrable, inescapable, would be to destroy its *religious* character, and make it 'worthless because compulsory'. The Christian then 'grounds his philosophy on assertions', but has the very good reason for making them—namely, that he *ought* to do so. These assertions are not baseless, either: they are grounded upon 'three ultimate *facts*': 'the Reality of the LAW OF CONSCIENCE; the existence of a RESPONSIBLE WILL, as the subject

[1] *Aids*, p. 89 (Bohn. ed).   [2] *Ibid.*, p. 177 (footnote).

of that law; and lastly, the existence of Evil. . . . The first is a Fact of Consciousness; the second a Fact of Reason necessarily concluded from the first; and the third a Fact of History interpreted by both.'[1]

Coleridge thus sets himself in avowed opposition to Hobbes and all Necessitarianism (a doctrine to which he had for a short time adhered, see above p. 48)—all, that is, who say that mind and matter are 'alike under one and the same law of compulsory Causation'. But at the same time he also opposes Shaftesbury and his followers, who view human nature through rose-tinted spectacles and virtually deny Original Sin and The Fall. For Coleridge, man was essentially a 'fallen' creature, in the sense that his Will, his inmost essence and Self, was blighted by a disease which only Reason and Redemption could control. Finally he dissociates himself from the Calvinists who press the doctrine of the diseased Will into a denial of all freedom, and who in their image of God see Power and Will to the exclusion of Wisdom and Goodness. Man is fallen indeed, but not so far as to render worthless the God-given faculty of Reason.

He continues, in the 'Aphorisms on Spiritual Religion', to insist upon the 'perfect rationality' of the Christian doctrines 'when examined by their proper organs, the Reason and Conscience of Man'. What to the Greeks was *Nous*, Ideas, St Paul calls Spirit, Truths spiritually discerned. The Spirit heard in Reason and Conscience, confirmed and supported by Scripture, is not to be confused with any 'Inner Light' alleged by the fanatics. He will not now, he says, deal with the mysteries of the Trinity or the Origin of Moral Evil (this will all be made clear in his *Magnum Opus*, which he is 'now preparing for the press'); but he must deal with objections springing from the moral feelings —objections to such doctrines as Arbitrary Election and Reprobation, or to that of Vicarious Atonement. It was this last objection which, amongst other things, had once made Coleridge a Unitarian. As for the modern Calvinists, such as Jonathan Edwards and Dr Williams, he is content to vindicate the freedom of the will again, stressing that this

[1] *Aids*, p. 91.

freedom is perfected in union with the will of God, and that salvation is attainable not by the human will alone, but at the same time not without the will.

The discussion of these mysterious—and to some obnoxious—tenets broadens out (Comment to Aph. II, pp. 166 ff.) into twenty or so of the most luminous pages ever written on the nature and grounds of religious belief. Nothing is more difficult to convince men of than the doctrines of Election and Redemption. But are they more difficult to accept than the existence and personality of the living God? Or rather if we accept God, have we any right to reject associated corollaries of this belief for reasons which, if valid, would also undermine theism itself? As a Christian apologist (which by now he is) Coleridge has a more difficult task than when he was merely defending the religious world-view in general. Then, he could say that Conscience commands the belief in God, because without it conscience would be baseless. But does it equally prescribe belief in Election, Atonement, the Trinity? Does it involve belief in the Redemption of Mankind by Jesus Christ?— specifically, by his death upon the Cross? This is the heart of the conflict between Socinianism and orthodoxy, between Coleridge young and Coleridge old. My own feeling is that he was never quite so fully reconciled as he tried to be to historical Christianity. It is one thing to hold that 'Redemption' by divine grace is a religious need arising from the original sinfulness of man; it is not quite the same to hold that such redemption was historically effected on a certain Friday at Calvary, by one who was miraculously both God and man. Coleridge certainly thought he had discovered how to hold both, and perhaps we must agree that he had. If so, he was probably helped by his reverence for Scripture as 'revelation'—an attitude or feeling which, in spite of his very advanced views on scriptural inspiration (see below, pp. 242-5), he retained to the last, and which separates him to some extent from us now. My impression is confirmed by the way in which, in the present passage, he avoids a direct confrontation with 'Redemption', and widens the discourse till it recovers the generality with which he is more at home.

The marvel is, I think, not that there are unassimilable ingredients left in his argument, but that so much of it is valid for all time—and not only so, but even *ahead* of our own times in these 1970s.

The argument turns mainly upon the distinction between Reason and Understanding which runs like a *leit-motiv* all through Coleridge's religious writings, and which is stated *fortissimo* later on in *Aids*. I will now briefly try to indicate his drift at this point.

Religious beliefs, as he has already said, differ from mathematical certainties in that they require a leap of faith and not merely intellectual assent. But furthermore, they must not, 'like theoretical or speculative Positions, be pressed onward into all their possible *logical* consequences'. These beliefs arise from our experience as *moral* beings, and it is by practical interests, not speculative, that we are constrained to adopt them:

> The Law of Conscience, not the Canons of discursive Reasoning, must decide in such cases. At least, the latter have no validity, which the single *veto* of the former is not sufficient to nullify. The most pious conclusion is here the most legitimate.[1]

To guard against the possible anarchy of such 'pious conclusions'—for what devotional crotchet or fantasy might not justify itself on these lines?—Coleridge subjoins:

> Where the evidence of the senses fails us, and beyond the precincts of sensible experience—there is no *reality* attributable to any notion, but what is given to it by Revelation, or the Law of Conscience, or the necessary interests of Morality.

For instance, Reason demands the hypothesis of a unity, a 'One', as the ground and cause of the Universe. So does Religion, but religion needs more than this; it raises the hypothesis of The One into the Idea of the living God, the personal object of our devotion, love, fear and worship. The 'notional ONE of the Ontologists' is not the same as the living God of religion, and Coleridge insists that we must not allow logical deductions from 'the One' to interfere

[1] Pp. 108-9.

with our religious relationship with God. We must not be
frightened by speculative objections (or by the glib infidel
who uses them) if their upshot is repugnant to Conscience—
as would be the case, for example, if we were told that the
Eternity of God precludes a 'Creation', or that the World
must be co-eternal with him; or that the Immutability of
God makes all prayer vain and superstitious. Such conclusions may seem logically inescapable, but they are false
for *religion*, because they are deduced from the wrong pre-
misses: the *entia* of logic, and not the object of religious
devotion. If we lose sight of this vital distinction, we risk
losing touch with the God 'in whom we *believe*', and finding
Him supplanted by 'a stoical Fate', or 'the superessential
One of Plotinus'—without intelligence, self-consciousness,
life or even *Being*; or the *substantia una et unica*, the indivisible world-substance, of Spinoza.

And so with Election and Redemption: we are not to try
and read the mind of God, or to imagine how *from his point of
view* these mysteries might be set in motion. We are to start
from our own experience and need: our experience that 'the
best of men are what they are through the grace of God';
and our need for redemption from sin and all the imperfec-
tions of our fallen nature. It is the part of Reason always to
keep theological ideas alive by close contact with our
practical living, and not to allow the Understanding to pry
into them and dissect them with logical tools not applicable
to them.

But if not the abstract or speculative reason, and yet a reason
there must be in order to a rational belief—then it must be the
practical reason of man, comprehending the Will, the Conscience,
the Moral Being with its inseparable Interests and Affections—
that Reason, namely, which is the Organ of *Wisdom*, and (as far as
man is concerned) the source of living and actual Truths.[1]

Coleridge tries also to show (here again, as already
foreshadowed) that 'the scriptural and only true Idea of God'
involves the idea of the Trinity ('Tri-unity'). Only this
image is consistent with the divinity of Christ, and only

[1] P. 115.

this guards us against either pantheism, which identifies the Creator with the Creation, or the misrepresentation of God as mere impersonal Law. It must not be supposed, Coleridge remarks here, that he regards the Trinity as a doctrine attainable by mere reason, independently of Revelation. On the contrary, 'a religion not revealed is, in my judgment, no religion at all'. The so-called 'demonstrations' of God's existence 'either prove too little, as that from the order and apparent purpose in Nature; or too much, namely that the World is itself God'. The Cosmological 'proof', too, really presupposes the Ontological—'that is, the proof of a God from the necessity and necessary *Objectivity* of the Idea'. Otherwise where do the Cosmological 'provers' get their idea of God from? If one has already absorbed the ontological presupposition (consciously or not), then doubtless Nature will seem largely to confirm it. But the fact is that this truth, though the hardest to 'demonstrate', does not need 'demonstration':

> though there may be no conclusive demonstrations of a good, wise, living, and personal God, there are so many convincing reasons for it, within and without . . . that for every mind *not* devoid of all reason, and desperately conscience-proof, the Truth which it is the least possible to prove, it is little less than impossible not to believe!—only indeed just so much short of impossible, as to leave some room for the will and the moral election, and *thereby to keep it a truth of Religion, and the possible subject of a Commandment* [my italics].[1]

A deist might excusably reject the Trinity, because he cares nothing for Scripture or redemption, and relies entirely on Nature. But a Christian, who accepts the Scriptures as 'revelation', has no pretext for rejecting it, especially as the doctrine of redemption, on which he relies, is the main argument for the divinity of the Redeemer.

Coleridge's strong moral bent, and his dislike of getting trapped by the theological cobweb-spinners, continues to predominate in the next few Aphorisms. Religion, he says in the spirit of Whichcote or John Smith, is meant to improve

[1] P. 121.

our Nature, faculties and temper: well, in the light of that, just consider the Synod of Dort, lost in wandering mazes of fix'd fate, foreknowledge absolute; or the Council of Trent, distinguishing two kinds of transubstantiation, and ask yourself: Will such beliefs 'tend to the improvement of my moral or intellectual faculties?' Ancient philosophy sought to purify and elevate the moral character through the intellect; Christianity reversed that order: 'her first step was to cleanse the heart'. But in the very act of so doing, she was also clarifying the mind by freeing it from 'the rank vapours that steam up from the corrupt heart'. Alas, however, this original divine policy was not afterwards maintained:

> Too soon did the Doctors of the Church forget that the *heart*, the *moral* nature, was the beginning and the end; and that truth, knowledge, and insight were comprehended in its expansion. This was the true and first apostasy—when in council and synod the Divine Humanities of the Gospel gave way to speculative Systems, and Religion became a Science of Shadows under the name of Theology, or at best a bare Skeleton of Truth, without life or interest, alike inaccessible and unintelligible to the majority of Christians.[1]

We must begin in humility: like children, believing first, that we may understand later.

In Aphorisms VII and VIII of this section, and in the ensuing section on the difference between Reason and Understanding, we meet with some of Coleridge's most important affirmations. First, he contrasts Judaism with Christianity, claiming that Judaism provided the 'groundwork': One God the Father Almighty, the Moral Law, a state of retribution after death and the Resurrection of the dead (the latter a disputed point, however)—but not the peculiar and characteristic doctrines of Christianity. These are: first, that mankind has been redeemed by the Incarnation of the Son of God in Jesus Christ; that his life, death and resurrection are not only manifestations and proofs, but essential parts of the great redemptive act which has rendered the corruption of our nature no longer insurmountable.

[1] P. 126.

Next, the belief in the 'possible appropriation of this benefit by Repentance and Faith'; the belief that some at least of us shall survive mortality; the belief in the communion of each awakened spirit with the Holy Spirit; the belief in gifts of the Spirit, showing themselves in work of love; the belief that these works are signs and evidences of our faith, and that God will judge us mercifully through Christ's mediation.

All this seems orthodox enough, though perhaps the phrase 'incarnation of the *Son* of God' is a significant Coleridgean gloss; and later on in the book he clarifies and re-interprets several of his statements. But the first development of his thought, which follows immediately, is the important plea about the insufficiency of morality without religion—which Coleridge has learnt from his own bitter experience. He turns to his reader and asks him, varying the stress in a series of questions, whether Morality and Prudence are likely to be enough for him:

> From what you know of yourself . . . and of mankind generally; dare you *trust* to it? Dare *you* trust to it? To *it*, and to it alone? If so, well! It is at your own risk. . . . But if not, if you have had too good reason to know, that your heart is deceitful and your strength weakness: if you are disposed to exclaim with Paul—the Law indeed is holy, just, good, spiritual; but I am carnal, sold under sin: for that which I do, I allow not; and what I would, that I do not!— in this case, there is a voice that says, *Come unto me: and I will give you rest*. . . . You are, in short, to embrace the *Christian* Faith as your Religion. . . .[1]

And to anyone who demands further elucidation and 'proof' of the Christian tenets, he replies in the celebrated and oft-quoted words:

> Christianity is not a Theory, or a Speculation; but a *Life*;— not a *Philosophy* of Life, but a Life, and a living Process. . . . TRY IT.

Most infidelity is due, not to 'the strong free mind', but to 'the enslaved will'. In like manner, the Gospel is not a

[1] Pp. 131-2.

'system of Theology', but a history —though one involving doctrinal truths. It is quite possible to believe too much ('Ultrafidianism'), like Sir Thomas Browne who thought there were not mysteries enough in religion for an active faith, and loved to echo Tertullian's *Certum est quia impossibile*. But by far the commoner excess is 'Minimifidianism', which tries to 'draw religion down to the believer's intellect, instead of raising his intellect up to religion'. It is this that makes the fundamental mistake of allowing the Understanding, the faculty which judges 'according to sense', to intrude into regions beyond its scope, where Reason and spiritual discernment alone are competent.

Coming now to Reason and Understanding (pp. 142 ff.), Coleridge begs for special attention, as he rests all his hopes on the success of that distinction. He had already published views on this subject (in the *Statesman's Manual* and the 1818 *Friend*), but he elaborates them further here.

Reason, then, he now defines as 'the Power of Universal and necessary Convictions, the Source and Substance of Truths above Sense, and having their evidence in themselves'; the Understanding judges authoritatively only in reference to sense-data. Reason is a direct beholding of Truth, bearing the like relationship to the intelligible and spiritual as sense has to the material or phenomenal; the proper function of Understanding is 'generalizing the notices received from the senses'. It was the Understanding, generalizing from the senses, that gave us the Ptolemaic cosmology; Reason, overriding the senses, gave us the Copernican and Newtonian.

The truths of religion, he observes—truly enough for his own times though apparently not for ours—are so impressed upon us in childhood that we grow up taking them for granted. Thus, if later we come across 'proofs' of God from Nature, as in Ray, Derham etc., we find their arguments otiose because we already believe in God for other reasons. On the other hand we shall be confronted with 'all the doubts and difficulties, that cannot but arise where the Understanding, *the mind of the flesh*, is made the measure of spiritual things'. The special danger here is that these doubts are mistakenly supposed to apply only to the superstructure of Christian beliefs, whereas in truth 'natural religion' is open to the very same kind of analysis. The only way to non-suit the infidel is to remove the cause from the Court of the Understanding and appeal to the Higher Court of Reason. 'Placing' the Understanding in this way is, he explicitly says, 'an indispensable preliminary to the removal of the most formidable obstacles to an intelligent belief of the . . . characteristic Articles of the Christian Faith'.

> Wherever the forms of reasoning appropriate only to the *natural* world are applied to *spiritual* realities, it may be truly said, that the more strictly logical the reasoning is in all its *parts*, the more irrational it is as a *whole*.[1]

Don't, for instance, get caught in the spider-web of speculations about the 'origin of evil'; this will only imprison you in barren paradoxes. It is far more profitable, and our religious duty, to examine the evil in our own hearts and try to eradicate it.

Coleridge gives an acceptable meaning to the tenet of 'Original Sin'. He simply sweeps aside all crude notions about Adam's fall as the first or 'original' case of sin, which by inheritance has infected the whole human race ever since. Original sin is sin having its cause or 'origin' in the 'corrupt nature of the will'; it is sin ever-originating in that corruption. And however symbolized or mythologized, it is admitted as a fact in all the higher religions; in Christianity it is the disease which calls for the cure, namely the Redemption. Coleridge is quick to see that this doctrine presupposes a Will that is free, responsible and autonomous; and in a lengthy footnote (pp. 176 ff.) he tries to convince a sceptical 'young friend' that this is true. It is contrary to reason to contradict your own consciousness of freedom ('Sir, we *know* our will is free') in defiance of conscience. And here Coleridge repeats one of his profound observations: I cannot, he says,

> as I could in the case of an arithmetical or geometrical proposition, render it *impossible* for you to suppose it [i.e. that freewill is a delu-

[1] P. 168.

sion] . . . it is doubtless in your power to suppose this. Were it not, the belief of the contrary would be no subject of a *command*, no part of a moral or religious *duty*.

'The Fall', too, is thus philosophized by Coleridge: it occurs whenever the Will, by definition free and self-determined, submits to 'nature', i.e. the mechanism of cause and effect:

> . . . if by an act, to which it had determined itself, it has subjected itself to the determination of nature (in the language of St Paul, to the law of the flesh), it receives a nature into itself, and so far it becomes a nature, and this is a corruption of the Will and a corrupt nature. It is also a *Fall* of Man, inasmuch as his Will is . . . the ground and condition of the attribute which constitutes him *man*.[1]

Don't fancy that you can escape from this into some non-Christian kind of 'religion'—you will find it a universal truth, always applicable to our plight. Beware of arguments against Christianity 'which, if valid, are valid against all religion'—arguments against Christianity 'which cannot stop there, and consequently ought not to have commenced there'. And do not be misled by Paley and other Utilitarians into accepting the 'prudential calculus'—i.e. judging the morality of actions by their alleged consequences. They are to be judged only by the Will and Heart from which they spring:

> Whatever springs out of the *perfect law of freedom*, which exists only by its unity with the Will of God . . . *that* is GOOD. Whatever seeks to separate itself from the Divine Principle, and proceeds from a false centre in the agent's particular will, is EVIL. . . .[2]

The argument now broadens, in a way which I find fascinating, to include what one might call the sociology of religion and a philosophy of history. Once again, the insight and prescience of Coleridge are astonishing. First he asks, what are the signs that religion is alive and operative in any society? He answers, wherever it is the prevailing habit

[1] P. 190.   [2] P. 197.

to regard the present life as subordinate to a life to come, and to mark the present state, *the World of their Senses*, by signs, instruments and mementos of its connexion with a future state and a spiritual world;—where the Mysteries of Faith are brought within the *hold* of the people at large, not by being explained away in the vain hope of accommodating them to the average of their understanding, but by being made the objects of their love by their combination with events and epochs of history, with national traditions, with the monuments and dedications of ancestral faith and zeal, with memorial and symbolical observances, with the realizing influences of social devotion, and above all, by early and habitual association with Acts of the Will, *there* Religion is.[1]

The thought, though not the prose rhythm, is Burkean. How would our present society stand up to this test?

Anticipating a leading theme in his later *Church and State* (cf. below, Ch. XVII) he next affirms that where there is 'a permanent learned class' ('clerisy' in the later work), 'possessing the respect and confidence of the country', the article of Original Sin will be 'an Axiom of Faith in *all* classes'. With the learned themselves this will be so, because (and who before Coleridge could have put it this way?) this article is 'the first—I had almost said *spontaneous* —product of the application of moral science to history, of which it is the interpreter'.

In the aftermath of the 'Godless revolution', reaction seemed to have brought about a revived zeal for religion. We saw something like this in the decade following the Second War of this century. But Coleridge doubts the genuineness of the 'revival' in his own time—and this leads him to one of his famous outbursts against the *Zeitgeist*, familiar to readers of *The Friend* and other works, but too characteristic to be omitted here. Where religion is patronized as a supplement to law and the police force,

where Moral SCIENCE is exploded as the mystic jargon of dark ages; where a lax System of Consequences . . . is publicly and authoritatively taught as Moral Philosophy, where the mysteries of religion . . . are either cut and squared for the comprehension of

[1] Pp. 195-6.

the understanding, 'the faculty judging according to sense', or desperately torn asunder from the reason . . . lastly, where Private Interpretation [of Scripture] is everything and the Church nothing —*there* the mystery of Original Sin will be either rejected, or evaded, or perverted into the monstrous fiction of Hereditary Sin . . .; in the mystery of Redemption metaphors will be obtruded for the reality; and in the mysterious appurtenants and symbols of Redemption (Regeneration, Grace, the Eucharist, and Spiritual Communion) the realities will be evaporated into metaphors.[1]

There is an interesting footnote to this passage disclaiming (how needlessly for any who know his prejudice against Rome) any supposed Papist leanings, but at the same time explaining very forcibly what qualifications are needed in anyone venturing to interpret the Scriptures (and they are qualifications rare and high), and affirming—as no doubt the leaders of the Oxford Movement noted with approval— that a Christianity 'without a Church exercising spiritual authority (though *not* Rome) is vanity and dissolution'.

The two great 'Moments' of the Christian religion, then, are Original Sin and Redemption—indeed, 'Christianity' and 'Redemption' are equivalent terms. Against 'Redemption' the only valid objection would be a moral one: that the whole concept imputed to God a vindictiveness and injustice foreign to the idea we ought to entertain of him. It was some such obstacle which had kept Coleridge amongst the Unitarians in his youth. But now that Coleridge can see 'Redemption' as 'restored possibility of overcoming the corruption of our Will', the obstacle has vanished. He clearly shows the blasphemous irrationality of the crude theories of 'vicarious atonement'; the redemptive act itself was transcendent, and not to be confused with its effects, expressed metaphorically as 'payment of debt', 'ransom', etc., or with outworn notions like 'blood-sacrifice'. The real, spiritual effect of Redemption is Regeneration, Rebirth to new life in the Spirit. So-called 'baptismal regeneration', like the Romish 'extreme unction', is magic.

Much of Coleridge's teaching is in accord with the most

1 Pp. 199-200.

advanced theology of today. He knows well how to keep a doctrine alive as a 'truth of faith', instead of killing it by alleged 'evidence'. Consider for example his refutation of Paley, who in a famous paragraph claimed that Christ had *proved* the future life by his own words, supported by that 'splendid apparatus of prophecy and miracles'. Coleridge on the other hand, backed by Jeremy Taylor, believed that 'true Christian faith must have in it something of in-evidence, something that must be made up by duty and by obedience'. Coleridge does indeed marshal an impressive collection of the arguments in favour of a future life; but his wisest comment is, I think, that the important thing in Christian teaching is not *that* there is life after death, but that there is a state of being for which we must aspire, and which we can already sometimes feel. 'This alone is the essential in Christianity, that the same spirit should be growing in us which was in the fulness of all perfection in Christ Jesus'. He knows that it is safest to ground religion on experience and need, not on traditional and shaky 'evidences':

> *Evidences* of Christianity! I am weary of the word. Make a man feel the *want* of it; rouse him, if you can, to the self-knowledge of his *need* of it; and you may safely trust it to its own Evidence. . . .[1]

And yet, of course, his positions are not always unassailable, and if I still recommend *Aids* to the 'young reader' of today I must forewarn him of some of the slippery places. For instance, take this whole question of Redemption: what is it that he is asking us to accept? Not vicarious atonement, not 'paying the price of sin'—no, no, of course not. Then is it just that Christ's noble life, spirit and teaching can so inspire us that we are enabled to live a better life ouselves? One might suppose so from the phrase I quoted just now: 'this alone is the essential in Christianity, that the same spirit should be growing in us which was in the fulness of all perfection in Christ Jesus'. But if so, if Christ redeems by his example, by winning us to try and be like him, what becomes of the 'transcendent act' on which Coleridge also insists? He would have regarded 'redemption by example', I think,

[1] P. 272.

as a fatal piece of Socinian watering-down of doctrine—the true (and orthodox) doctrine being that the Son of God was incarnate in Jesus, and that his death and resurrection (not his life and teaching) were the agents of Redemption. In other words, Coleridge seems to want it both ways: the saving act was objective, transcendent, cosmic, mysterious: *it happened!* and we are thankfully to appropriate its benefits; but also, alternatively, we are saved if and when the spirit of Christ is growing in us.

Coleridge will sometimes offer paragraphs of embarrassingly orthodox language, as if to appease his clerical readers who might with good reason suspect him of being too enlightened. And all the while we know that he understands much more by his terms (if not something quite other) than most clerical readers of those days would have done. Again, it is one of his charges against his wicked opponents that they 'evaporate realities into metaphors'. I suppose this means that they interpret metaphorically what was meant literally—an immemorial and very dangerous procedure when applied to scriptural interpretation, but one on which orthodox scholars themselves often have to rely. No doubt, in making this accusation, Coleridge is remembering the glib Socinian reductions of gritty texts to something more suited to their taste. But what is Coleridge's own method, for instance, in dealing with Original Sin and Redemption, but the 'evaporation' of stories meant literally into 'metaphors' far more meaningful and profound? 'No', he might reply, 'what I condemn is evaporating *realities* into metaphors. But I am doing the opposite: I am presenting the realities of which the Scripture-stories are metaphors—symbols, rather.' Here too, however, I think Coleridge is 'having it both ways'. He recommends his reader to translate theological terms into their spiritual and moral equivalents, but warns him that they mean more than those equivalents. He will give us 'acceptable' and 'enlightened' interpretations of doctrine, yet leave us feeling that the doctrines were truer than we thought or could conceive, all the time. Great demythologizer as he was, he would not have gone all the way with some of the demythologizers of

our own century—perhaps because, being a poet (yes! let
us not forget, as in a study of this kind we too easily may,
that it is a *poet* we have to do with) he knew that symbols
partake of the reality they represent. The classic case, including all others, of the infection of the modern mind by the
mechanical philosophy of the eighteenth century, has been
the evaporation of God himself into a metaphor—'reducing
the Creator to a mere *anima mundi*', a personification of the
force of gravity. Modern 'enlightenment' shows 'an increasing unwillingness to contemplate the Supreme Being in his
personal attributes: and thence a distaste to all the peculiar
doctrines of the Christian Faith, the Trinity, the Incarnation
of the Son of God, and Redemption'. 'I speak feelingly', he
says,

> for I speak of that which for a brief period was my own state.

'Some I have known', he adds,

> who under this unhealthful influence have been so estranged from
> the heavenly *Father*, the *Living* God, as even to shrink from the
> personal pronouns as applied to the Deity . . . many, who find the
> God of Abraham, Isaac and Jacob, far too *real*, too substantial;
> who feel it more in harmony with their indefinite sensations
>> To worship Nature in the hill and valley,
>> Not knowing what they love—
> and (to use the language, but not the sense or purpose of the great
> poet of our age) would fain substitute for the Jehovah of their Bible
>> A sense sublime
>> Of something far more deeply interfused,
>> Whose dwelling is the light of setting suns,
>> And the round ocean and the living air;
>> A motion and a spirit, that impels
>> All thinking things, all objects of all thought,
>> And rolls through all things![1]

Coleridge's comment is: 'And this from having been educated to understand the Divine Omnipresence in any sense
rather the alone safe and legitimate one, the presence of all
things to God!' Our own first comment, at least on his way

---

[1] Pp. 270-1.

of quoting *Tintern Abbey*, might rather be: 'How kind he is still being to Wordsworth, to exonerate him from having meant what he said when he wrote that poem!'

Much more might be said about this rich and extra-ordinary book. I will conclude where Coleridge himself con-cludes, with his final attack upon his arch-foe: Materialism —'the Source, the spring-head' of all the opposition he expects to meet. True, he thinks the 'dogmatism of the Corpuscular School' has been recently undermined by 'the increasingly *dynamic* spirit of the physical sciences now highest in public estimation'; by the work of Davy, Oersted and John Hunter, and by the new predominance of organic over mechanical concepts in biology and anatomy. Neverthe-less 'only not all are materialists', and it is the legacy of the Mechanico-corpuscular scheme, beginning with Descartes, which has all along been the enemy of all he cares for and stands for. I will end by quoting a passage in which Cole-ridge astonishes me once again by anticipating the insights of men like Whitehead in criticizing the effects of modern science:

> In order to submit the various phenomena of moving bodies to geometrical construction, we are under the necessity of abstracting from corporeal substance all its *positive* properties, and obliged to consider bodies as differing from equal portions of space only by figure and mobility. And as a *fiction of science* [S. T. C.'s own italics, but I should in any case have underlined it], it would be difficult to overvalue this invention. . . . But in contempt of common sense, and in direct opposition to the express declarations of the inspired his-torian . . . and to the tone and spirit of the Scriptures throughout, Des Cartes proclaimed it as *truth of fact*: and instead of a World *created* and filled with productive forces by the Almighty *Fiat*, left a lifeless Machine whirled about by the dust of its own Grinding: as if Death could come from the living Fountain of Life; Nothing-ness and Phantom from the Plenitude of Reality! the Absoluteness of Creative Will![1]

[1] See pp. 264-9.

CHAPTER XVII

ON THE CONSTITUTION OF CHURCH AND STATE ACCORDING TO THE IDEA OF EACH

THIS book, published in 1830, 'was the only one of his works which achieved anything like a popular success' —says Dr J. Colmer. Coleridge may have felt, after the Reform Bill, that 'he had lived and written in vain'; but as the same writer goes on,

> He could not be expected to be able to foresee that his last political work . . . would leave a permanent mark on the thought of the nineteenth century, that slowly and working in an unobtrusive fashion it would lead men to re-examine the function of the Established Church . . . and would reawaken a sense of social responsibility in the Whig and Tory parties.[1]

Having already said what I could of *Church and State* in a book called *Nineteenth Century Studies* (1949), I shall not need to add much here. In a book like the present one, which aims to trace the development of Coleridge's religious thought, *Church and State*, belonging mainly to the story of his political thinking, does not claim a large place. Still, it is of great interest as showing (like *The Friend* and the *Lay Sermons*) how his mind worked when he turned from the formulation of general principles to their application in contemporary society. As I said in the book just mentioned, Coleridge's 'politics are religious, and his religion (is) political':

> For this very reason he was able to survey the whole human scene from an elevation above the reach of his English contemporaries, and to subject it to a critique more searching and comprehensive . . . than any it could receive from the Utilitarians or Evangelicals, or indeed had received since the seventeeenth century. He was the first of the nineteenth century 'prophets', and if not (because of

[1] J. Colmer, *Coleridge, Critic of Society* (1959), p. 165.

his incomplete achievement) actually the greatest, yet potentially so, for he combined with the prophetic animus the philosophic vision of the schoolman.[1]

The composition of *Church and State* arose from Coleridge's need to declare his reasons for approving in general (though deploring the absence of safeguards) the Acts for Catholic Emancipation, in particular that of 1829. Emancipation itself he regarded as an act of mere justice to His Majesty's Roman Catholic subjects, above all those in Ireland. The 'safeguard' he wanted was a solemn declaration that no particle of the national wealth should be diverted to the support of a priestly caste owing allegiance to a foreign potentate. But this exclusion had nothing to do with doctrine. So long as he was a loyal British subject, the beliefs of a Roman Catholic, priest or layman, should matter nothing in the eyes of the law. The important thing about *Church and State*, however, the thing that makes it Coleridgean and therefore puts it (in spite of its slender bulk) in the same class as Hooker's *Laws of Ecclesiastical Polity*, is that what might have been a mere leading-article on a current issue becomes in Coleridge's hands a profound enquiry into the very meaning and purpose of both Church and State. He is not writing history, though his terminology —'Major and Minor Barons', 'Franklins', 'Burgesses', etc. —and his mode of thought, are often feudal in character. Nor is he merely writing a tract for his own times, although the contemporary bearings of his argument are clear. What we can say is that, with England, English history and the English social organism in the forefront of his mind as typical and perhaps exemplary, he writes of what a State should be, and a Church should be, if it realized its own 'Idea'. 'By "Idea" he means, not the conception of a thing abstracted from its particular form at any given time, but that which is "given by the knowledge of its ultimate aim".' The 'Idea' of a State 'consists in the balance or equilibrium of two main antagonists or opposite interests: *permanence* and *progression*'. Permanence is represented by the landed

[1] *Op. cit.*, pp. 44-5.

interest, progression by the mercantile and professional classes; and even though the proper balance between these forces is imperfectly realized in fact and in history, yet this is the 'idea' which gives purpose and meaning to the whole.

When we come to the Church, we find that Coleridge distinguishes rather confusingly between the National Church and the Christian Church; and what is more, the 'National Church' is not the same thing in all respects as the 'Established Church'—the Church of England. The 'National Church' in Coleridge's parlance means a Third Estate of the Realm, 'whose concern is with the ground, the necessary antecedent condition of the other Estates, namely *cultivation*, "the harmonious development of those qualities and faculties that characterize our humanity".' In this is vested 'a portion of the national wealth ("Nationalty") for spiritual and cultural ends. This "Nationalty" is intended to support "The Clerisy", that is, all the clerkly persons whose functions are spiritual and educational: the learned (a small class devoted to advanced academic teaching and enquiry) and a numerous body of clergymen and teachers so distributed as to leave no corner of the country "without a resident guide, guardian, and instructor".'[1] 'We must be men in order to be citizens', and it is for the 'clerisy' to ensure that this is observed.

Coleridge's use of specially coined words like 'Nationalty' and 'Clerisy' contributes to the feeling of double-vision which comes over me as I read this part of the book. This is, and is not, England! I say to myself, not without some perplexity. What he has said about the National Church reads very much like a description of the Church of England as by Law established; yet he will not allow the identification. The National Church is the State Department of Divine and Humane Affairs, but not, by definition, of *Christian* Affairs. Moreover, it includes more than the C. of E., viz. Universities, schools, etc. In 'idea' it need not necessarily be Christian at all, though *religious* it must necessarily be.

The enduring significance of all this, namely the insis-

---

[1] I have here been quoting from, or paraphrasing, p. 46 of my *Nineteenth Century Studies*.

tence that the State is responsible for the spiritual and educational welfare of the nation, even more than for its material prosperity and military defence, is somewhat obscured now that the State has in fact assumed responsibility for education, and national health, and given support to the arts. But even in Coleridge's time it was already clear —to him at least, as it is now to us all—that the State would really care only for 'inventions, discoveries, public improvements, docks, railways, canals and the like', and that the Church, so far from being National or Established, was diminishing in importance, losing its influence, and becoming a 'sect' instead of an 'Estate of the Realm'. The Church of England has of course remained 'national' in so far as it is 'established', but it would be needlessly confusing and meaningless to apply the word 'Church' to the Ministry of Education, the Local Education Authorities, the Arts Council and other secular cultural bodies recognized by the State.

And what of the 'Christian' Church? In explaining this, Coleridge seems to me to be conveying important truths in a needlessly paradoxical and even enigmatic way. In relation to the national Church, he says,

> Christianity, or the Church of Christ, is a blessed accident. . . . Let not the religious reader be offended with this phrase [he adds in a footnote]. I mean only that Christianity is an aid and instrument which no State or realm could have produced out of its own elements, which no State had a right to expect. It was, most awfully, a GODSEND![1]

To me this seems an exasperating pose: God *did* 'send' it, and the Third Estates, wherever they existed, came into being *because* of it. But Coleridge speaks as if we had started off with full-blown Departments of Divine Affairs, and then one day noticed, with amazement, gratitude and joy, Christianity appearing out of the blue for our encouragement and extra support. Of course this is not what he meant,[2] but his language is open to that interpretation. He

[1] *C. and S.*, pp. 65-6 (1852 ed.).
[2] As if to justify himself historically, he points (p. 67) to the Levitical and Druidical 'Churches' before Christ.

is on safer ground when he declares that the Church of
Christ is not a kingdom of this world, nor an estate of any
realm, but

> the appointed opposite of them all collectively—the sustaining,
> correcting, befriending opposite of the world; the compensating
> counterforce to the inherent and inevitable evils and defects of the
> State.[1]

Presumably then, it includes all Churches and sects which
are truly Christian in faith; and all Christian souls belong
to it in spirit. Coleridge will not allow Socinianism to count
as Christianity, though he will not deny the name of Christian to individual Socinians whose lives are better than their
creed. It is a mark of the Christian Church to be universal,
that is, neither Anglican, Gallican, Roman or Greek, but
'Catholic' under Christ. The Roman Church transcends
frontiers, and so is not a 'national' Church; but it pays
homage to the Bishop of Rome, and so is not 'universal'.
Coleridge never overcame his ingrained dislike of Popery,
but he would never have denied that the Roman Catholic
Church was part of the universal 'Christian' Church, and
was ranged with it in opposition to the World and to
Mammon. This aspect of Christianity—its function as
counterpoise to the commercial spirit, and worldliness in
every form—although emphasized here, had been most
fully developed in the second *Lay Sermon* (1817), where
(as we saw, cf. above, pp. 183-7) he laments that we do not
find in contemporary England 'Christianity tempering commercial avidity, and sprinkling its holy damps on the passion
of accumulation'.

I will conclude this section with another quotation from
Nineteenth Century Studies:[2]

> It was this distinctive blend of religion with politics and education
> which made Coleridge's teaching so influential, first with Thomas
> Arnold for whom . . . the Church *was* the State viewed in its
> spiritual aspect, and who wished to include all Christian denomina-

---

[1] *C. and S.*, pp. 138-9.   [2] P. 49.

tions within the 'established' Church; and later, with F. D. Maurice and the Christian Socialists, who, starting from the Idea of the Kingdom of God as real, believed it to be the Church's duty to actualize it, and make that Kingdom come on earth as it is in heaven.

CHAPTER XVIII

CONFESSIONS OF AN INQUIRING SPIRIT

OR

LETTERS ON THE INSPIRATION OF THE SCRIPTURES

THIS book was published in 1840 (i.e. six years after Coleridge's death), and bore the following 'advertisement' by Henry Nelson Coleridge:

> The following Letters on the Inspiration of the Scriptures were left by Mr Coleridge in MS. at his death. The Reader will find in them a key to most of the Biblical criticism scattered throughout the Author's own writings, and an affectionate, pious, and, as the Editor humbly believes, a profoundly wise attempt to place the study of the Written Word on its only sure foundation—a deep sense of God's holiness and truth, and a consequent reverence for that Light—the image of Himself—which He has kindled in every one of his rational creatures.

With such circumlocution did the pious editor of 1840 think fit to clothe his meaning; and this fact itself illustrates the strength of adverse feeling in the England of that time—adverse, that is, to any free application to the Bible of the accepted methods of historical, textual and literary research. Nowadays, of course, the results of two centuries of 'higher criticism' have been so thoroughly absorbed that they are taken for granted (except in 'fundamentalist' circles) by learned and unlearned alike. Ever since the Reformation the Bible had been for Protestants, quite simply, the 'Word of God', or 'Revelation'; the source of all saving truths, the arbiter of faith and doctrine, the guide, mentor, and consoler of the faithful. In all the 'Reformed' Churches it had replaced Church and Pope as the final authority and court of appeal.

It is difficult now to assess how widespread, in the England of 1830-40, was the belief in the 'verbal inspiration' of the biblical writings. We can safely assume, however, that it was both widely held and deeply rooted: so deeply as to be held as a fact and not a doctrine. We remember with what howls of execration Benjamin Jowett was greeted when he said (in *Essays and Reviews,* 1860) that the Bible should be treated 'like any other book'. A few scholars knew about the textual problems, and were alive to what was going on in Germany; but the prevailing view undoubtedly was that God through the Holy Spirit had in some sense composed the Bible himself as an authoritative theological and spiritual textbook for Christians, and that the sacred writers had taken the Word (even the *words*) from him by inspiration. So excellent was the English style of the Authorized Version (or at least, of its best-known passages), and so hallowed had this Bible become through centuries of holy usage in Church and home, that many—without perhaps knowing it or acknowledging it—felt that God himself had spoken in Tudor English. Hence the dismay and outcry in 1881, when the Revisers introduced alterations with a view to rendering the original texts more accurately. Hence, even in 1961 and 1970, the complaints (less fanatical and more 'literary' in tone), that the translators of the New English Bible had wantonly 'altered the Bible'. This phrase could only mean 'departed from the A.V. wording', but those who used it were betraying their belief that 'the Bible' *was* the Authorized Version' It did not occur to some of these malcontents that 'the Bible' was 'what the Hebrew and Greek originals had said', and that the N.E.B. was an attempt to put those originals straight into modern English, without any reference to the A.V. whatever.

I merely mention this point to demonstrate that, nearly a hundred and forty years after Coleridge's death, the 'talismanic' view of Scripture still lives on. Witnesses still take their 'Bible Oath' in the law courts, and in many churches the readers of lessons, after opening the numinous volume on the lectern, still begin with the phrase 'Hear the word of God!'

Coleridge, as we have abundantly seen, was second to none in his reverence for Scripture, but as a critic and interpreter of the sacred writings he was far ahead of his times. As I have elsewhere said:

Coleridge's literary and spiritual insight placed him upon a point of vantage from which he could overlook the nineteenth century country in front of him, and reply in advance to all that the *Zeitgeist* would thereafter bring forward. The standpoint of the *Letters* transcends the level of the later Science-and-Religion controversies, none of which need have arisen had his ground been firmly occupied from the beginning.[1]

Briefly, what he urged was the replacement of 'Bibliolatry'[2] (Bible-worship, making a book into an idol) by reverent and living contact with the great spiritual literature. He places the 'authority' of the Bible, not in any alleged supernatural origins, not in any divine ventriloquism mediated by inspired writers, but simply in its intrinsic truth and worth, and its power to meet the profoundest needs of the human soul:

> In short whatever *finds* me, bears witness for itself that it has proceeded from a Holy Spirit.[3]

This might blur the line between Scripture and other literature, robbing the Bible of its uniqueness. As if feeling this, Coleridge goes on to say that

> in the Bible there is more that *finds* me than I have experienced in all other books put together; that the words of the Bible find me at greater depths of my being; and that whatever finds me brings with it an irresistible evidence of its having proceeded from the [note the silent transformation of 'a' into 'the'] Holy Spirit.[4]

But, he continues, the doctrine of verbal inspiration requires me to believe that not only what finds me, but *everything* contained in the Holy Book, was dictated by an 'Infallible Intelligence', and that the sacred writers were 'divinely informed as well as inspired'. This is what Coleridge rejects. The Bible contains much that is 'word of God'—more than any other book, or all other books put together—but it also contains much else. And we are not to read the 'much

---

[1] *Nineteenth Century Studies*, p. 40.
[2] For a note on the origin of this word see above, p. 75.
[3] In *Aids* (Bohn ed.), p. 295. (The *Confessions* are printed in this same volume.)
[4] *Ibid.*, p. 296.

else' as though it were all of a piece with the rest. If this is now an accepted commonplace, hardly in need of mention, let us not forget that we owe such emancipation to Coleridge and to those others, whether in Germany or here, before and after his time, who first spread light amid the encircling gloom.

As we have seen (cf. above, p. 75) Coleridge had long ago found a kindred spirit and outlook in Lessing, and drew largely from him in the *Confessions*. Of the official German theologians and biblical scholars it is to Johann Gottfried Eichhorn (1752-1827) that he refers most frequently. He met Eichhorn at Göttingen in 1799, and told Poole (in a letter of May 6 of that year) that he had received from him, and from Blumenbach, 'the most *flattering* attention'. In his Letters between 1799 and 1833 I have counted eight references to Eichhorn, mostly implying guarded approval. For example, writing to W. Hart Coleridge on January 16, 1818, he proposes the notion of a translation of Hebrew prophecy and poetry comprising 'all that is valuable in Eichhorn, Paulus, Rosenmüller and the other German "Neologists" ', 'free from the Poison of their Peculiarities'. And writing to his son Derwent (March 28, 1819) he recommends him to read Richard Field's *Of the Church* (1635), Baxter's *Life* and Eichhorn's *Introductions to the Old and New Testaments*—'to all which my notes and your own previous studies will supply whatever antidote is wanting'. On May 25, 1820 he tells J. H. Green that he has just read Bishop Marsh's Divinity Lecture (3) on the authenticity and credibility of the New Testament books, knowing Marsh's acquaintance with Eichhorn, Paulus, etc., and being himself familiar with the work of Eichhorn, whom he calls 'founder and head of the daring school'. He goes on to state his own conclusion that the Gospel history (in the Synoptics), and the doctrines contained in the Fourth Gospel and the Epistles, 'truly represent the assertions of the Apostles and the faith of the Christian Church during the first century'; and that there is no reasonable ground to doubt 'the *authenticity* of the Books ascribed to John the Evangelist, to Mark, to Luke, and to Paul; nor the *authority* of Matthew and the author of the Epistle to the Hebrews'. We can be confident, at least, that 'these Apostles and Apostolic men wrote nothing but what they themselves *believed*'. And yet, he goes on very characteristically and revealingly,

> I have no hesitation in avowing that many an argument derived from the nature of man, nay, that many a strong, though only *speculative* probability, pierces deeper, pushes more home, and clings more pressingly to my mind than the whole sum of merely *external* evidence, the *fact* of Christianity itself alone excepted. Nay, I feel that the external evidence derives a great and lively accession of force, for my mind, from my previous speculative convictions or presumptions; but that I cannot find that the latter are at all strengthened or made more or less probable to me by the former. Besides, as to the external evidence I make up my mind *once for all*, and merely *as* evidence think no more about it; but those facts or reflections thereon which tend to change belief into insight, can never lose their effect. . . .

It is interesting and moving to find Coleridge, in 1820, still virtually putting the light of Nature ('my previous speculative convictions') above historical 'revelation' in order of convincingness. 'Know then thyself, presume not God to scan'—yes indeed, Know Thyself! Has anyone ever quoted that maxim more often than Coleridge? But as for scanning God—how could this man, with the intellect of an angel and the soul of a poet, do otherwise? And how could he, with such profound self-knowledge as he had, scan God without bringing to life, making real, truths which had long 'lain bed-ridden in the dormitory of the soul'? History was never of first importance to Coleridge (we remember that historical sightseeing always bored him); it was *natura naturata*, *fait accompli*, 'fixed and dead'. What mattered was the living moment, the *natura naturans*, the living and ever renewed interchange between Nature and Thought, between God and the Soul. In this same letter, speaking of the Redemption (yes! he is still toiling to make that idea real and meaningful), he says that though a 'redemptive power' is necessary for fallen man, it must act 'in my will and not merely *on* my will'. 'Christ must become man, but he cannot become *us*, except as far as we become *him*, and this we cannot do but by *assimilation*; and assimilation is a *vital real* act, not a notional or merely intellective one.'

His last reference to Eichhorn is in a letter (Oct. 30, 1833) written to John Sterling less than a year before his death. He is thinking of 'preparing for the press', 'if I find it practicable' (he is Coleridge to the last), a metrical translation of the Apocalypse, with an Introduction on the 'Use and Interpretation of Scriptures'. 'I am encouraged to this', he says, 'by finding how much of *original* remains in my views after I have abstracted all I have in common with Eichhorn and Heinrichs.'[1]

What, then, was the significance of Eichhorn for Coleridge and for us? Cheyne calls him the founder of modern Old Testament criticism, and says that he established the method of studying the Bible not merely as the vehicle of Revelation, but as a collection of oriental books, to be interpreted according to what we can learn of the mental habits of Semitic peoples.[2] One of the most interesting sidelights on the background of Coleridge's biblical studies comes from an unexpected source: R. W. Mackay, formerly celebrated as the author of one of the 'advanced' books of the mid-nineteenth century—*The Progress of the Intellect* (1850), reviewed for the *Westminster* by Miss Marian Evans. The references to Eichhorn and Coleridge occur in an essay called *The Tübingen School and its Antecedents, a Review of the History and Present Condition of Modern Theology* (1863). This essay was written in the full flush of the Victorian rationalist and scientific 'enlightenment', and one must bear in mind Mackay's 'liberalism' while reading him. While this ensures from him a favourable estimate of the Higher Criticism, it makes him less than just to Coleridge himself. Yet Mackay is no blinkered fanatic; for example, following Baur, he is prepared to give a sympathetic reading to the Fourth Gospel—not as 'history', but as the spiritual drama of the Logos.

Before we could have anything like an objective, scientific

---

1 I have not been able to identify 'Heinrichs'.
2 See T. K. Cheyne, *Founders of O.T. Criticism* (1893).

study of the Bible, says Mackay, the old Protestant
notions of its inspiration and infallibility had to be exploded.
The work had been begun long ago by the 'fathers' of biblical
criticism: Simon, Spinoza, Bayle, etc.; and more recently
Michaelis had reduced the 'inspiration' to a minimum. But
the final stage was hardly reached before Eichhorn, and even
after him a lingering spectre of 'special divinity' still haunted
the Bible, especially certain parts of it. Eichhorn was 'the
first among professional theologians to deal with Scripture
freely on the footing of a mere literary work':

> instead of commencing as heretofore with an ideal theory about
> the Canon anticipating the facts . . . he begins inductively with
> special enquiries about particular books . . . and while reserving a
> generally divine element in Scripture, he makes the human agencies
> so prominent that, instead of pursuing an ignis fatuus of super-
> naturalism which vanishes on approach, we are made to feel our
> real business to be with the substance of the writings as given, i.e.
> as modified by the peculiar individualities of the writers, and as
> amenable to the same rules as other books. Hence his solemn
> apostrophe to the Bible writers—'However great my respect for
> ye, ye holy men, never let me fall into the superstitious idolatry
> already deprecated by yourselves, or deem it irreverent to submit
> your productions to the strictest rules of human criticism!'

There is no need here to go into Eichhorn's treatment of the
synoptic problem, although this engaged Coleridge's attention a good deal. Formerly, as long as 'plenary inspiration'
was believed in, the discrepancies between the gospels had
to be 'harmonised' so as to preserve the appearance of
'absolute gospel agreement'. But now, real differences and
disagreements could be recognized, and theories devised to
account both for them and for the similarities in the gospel
accounts. Minute agreement indicated a common original,
perhaps an *Urevangelium* (written or oral). But the differences? Were there a number of possible transcribers or
translators from an Aramaic original? The evangelists must
have copied each other or a common source (one or more?).
When all was said, however, Eichhorn finally claimed that
the synoptic gospels were 'virtually' the works of the apos-

tolic authors (cf. Coleridge's view given above, pp. 245-6). The Fourth Gospel he regarded as a revision of the 'original gospel' for the benefit of Hellenized readers; the long speeches in it being 'free invention'.

Mackay makes Schleiermacher sound very close to Coleridge when he says that, for the former, the 'inspiration' of any part of the Bible was a matter to be 'proved by the inner witness of the Christian consciousness'. Yet he accuses Coleridge of sitting on the fence between the old and the new, and wanting the best of both worlds—that is, to base the claims of the Bible on its moral authority, and yet to preserve its numinous prestige. There is some truth in his remark about

> the fastidious delicacy of those who, acquiescing like Coleridge and others, in the great historic change from outer to inner criteria, have in later times left the door open to reactionary follies [by treating the Bible, not only as its own evidence, but also as], the surest reflection of the inward word, the appointed conservatory, indispensable criterion, and continual source and support of true belief.

Coleridge would have said that the two views were not incompatible: at any rate he held them both at once. 'I take up this work with the purpose to read it for the first time as I should read any other work'—yet he immediately adds,

> as far at least as I can or dare. For I neither can, nor dare, throw off a strong and awful prepossession in its favour—certain as I am that a large part of the light and life, in and by which I see, love and embrace [the cardinal truths of faith and knowledge] has been directly or indirectly derived to me from this sacred volume—and unable to determine what I do not owe to its influence.[1]

Perhaps the most singular example of a surviving traditionalism, and one which may well disconcert the modern reader who has otherwise been following Coleridge with admiring approval, is his statement that all passages in Scripture

---

[1] *Confessions, loc. cit.*, p. 294.

in which the words are by the sacred historian declared to have been the Word of the Lord supernaturally communicated, I receive as such. . . .

—even though he adds, as an escape clause, 'with a degree of confidence proportioned to the confidence required of me by the writer himself, and to the claims he himself makes on my belief'. And this statement comes in the same letter as the more acceptable 'the Bible and Christianity are their own sufficient evidence'.[1]

Another interesting sidelight on the state of biblical criticism in Coleridge's later years is provided by Connop Thirlwall (1797-1875),[2] one of that small group through whom, in the early decades of the nineteenth century, German ideas were trickling through to this country. In 1825 he published a translation of Schleiermacher's *Critical Essay on the Gospel of St Luke*, adding an Introduction in which he appraises the work done on the synoptic problem, mainly in Germany, during the preceding twenty years. It is not his views on the Gospels which concern us here, but his general remarks about the climate of opinion in Coleridge's time. 'It cannot be concealed', he says

> that German theology in general, and German biblical criticism in particular, labours at present under an ill name among our divines [he refers, in illustration, to Conybeare's Bamptom Lectures of 1824].

Their main objection, he goes on, is that these scholarly discussions tend to 'destroy the reverence with which Christians are accustomed to regard these works as Holy Writ, and containing the word of God'. This sort of objection is so prevalent that we must consider carefully how biblical criticism is likely to affect the traditional notions of 'inspiration'. It is incompatible, he declares,

> with that doctrine of inspiration once universally prevalent in the Christian church, according to which the sacred writers were

---

[1] *Ibid.*, pp. 297 and 300.

[2] Fellow of Trin. Coll., Cambridge; afterwards Bishop of St David's. S. T. C. met him at Cambridge in 1833.

merely passive organs or instruments of the Holy Spirit. This doctrine however has been so long abandoned that it would now be a waste of time to attack it.

Long abandoned? A waste of time to attack it? How often, in the history of thought, have not the 'enlightened' said goodbye to old errors (sometimes truths as well) which in fact had never died at all! Thirlwall remembers this at once, for he adds:

> When I say it has been abandoned, I mean of course only by the learned; for undoubtedly it is still a generally received notion.

However, a softened version of 'inspiration' is now prevailing, says Thirlwall, which interprets it as working merely by 'suggestion' or 'superintendence'. This enables the Church of England to say that 'the inspiration of Scripture is a fundamental tenet on which she (the Church) absolutely insists: but as to the nature and mode of that inspiration she allows her members full liberty of private judgment.' A masterly formula, indeed!—which Thirlwall may have stated in good faith, but of which we should have savoured the irony if we had met with it in Voltaire, Mallock or Samuel Butler. We can sense what 'true inspiration' must be, says Thirlwall, if we compare the apocryphal with the canonical books: in the latter alone do we feel the 'continual presence and action of what is most vital and essential in Christianity itself'.

I want also to draw attention to some remarks by Otto Pfleiderer in his *Development of Theology in Germany since Kant, and its Progress in England since 1825* (1893). After a very able survey of the German field from Semler, Lessing and Herder (who first declared that the biblical books were to be read as human productions) to Baur and his Tübingen disciples, he comes on to England since 1825. First he gives a brief and clever summary of Romanticism as a European movement, and then of the intellectual state of England in 1825. His analysis of this latter, which virtually gives the background to *Aids to Reflection*, and may have been influenced by Coleridge, corresponds roughly with

Coleridge's own: the country was divided, he says, between the party of the Lockean rational-supernaturalists (light without heat) and that of the Evangelicals and Methodists (heat without light). Coming next to Coleridge himself, he shows that rather cool, patronizing attitude often found in those who have not lived long enough in Coleridge's company. Still, he allows that the Reason-Understanding distinction, for example, has 'a certain meaning' as a protest against shallow 'rationalism', but thinks that Coleridge's use of it, and of its corollaries, betrays an 'inclination to suppress intelligent criticism in religious questions'. Who that has followed Coleridge's spiritual pilgrimage at all closely could possibly agree with Pfleiderer here? Others might misuse Coleridge's ideas to that end, but the author of the works we have here been studying—the thinker and prophet who thought Doubt nearer to faith than Acquiescence—could never have had any such 'inclination'.

Pfleiderer admires *Confessions of an Inquiring Spirit*, comparing Coleridge's 'reverent freedom' with that of Lessing, Herder and Schleiermacher. He notes that it has influenced the Church of England through the leaders of the 'Broad Church' movement. Most interesting of all are his quotations from Thomas Arnold on Coleridge:

> His mind is at once rich and vigorous, and comprehensive and critical; while the ’ῆθος is so pure and lively all the while (Letter to Mr Justice Coleridge, Sept. 25, 1839).

—and on the *Confessions*, which Arnold read in manuscript as 'Letters on the Inspiration of the Scriptures':

> [the Letters, says Arnold, are] well fitted to break ground in the approaches to that momentous question which involves in it so great a shock to existing notions . . . but which will end, in spite of the fears and clamours of the weak and bigoted, in the higher exalting and more sure establishing of Christian truth.

My last reference in this context is to the 1847 edition of the *Biographia*, Vol. II. Here, in the 'Biographical Supplement', there is an extract from Archdeacon Julius Hare's preface to his *Mission of the Comforter* (1846), a work dedicated to the memory of Coleridge. He calls Coleridge

the great religious philosopher to whom the mind of our generation in England owes more than to any other man.

The main work of his life, says Hare,

was to spiritualize, not only our philosophy but our theology, to raise them both above the empiricism into which they had long been dwindling, and to set them free from the technical trammels of logical systems. . . . The third and fourth volumes of his *Remains*, though they were hailed with delight by Arnold on their first appearance, have not yet produced their proper effect on the intellect of the age . . . [Coleridge had] a few opinions on points of Biblical criticism, likely to be very offensive to persons who know nothing about the history of the Canon. Some of these opinions, to which Coleridge himself ascribed a good deal of importance, seem to me of little worth; some, to be decidedly erroneous. Philological criticism, indeed all matters requiring a laborious and accurate investigation of details, were alien from the bent and habits of his mind; and his exegetical studies, such as they were, took place when he had little better than the meagre Rationalism of Eickhorn [*sic*] and Bertholdt [*sic*] to help him. Of the opinions which he imbibed from them, some abode with him through life.[1]

Though he is right about the 'bent and habits' of Coleridge's mind, Hare does far less than justice to the *Confessions*. He fixes on errors in exegetical details, but ignores the commanding sweep of the main argument. Still, his general estimate of Coleridge's work and influence is just and fine.

In Vol. I of the same edition, S. T. C.'s daughter Sara writes of the effort of his later years, in a style strongly marked by hereditary traits. He sought, she says,

to construct a system really and rationally religious; and since, in his philosophical inquiries, he 'neither could nor dared throw off a strong and awful prepossession in favour' of that great main outline of doctrine which came to us from the first in company with the highest and purest moral teaching which the world has

---

[1] *Op. cit.*, p. 426.

yet seen . . . and had actually been to himself the vehicle of all the light and life of the higher and deeper kind, which had been vouch-safed to him in his earthly career;—he therefore *set out* with the desire to construct a philosophical system in which Christianity —based on the Tri-une being of God, and embracing a Primal Fall and Universal Redemption—Christianity ideal, spiritual, eternal, but likewise and necessarily historical—realized and manifested in time—should be shown forth as accordant, or rather as one with ideas of reason; and the demands of the spiritual and of the speculative mind, of the heart, conscience, reason, should all be satisfied and reconciled in one bond of peace.

To purge our bosoms of this perilous stuff, let me end with two short sayings of Coleridge himself illustrating his pre-science on what one might call the Moses-Geology issue:

(i) the Pressing of Moses into the Service of Geological theory (by would-be 'harmonisers') . . . must end in the triumph of Infidels. If there be one sure Conclusion respecting the Bible, it is this—that it not only uniformly speaks the language of the Senses, but adopts the inferences which the Childhood of the Race drew from the appearances presented by the Senses. The Bible must be interpreted by its known *objects*, and *ends*, and these were the Moral and spiritual Education of the Human Race. The ends secured, the truths of Sciences follow of their own accord.[1]

(ii) [The first Chapter of Genesis is, in effect, saying:] The literal fact you could not comprehend even if it were related to you; but you may conceive of it as if it had taken place thus and thus.[2]

[1] *UP*, 336, July 1824 (to Mrs W. Rogers).
[2] *Literary Remains* (1838), Vol. III, p. 319.

CHAPTER XIX

CONCLUSION

AS I have said more than once in this book, the last hurdle that Coleridge had to o'erleap in his return to orthodoxy was the *historical* aspect of Christianity. The Trinity he had long ago accepted as a necessary speculation, but the incarnation of the Logos in a particular man, in a particular place, and at a particular point of history, was a doctrine less congenial to his mental habit. Nevertheless he did come to accept it. The following extract from the *Literary Remains* summarizes how he did it:

> To know God as God (τὸν Ζῆνα, the living God), we must assume his personality: otherwise what were it but an ether, a gravitation?—but to assume his personality, we must begin with his humanity, and this is impossible but in history; for man is an historical—not an eternal being. *Ergo*, Christianity is of necessity historical and not philosophical only.[1]

In May 1825 Coleridge wrote to his nephew J. T. Coleridge enclosing 'the first third' of *Aids*, and discussing the plan of the whole work. He says he has 'touched on the mystery of the Trinity only in a *negative* way'—that is, he has exposed the weakness of the usual arguments against it, and shown that Christianity is nothing without it. But he is reserving for 'my large work' the 'positive establishment of the Doctrine as involved in the Idea of God'. He claims to have finished the first division of this, 'namely the Philosophy of the Christian Creed, or Christianity true in *Idea*. The 2nd Division will be Christianity true in *fact*—i.e. historically. The third and last will be Christianity true in *Act*, i.e. morally and spiritually.' But he thinks (and surely we can agree) that in *Aids* (supplemented by some projected essays not all completed, but including the Letters on Inspiration) he has given a pretty complete account of his position. 'At

[1] *Ibid.*, Vol. IV, p. 12 ('Luther's Table Talk').

all events', he concludes,

> no one hereafter can with justice complain that I have disclosed
> my sentiments only in flashes and fragments—and that no one can
> tell what the opinions and Belief are of your affectionate uncle and
> Friend, S. T. Coleridge.[1]

In the last month of his life, Coleridge is reported to have
said:

> The metaphysical disquisition at the end of the first volume of the
> 'Biographia Literaria' is unformed and immature—it contains the
> fragments of the truth, but it is not fully thought out. It is wonder-
> ful to myself to think how infinitely more profound my views now
> are, and yet how much clearer they are withal.[2]

If so, I must leave it to others to plumb these depths.
Within the limits of this book there is no more that can or
need be added. Coleridge's later letters and notebooks—
so far, that is, as they are as yet available to the general
reader[3]—are full of references to his projected *Opus
Maximum*, which was to crown his life's work and unify his
multitudinous thinking and reading in one vast synthesis.[4]
We shall not properly know, until the existing portions of
the *Opus* are published, how much more we shall have to
learn. But we do know, and have seen, that hints towards it
are scattered throughout his writings, and indeed that all
his prose works are fragments not yet built into the total
structure. Perhaps, in those fragments, we have enough to
account for the great influence Coleridge exerted over some
of the best minds of the nineteenth century. Everyone knows
that J. S. Mill, a man of totally opposite views, called
Coleridge one of 'the two great seminal minds of England
in their age' (the other being Bentham), and added that
'there is hardly to be found in England an individual of any
importance . . . who did not first learn to think from one of
these two'. Of those who did learn from Coleridge, it is

---

[1] *UP*, 349.   [2] *Table Talk* (1851 ed.), p. 330.

[3] At the time of writing (Oct. 1970), the last vols. of E. L. Griggs's ed. of the
Letters are still awaited, also K. Coburn's ed. of the later Notebooks, and nearly all
of the 'Collected Coleridge'.

[4] We await also G. N. G. Orsini's ed. of what exists of this.

enough to mention Sterling, Carlyle, J. S. Mill, J. C. Hare, Thomas Arnold, J. H. Newman, James Martineau, F. A. J. Hort, F. D. Maurice, Charles Kingsley, Matthew Arnold, Walter Pater and many others. A good deal has been written about Coleridge's influence on the Broad Church movement (mainly through Maurice) and upon 'Christian Socialism'. But I think that if we live with him long enough, share his valiant struggles for Faith against heavy odds, and watch his final attainment of it, we shall be inclined to see him rather as the prototype of those—like Kierkegaard perhaps, or the best of the Christian existentialists of the present century— who have sought to renovate the Faith, not only by re-stating it intellectually, but by living it out into reality themselves. *Aids to Reflection* is still a book which can speak straight to the condition of any well-disposed young pagan of today (if he would ever read it); and the *Confessions*, as I have said, laid down nearly all the positions about biblical interpretation which are now taken for granted by everyone.

In his later years Coleridge often regretted that he had not taken Holy Orders, and no doubt (since he had become orthodox) he would have been happier as a parson. Happier still, perhaps, if he had been a College don, where he could have spellbound generations of the best young (and older) men without having to worry about money matters or—in those days—the writing of books. But we may be thankful that he never took Orders, for his defence of the Faith is much more impressive as the work of a layman—of one, that is, who is not professionally committed to the defensive side, but has embraced the Faith through intellectual conviction and emotional need.

I conclude with two brief extracts from the as yet unpublished Third Volume of Coleridge's *Notebooks*. The first is taken out of context, but may serve as a motto for his religious work:

(i) To make the intellectual Faith a fair analogon and unison of the Vital faith . . . (3278).

(ii) But O! not what I understand, but what I *am*, must save or crush me! (3354).

INDEX